The Federal Budget: Economics and Politics

THE FEDERAL BUDGET:

ECONOMICS AND POLITICS

Aaron Wildavsky, *Editor*

Michael J. Boskin, *Editor*

James W. Abellera

Marcy E. Avrin

George F. Break

Alain C. Enthoven

Robert W. Hartman

Herschel Kanter

Melvyn B. Krauss

Roger P. Labrie

Arnold J. Meltsner

Rudolph G. Penner

Alvin Rabushka

Robert D. Reischauer

Laurence S. Seidman

Institute for Contemporary Studies
San Francisco, California

Distributed by Transaction Books
New Brunswick (U.S.A.) and London (U.K.)

Inquiries, book orders, and catalog requests should be addressed to the Institute for Contemporary Studies, Suite 811, 260 California Street, San Francisco, California 94111—415—398—3010.

Library of Congress Catalog No. 81—86378.

Library of Congress Cataloging in Publication Data
Main entry under title:

The Federal budget.

     Bibliography: p.
     Includes index.
     1. Budget—United States—Addresses, essays, lectures.
I. Wildavsky, Aaron B. II. Boskin, Michael J.
III. Abellera, James W. IV. Institute for Contemporary
Studies.
HJ2051.F39 1982   353.0072'2   82—11690
ISBN 0—917616—49—9
ISBN 0—917616—48—0 (pbk.)

CONTENTS

III

Current Budget Problems

IV

Structural Reforms

V

Conclusion and Summary

CONTRIBUTORS

JAMES W. ABELLERA
Managing editor, AEI Foreign Policy and Defense Review

MARCY E. AVRIN
President, Avrin Economics, Inc.; research associate,
National Bureau of Economic Research

MICHAEL J. BOSKIN
Director, Palo Alto office, National Bureau of Economic Research;
senior fellow, Hoover Institution; professor of economics,
Stanford University

GEORGE F. BREAK
Professor of economics, University of California, Berkeley

ALAIN C. ENTHOVEN
Marriner S. Eccles Professor of Public and Private Management,
Graduate School of Business; professor of health care economics,
School of Medicine, Stanford University

ROBERT W. HARTMAN
Senior fellow, The Brookings Institution

HERSCHEL KANTER
Staff member, Institute for Defense Analyses

MELVYN B. KRAUSS
Senior fellow, Hoover Institution; professor of economics,
New York University

ROGER P. LABRIE
Research associate, American Enterprise Institute for
Public Policy Research

ARNOLD J. MELTSNER
Professor of public policy, University of California, Berkeley

RUDOLPH G. PENNER
Director of tax policy studies and resident scholar,
American Enterprise Institute

ALVIN RABUSHKA
Senior fellow, Hoover Institution

ROBERT D. REISCHAUER
Senior vice-president, The Urban Institute

LAURENCE S. SEIDMAN
Associate professor of economics, University of Delaware

AARON WILDAVSKY
Professor of political science, University of California, Berkeley

PREFACE

Spending by the federal government has been a growing concern to analysts and policymakers since the mid-1970s, when federal budget deficits began rising to levels unknown since the end of World War II. The reasons behind the spending increases involved a combination of economic theories that played down the importance of budget deficits and steadily growing revenues made available because of "bracket creep"—tax increases caused by inflation and the unindexed tax code.

In the last two years of the Carter administration, anxiety about spending and the budget reached fever proportions. However, worries about the overall budget—including both spending *and* taxing—have dominated public policy headlines throughout most of 1982. One reason for the concern is that unlike original projections, which showed a real decline in deficit spending, the Reagan administration is currently projecting *increasing* deficits, exceeding $100 billion, for each of the next several fiscal years.

The short-term problem arises from a combination of large tax cuts enacted in 1981, substantial increases in the defense budget projected over the next couple of years, and ongoing increases in many other parts of the budget, following patterns begun in the last half-decade.

This study, which considers both taxing and spending but emphasizes the spending side of the budget, follows an earlier study published in 1978—*Federal Tax Reform.* Since the budget problem involves important economic *and* political issues, we asked an economist, Michael Boskin, and a political scientist, Aaron Wildavsky, to coedit the book.

The issues considered are fairly straightforward. We wanted to examine options for controlling the budget as well as specific spending programs (defense, social security, health care, and subsidies for the well-to-do). And above all, since the problem of controlling federal spending will be with us for a long time, we wanted to publish a study that would be helpful in analyzing and understanding broad issues of taxing and spending beyond the next couple of budget years.

The result is a book that has two essential subjects. It is an economic study of the federal budget as well as a political and institutional study of the budget process. In this sense, it fits into the pattern of several recent Institute studies—particularly *Politics and the Oval Office* (1981, a study of presidential governance edited by Arnold J. Meltsner) and *Social Regulation: Strategies for Reform* (1982, edited by Eugene Bardach and Robert A. Kagan).

We hope this book will make an important contribution to the ongoing debate on the federal budget.

A. Lawrence Chickering
Executive Director
Institute for Contemporary Studies

San Francisco, California
June 1982

I

Introduction and History

1

AARON WILDAVSKY

Introduction: Toward a New Budgetary Order

Fighting the deficit. Socialism, subsidies, and the welfare state. Market, hierarchical, and egalitarian approaches. Uncontrollability as control. Constitutional amendments. Spending and ceilings.

The doctrine of the balanced budget that became so powerful over the course of U.S. history stood for a social as well as a financial equilibrium. The balance referred to was not only one between revenue and expenditure but between social orders. The fundamental compromise that established and

3

maintained American democracy, a compromise between
economic individualism, political egalitarianism, and social
hierarchy, was based on balance. Americans believed,
though they need not have been able to specify exactly how,
that because their society was so finely equilibrated, satisfactory outcomes acceptable to diverse forces would emerge. In
a word, "balance" meant that things would be all right. For
the budget to be unbalanced, therefore, meant that society
was out of kilter. That is why, in defense of this moral bound-
ary, terrible things were supposed to happen (or were retro-
spectively attributed to events) when the budget became
unbalanced in peacetime.[1]

THE DEMISE OF THE
BALANCED BUDGET

When things go well, one tends to credit the doctrines and
practices that one has followed; when things go badly, one
may still hope to recover by doing more of the same. Though
his administration urged a variety of methods to enhance
business activity, President Hoover insisted that "we cannot
squander ourselves into prosperity." To Herbert Hoover, a
balanced budget was the "very keystone of recovery," without which the depression would continue indefinitely. He
stressed lowering federal expenditures and, if that failed,
raising taxes (Kimmel 1959, p. 160; Dorfman 1959, pp.
610–16).

The Democratic opposition firmly shared his opinion that
achieving a balanced budget was essential to ending the
depression (Kimmel 1959, p. 148). The new president,
Franklin D. Roosevelt (1933–1945), was so concerned about
the near $1.6 billion deficit—"a deficit so great that it makes
us catch our breath"—that he promised in both his campaign and his inaugural address to make a balanced budget
top priority.

Gradually, however, the federal government's goal of achieving a balanced budget during a depression came under attack. Waddill Catchings and William Trufant Foster wrote against the idea of a minimal government that relied on the private sector to generate income and employment; instead, they advocated maintaining employment through long-range public works. Though new debt would be created, the additional economic activity and increased revenue would make repayment of the debt easier than an ongoing depression. "We must conquer the depression by collective action," Foster insisted in 1932 (Kimmel 1959, p. 155).

This necessarily means the leadership of the federal government— the only agency which represents all of us. . . . We must abandon our policy of defeatism, our worship of the budget, our false economy program. . . . Instead, we must collectively put into use enough currency and credit to restore the commodity price level of 1928.

As the depression deepened, economists and publicists began to talk about "spending" the nation out of the depression. The publishing magnate William Randolph Hearst promoted a "prosperity" bond issue in the then unheard-of amount of $5.5 billion. The philosopher John Dewey, president of the People's Lobby, asked for $3.5 billion for public works and relief. However, instead of debt financing which might be inflationary, he proposed that debts be written down and interest rates reduced (Dorfman 1959, pp. 617, 637). Yet there were still those to counter with the traditional belief that continuously unbalanced budgets lead to inflation, and that this could only weaken an already depressed economy (Kimmel 1959, pp. 157, 222–23). Petitions of all kinds, signed by economists of all persuasions, both for and against increased government spending, proliferated (Dorfman 1959, pp. 659–75). Underlying these quarrels and rival economic theories was the shared sense of urgency that something had to be done, and that it had to be different from whatever was currently being done.

By the early 1930s a number of Americans in the Democratic party had begun to seek a rationale for encouraging the government to expand public works and thus increase employment. They found this rationale in the work of John Maynard Keynes and introduced his thought to key figures, including President Roosevelt.[2] Building on ideas advanced in 1931 by his collaborator, R. F. Kahn, Keynes argued that it was appropriate, in a deflationary period when vast economic resources went unused, for the government to create deficits as a means of expanding demand. When economic activity was slow, government should step in to speed it up; when the economy overheated and inflation resulted, government could decrease spending. In short, raising and lowering the deficit became a prime means of economic control. The important point, however, was not the practice of Keynesian doctrine—any student of politics knows that it would be much easier to raise than to lower spending—but that it provided a strong intellectual rationale for doing what many people wanted. At long last politicians could combine spending with virtue.

THE RISE AND FALL OF THE UNBALANCED BUDGET

The triumph of Keynesian doctrine marked both an end to the primacy of the balanced budget and a beginning of variable expenditure as an instrument of economic stabilization. The emphasis shifted from matching spending and revenue at the lowest possible level to manipulation of the difference between them. The Employment Act of 1946 brought a new equation focusing federal policy on the goal of full employment, with deficits and surpluses apparently left to vary in its wake. Spending and owing, instead of being the great enemies of economy, had become its greatest friends.

By the mid- to late 1960s a new budgetary compromise had been made. Its essence was the unbalanced budget (or, if one prefers, balance at the spending level necessary to achieve full employment, which mostly meant the same thing). Its principle was the change in belief among egalitarians (by then allied with the Democratic party) to the view that government spending was a good thing, especially if it was done in a redistributive direction. By taking from the rich and giving to the poor, they could at one and the same time help their friends, whom they hoped to recruit, and hurt their enemies. So far so obvious. The less obvious question is what was in it for the established forces favoring economic markets and social hierarchy? Belief in hierarchy, which is based on sacrifice of the parts in favor of the whole, goes along with a sacrificial ethic. So long as status distinctions are maintained (say, officers come from the upper class), hierarchs should be willing to do their all (say, lead the troops and thus suffer higher casualties). So long, therefore, as labor unions, racial minorities, and poor regions—the relevant disadvantaged interests—accepted the existing social structure, hierarchs were willing to buy them off. The other side of the establishment, the corporate and commercial interests, got their own quid pro quo: while everyone else was getting theirs, thus necessitating higher effective tax rates, the market men got direct subsidies like those for tobacco and shipbuilding, and indirect subsidies like loan guarantees and tax preferences. "Socialism for the rich" went hand in hand with redistribution to the poor. In case anyone was left out, the "middle masses" received medical and housing subsidies. And, most important, the elderly of whatever class, because they were numerous and organized, achieved a rapid growth in pension and medical payments. The point is that once the mutual restraint of the budget balance had been replaced by the free-for-all of the welfare state, the necessary social accommodations lacked the necessary income (spending increased as a proportion of national product while taxes went up faster than personal income, as the figures show), which explains why this arrangement lasted only a decade.

All this spending depended upon doing what was done without (a) decreasing the standard of living for most Americans, and/or (b) significantly disadvantaging the major participants in the political process. Within ten to fifteen years, however one counts (i.e., roughly from 1965 to 1980), both conditions were violated. The social order favoring equality found welfare insufficient and began a direct attack on corporate capitalism. To the social insurance state and the subsidy state (the old welfare state) was added the regulatory state. Eventually, corporations concluded that subsidy was not worth the cost of regulation. The amalgam of social orders that constituted American culture was coming apart. And this loosening of ties that bind was nowhere more evident than in budgeting.

As long as the rate of economic growth exceeded the rate of spending, government could be supported without increasing tax rates. The actual decline in growth and increase in spending, whatever the reasons, meant that this easy exit was closed. The next step (see figure 2) was to run down defense as a proportion of total spending from some 49 percent in 1960 to about 23 percent in 1978 (Ippolito 1981, p. 179). Such a reversal of priorities would work provided that the adherents of hierarchy did not become overly worried about the puncturing of their precious social system by foreign forces. This changed for any number of reasons, from the Soviet arms buildup to the invasion of Afghanistan to pure paranoia, but it changed. At the same time, whether the responsibility lies with oil price increases, declining labor productivity, lack of sufficient savings, overpopulation, deficit spending, or all or none of the above, inflation rose and take-home pay declined.

Figure 1
Federal Budget Outlays as Percentage
of Gross National Product
(fiscal years 1955–1981)

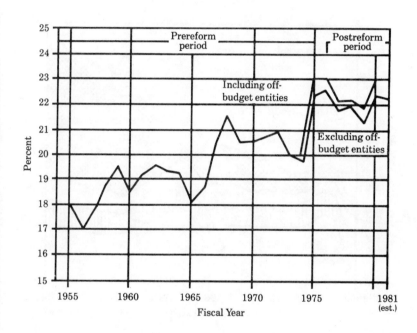

Source: Figures for 1955–1958 from *Budget of the United States Government, Fiscal Year 1978;* figures for 1958–1981 from *Budget of the United States Government, Fiscal Year 1981,* in Ippolito 1981, p. 205.

Figure 2
Federal Budget Outlays, Fiscal Years 1950–1982, by Category
(in constant 1982 dollars)

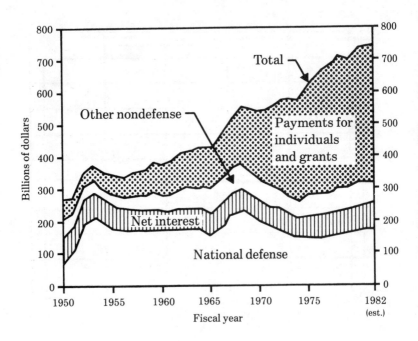

Source: *United States Budget in Brief, Fiscal Year 1982*, in Ippolito 1981, p. 27.

Table 1
Amount of and Increase in Per Capita Personal Income and Individual Income Tax 1970–1979

Year	Personal income Amount ($)	Increase (%)	Individual income tax Amount ($)	Increase (%)
1970	3,911	–	441	–
1971	4,149	6.1	416	−5.7
1972	4,513	8.8	453	8.9
1973	5,002	10.8	490	8.2
1974	5,449	8.9	561	14.5
1975	5,879	7.9	573	2.1
1976	6,420	9.2	611	6.6
1977	7,061	10.0	727	19.0
1978	7,856	11.2	828	13.9
1979	8,723	11.0	988	19.3

Source: Per capita figures calculated from data in *Economic Report of the President, 1980,* in Ippolito 1981, p. 210.

THE SEARCH FOR A NEW BUDGETARY ORDER

The budgetary crunch occurred because everyone wanted out. The hierarchical social order wanted to slow down domestic spending, speed up defense expenditure, and, if necessary, raise taxes—though this would be done sub rosa, in the manner of hierarchies, by "bracket creep" (as people were pushed into higher brackets), by social security increases, and by the excise taxes on oil. Egalitarians wished to expand domestic spending and keep defense down; they preferred higher taxes or bigger deficits to unemployment or income disparity. Competitive individualists wanted to give market mechanisms freer play by cutting both taxes and spending. When one arrays these preferences—raising versus reducing taxes and spending—their incompatibility becomes evident. So does the difficulty the major political parties have in coming to an internal accommodation. The Republican party of today is something like two-thirds market to one-third hierarchy (some would say 55–45). Its internal conflict is between the hierarchs, whose overriding consideration is social stability, and the market forces that want to expand the private and contract the public sectors. The quarrel of these semirival and semicooperative social orders—the quarrel within the establishment about budget balance—is not at all surprising, for one side cares about size and the other about the composition or balance among expenditures.[3] Because he takes a hierarchical, collectivist view of defense and a free market, individualist view of domestic policy, President Ronald Reagan encapsulates these conflicts within his own administration.

The Democratic party is divided in a different direction between its hierarchical and egalitarian wings. Once the restraint of budget balance was removed, these two groups came together in support of the welfare state. With the hierarchical elements returning to support higher defense and lower domestic spending in an effort to reestablish a social and financial equilibrium, the Democratic coalition is in danger of splitting.

Narrowly focused conflict over budgeting is best understood as part and parcel of a broader concern with the role of government in society. The rule that budget balance was desirable in peacetime (and that wartime debt was to be paid off in the next generation) enabled market, hierarchical, and egalitarian social orders to live with one another within the same political framework. The alternative rule, the unbalanced budget of the welfare state, created cohesion while it lasted but by 1980 had run its course. The question Americans must answer is whether any new rule will help create (or express) a social compact that the adherents of the various American social orders will find desirable or at least satisfactory. Let us begin looking at the implications of current choices by inquiring into possible pro- or anti-spending tendencies in the existing federal budgetary process. Then we can examine constitutional versus statutory approaches to improving the budgetary process—whether by making it more neutral or by giving it a different bias.

IS THE BUDGETARY PROCESS BIASED?

Is the congressional budgetary process as it now exists neutral in regard to claims for higher or lower spending? The Budget Reform Act of 1974 expressed Congress's desire to enhance its own power of the purse by giving it the ability to visibly relate revenue and expenditure. Since the broad coalition supporting the act was made up of both high and low spenders, however, the new process was not designed to favor either side.[4] On the one hand, the mere existence of budget committees raised another possible impediment to higher spending; on the other hand, the need for these committees to maintain collegial relations with the tax and spending committees as well as to remain subject to the will of Congress meant that they had to subordinate themselves to the rampant desires for higher spending. The evidence from Allen Schick's *Congress and Money* (1980, p. 313) is conclusive:

In almost a hundred interviews with Members of Congress and staffers, no one expressed the view that the allocations in budget resolution had been knowingly set below legislative expectations. "We got all that we needed," one committee staff director exulted. The chief clerk of an Appropriations subcommittee complained, however, that the target figure in the resolution was too high: "We were faced with pressure to spend up to the full budget allocation. It's almost as if the Budget Committee bent over backwards to give Appropriations all that it wanted and then some."

In considering the related question of mandatory spending, required by law and not subject to the annual appropriations process, Schick (1980, p. 571) makes a powerful plea to consider this a conscious choice: " 'Uncontrollability' is not an accident or an inadvertence of the legislative process but a willful decision by Congress to favor nonbudgetary values over budgetary control." Since budgeting, like history, is a matter of selectivity, Congress makes its most important choices by choosing what not to consider. Uncontrollability is a form of control. If much domestic spending is mandated and indexed and most defense spending is not, is that a bias in budgeting or just democracy at work?

Just as consumers find it more difficult to organize than producers, so spending interests are advantaged because their concern is concentrated and taxpayers' are diffused. A billion-dollar program has a greater effect on recipients than on taxpayers who contribute only a few hundred cents apiece. Are these advantages and disadvantages built into political life and thus part of a natural process like photosynthesis, or is the escalation helped along by voting on items rather than on totals? Is budgeting by addition of items rather than subtraction under ceilings the only natural way?

Reducing the total size of the budget not only requires eternal vigilance but *information* on where to cut and *coordination* among programs so that increases in some do not balance out decreases in others. Increasing spending is easy, requires little information (any area will do), and even less coordination. Without a spending limit, no spending agency has an incentive to cut its budget because the contribution to the total is small and uncertain (see Wildavsky 1980). Is that natural, as Mother Nature intended, or unnatural—i.e., a bias that explains why government grows?

NEW DIRECTIONS

One sign of the times is the proliferation of constitutional amendments designed, in the view of their sponsors, to remedy what James Madison referred to as the "discovered faults" in our basic political arrangements. Regardless of the remedy proposed, the terms of discourse—*defects* in the existing political process, *biases* in political arrangements, structural *impediments* to spending limits—suggest a renegotiation of long-standing arrangements.

The difference between the constitutional amendments mandating an out-and-out balanced budget and those requiring expenditure limitation is this: balance can take place at any level of spending, provided it is matched by revenues, whereas limits are designed to secure a specific (always lower) size of government. The balance people may wish to raise taxes; the limits people always want to lower spending. Thus the two pro-amendment sides would differ in the way in which they would answer a critical question: would they prefer a $600 billion budget with a $100 billion deficit or a $900 billion budget with no deficit? Is it the size of government or the balance between taxing and spending that matters?

The crucial character of the difference between size and balance is also apparent in consideration by Congress of further reforms in the budget process it recently reformed in 1974. Political life is speeding up. The seemingly obscure debates over the relative importance of the first and second budget resolutions are in fact over whether, by statute or by rule, Congress will impose on itself spending ceilings.

Nowadays budgeteers speak in strange tongues—e.g., "first resolution" and "second resolution" (the first setting a ceiling for total outlays; the second fixing allocations for specific categories). What would happen if the last became the first? That depends. The Budget Reform Act of 1974 did not decree lower spending, nor did it alter political incentives one whit. What the act did do was change calculations so that Congress could work its will, whatever that was, more effectively. The purpose of the second resolution, as I know from discussion at the time, was to legitimize "budgeting by addition" by formalizing the usual congressional tendency to lump together its item-by-item decisions and call this a budget, much as presidents do when the document has to be sent to the printer. Making the first resolution binding might signify a desire to introduce budgeting by subtraction (or "resource allocation," as the old-fashioned phrase had it), through which agencies and programs compete under a fixed total. It might, but it might not.

Those who wish to make the first resolution binding argue that the Budget Reform Act of 1974—setting up House and Senate budget committees and establishing the Congressional Budget Office—does not work well enough. There remains a lack of control over entitlements (see figure 3); the size of the budget has increased more afterwards than before; and the delays in passing the budget have, if anything, proved worse (see Fisher 1981, pp. 6–10). By setting a ceiling, by grasping the nettle of requiring competition among programs, the implication is that Congress would become financially responsible. But would it? An easy way out would be for Congress to set the ceiling so high that no increase in one place implied a decrease in another. The result of trying to make the first resolution all-important would be to make it trivial.

If the first resolution is to be meaningful, it must be at or below the level where the budget is today. If the resolution is to be helpful, it must be consistent over a period of years; otherwise the size of programs would vary in fits and starts, leaving everyone worse off. Willy-nilly, therefore, supporters of an effective first resolution must be interested in a semipermanent rule for setting ceilings. Tying spending to national product—the rule that the size of government should not increase faster than the growth of the economy—may

Figure 3
Entitlement and Other Uncontrollable Spending as Percentage of Federal Budget
(fiscal years 1967–1980)

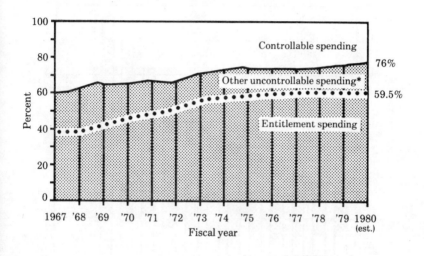

Source: *Congressional Quarterly Weekly Report*, 19 January 1980, in Ippolito 1981, p. 214.
*Spending required by contracts made in past years, borrowing authority, guaranteed loans, and other obligations.

Figure 4
Federal and Federally Assisted Credit Outstanding, Fiscal Years 1970–1981, by Category

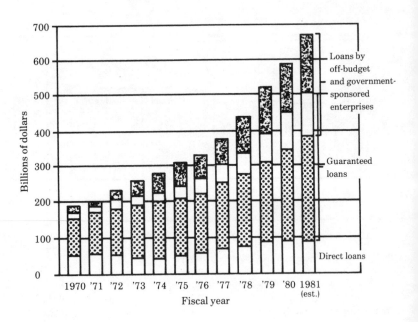

Source: *Special Analyses, Budget of the United States Government, Fiscal Year 1981*, in Ippolito 1981, p. 218.

not be the best rule, but it is hard to see how there could be a significant departure from it that would still leave a significant ceiling.

A major difficulty with a spending limit, whether constitutional or statutory (or by cabinet agreement, as in Canada), is that it does not include a commitment to a balanced budget —which, as it turns out, has most of the popular political support. In order to overcome this drawback, a substantial number of senators reached agreement on Senate Joint Resolution 58. Though it is called a "balanced budget" amendment, its title actually inverts the priorities. S.J.58 requires, insists upon, enforces expenditure limitation related to economic growth. Indexing for tax brackets is also mandated. But budget balance, though expected, is only suggested. According to the calculations of those who support a spending limit, it would lead to balanced budgets most of the time without demanding balance when the economy was in recession or increasing the size of government by raising taxes. Nevertheless, the adherents of hierarchy, and hence of social stability, prefer budget balance. In this scheme, balance becomes a kind of plan (nice if you can get it), while limits are actually the operative objective.

Thus far we have considered two alternatives — constitutional spending limits and congressional imposition of a binding ceiling—that in their own ways would be radical changes. The constitutional amendment would alter the very structure of the budgetary process, and the self-imposed ceiling would require central direction of a kind unknown in a fragmented legislature whose members have power bases largely independent of one another. What these proposals do have in common is their concern with ceilings, a sign of the belief that individual spending decisions add up to larger amounts than collective consideration of totals.

Aside from these radical proposals to readjust the relationship between budgetary parts and wholes, there is a more modest change that is coming under scrutiny: namely, indexing of social spending versus indexing of taxation. If the law requiring indexing of tax brackets against inflation takes effect in 1985 as scheduled, it will exert downward pressure on the budget. Indeed, the current situation—indexing some social spending, especially social security, while not indexing taxation—may be said to have driven the budgetary system for the past two decades. Were there a de-indexing of spending so that spending was eroded by inflation, and taxes were indexed so that revenue did not rise with inflation, the size of government would go down. Alternatively, both spending and taxing could be de-indexed, thus making the budgetary process more neutral and enabling high and low spenders to fight it out. All these possibilities would make a big budgetary difference.

It may be that the current budgetary disarray—the inability to agree on totals or their distribution so that large parts of the budget are left in limbo—may merely lead to more chaos. But it may also be that chaos will be the harbinger of opportunity to put the budget on a better track. Whatever happens—the changes or the chaos—will reveal whether and to what extent the different social orders that make up the United States will be able, in our time, to reconcile their visions of the good life and government's place in it.

2

AARON WILDAVSKY

Budgets as Compromises among Social Orders

Social hierarchies and market forces. A background in government finance. Budgetary equations. "A disreputable scramble for public money." The Civil War and debt reduction. The Budget Act of 1921.

In fine, taxation equal to the public expenditure is, in my opinion, the only method in nature by which our defence can be continued, our independence be preserved, a destructive increase of the public debt be avoided, our currency (hard or paper) be kept in a state of fixed value, the natural springs of industry be given to every profession of men, our supplies made plentiful, the public confidence be restored to the public counsels, the morality of our people be revived, and the blessings of heaven be secured to ourselves and our posterity.

—Webster 1791, p. 145

A successful financial system will conform to the political ideas which for the time being control society, and adjust itself to the political structure of the particular society to which it applies.
                                                —Adams 1899, p. 8

When you have decided upon your budget procedure you have decided on the form of government you will have as a *matter of fact.*
                                                —Fitzpatrick 1918, p. viii

Budgets reflect social orders; what is true of one is soon enough true of the other. Living one way and budgeting another is too contradictory to last.

The raising of revenue and the allocating of resources, year in and year out, constitute the most continuous record of collective concerns. These heightened moments of choice, in which not all desires may be accommodated, express public priorities better than any alternative mechanism or process or set of decisions. No doubt one can point to peculiarities in regard to particular times and programs. But over time, decade by decade from one century to the next, budgets are accurate indicators of what members of a polity wish to do (and not to do) together.

If budgets reflect social orders, they stand, as it were, for different ways of life. When we experience basic changes in budgeting, or we hear that radical changes in budgetary relationships are afoot, we know that society is not what it was or will be. Political cultures are in contention. Before beginning to discuss the potential for and desirability of budgetary change in the 1980s, therefore, it is worth understanding how this nation used to budget, why these budgetary relationships were transformed, and why Americans are now contemplating reforming their prior reforms. Knowing where we have been will help us understand today's choices about where we might go. This historical setting is especially necessary because earlier patterns of budgetary thought and action have been lost to our contemporary consciousness.

The winning side of the American Revolution was composed of three social orders—a weak social hierarchy that wanted to replace the English king with a native American variety better suited to colonial conditions, emerging market men who wanted to control their own commerce, and the heirs of a continental republican tradition that stressed small, egalitarian, voluntary associations (Pocock 1977). The compromises through which these social orders came to live together to form the American political culture are essential to understanding the unique form and content of federal budgeting in the United States.

At the outset, it is well to remember that the Revolution was fought against the power of the English king. Even the Federalists, who joined social hierarchy and market forces to form the first independent American establishment, had their qualms about how strong executives, like the president and departmental secretaries, should be. They wanted political unity and economic order, but on a minimal—not a maximal—basis. Republicans—first the social order, then the political party, originally known as Anti-Federalists—knew best what they were against: established churches, standing armies, and powerful executives. They were *for* life on a smaller scale and for limitations on status and economic differences so as to permit people to manage their own affairs (Storing 1981; Schambra 1981). Whether states (or colonies) were small enough or whether commerce could be limited without limiting liberty, they could not say. Presumably, local units would get together for the common defense, but the demise of the Articles of Confederation has left us unable to say whether and to what degree a more voluntary central system might have worked.

Left to their own devices, our social hierarchs would have wanted relatively high revenues and expenditures to support a stronger and more splendid central government. Since the market men would have to pay, they preferred a smaller central apparatus, except where spending and taxing provided direct aid. Together this establishment supported what, in American political life, were called "internal improvements"—subsidies for canals, harbors, railroads, and the like. But the establishment had to contend with the republican believers in small, egalitarian collectives who threatened to withdraw consent to union unless the size and scope of central government were severely limited. For these egalitarians did not believe that government spending was good for the common man, the small farmer and artisan of their day. Government took from the people (or so they believed) for the establishment. Limiting, not expanding, central government was the byword of republicanism.

Governments that ran deficits might have been acceptable to the hierarchical social order as a necessary accompaniment of domestic grandeur. The "public interest" was their phrase. But continuous deficits were unacceptable to market forces, who feared financial instability, debasement of currency, and inflation. So market men would pay more to balance the budget. It was the egalitarian republicans who insisted on lower levels of taxing and spending. Alone, they might have allowed imbalance—lower revenue than expenditure—since taxes discriminated against the ordinary citizen.

The balanced budget at low levels, except in wartime, was the crucial compromise that allowed the three social orders to coexist. Of course, unlike the signing of the Declaration of Independence, the compromise was not made on a single day, nor was there a formal declaration. The informal understanding, however, lasted for a century and a half: it was undone in the 1960s. Whether our generation can forge a new consensus that will do as well in our time and last as long as the old is being decided now.

What was this understanding? How was it verified and enforced? And what was in it for everyone concerned?

Market men—adherents of competitive individualism—won the opportunity to seek economic growth with governmental subsidy (i.e., internal improvements) and gained the stability that comes from knowing spending will be limited by willingness to increase revenues. Egalitarian republicans were able to place limits on the establishment. The supporters of social hierarchy obtained a larger role for collective concerns, provided they were able to gather sufficient revenue. No social order got purely what it wanted, but all got assurances that they would not be subject to severe disadvantages.

DEBT: THE GREAT EQUATION

The history of American attitudes toward public debt may be translated into formulas for relating revenues to expenditures that are no less powerful for being simple. The first of these budgetary great equations was simplicity itself: revenues minus interest on the public debt equaled allowable national government spending.* The new Constitution provided ample authority for all sorts of taxes including direct levies on individuals and internal excise taxes. In the debate over ratification, however, the proponents of the Constitution frequently insisted that the bulk of taxes be raised by customs duties and sale of public lands, with income and excise taxes reserved for emergencies. Despite Alexander Hamilton's major effort both to exert executive authority and simultaneously to give the government a sounder financial basis by invoking internal taxes (Forsythe 1977, p. 38), Thomas Jefferson and his republican followers soon reverted to their preferred version in which tariffs predominated. Given the widespread agreement on balanced budgets and parsimony in government as well as the desire to pay off the public debt, the first great equation had appeal.

Life soon provided the circumstances that lawyers say alter cases. In times of war, the second great equation prevailed: revenues, this time including internal taxes, equaled ordinary civilian expenditures minus wartime debt. When surpluses appeared or the attractiveness of internal im-

*See Huntington 1961 and Crecine 1961 for contemporary versions during the administrations of Harry S Truman and Dwight D. Eisenhower.

provements proved irresistible, or both, a third equation operated: revenues in surplus minus interest on debt, minus ordinary spending, minus internal improvements, equaled central government spending. It was only with the revolution in fiscal thought following the Great Depression of the 1930s that the fourth equation, sometimes called a full employment surplus, took center stage. The idea was to balance not the budget but the economy at full employment. The fourth great equation stipulated that revenues plus a deficit sufficient to secure full employment equaled spending. The formulation of a fifth equation is under discussion today.

The Constitution reacted against the Articles of Confederation. A major motivation behind the new governmental structure was to provide the national government with sufficient powers to levy taxes (without the direct concurrence of the states) so that the national credit might be placed on a firm foundation. In the first month after George Washington took office as president, and before a treasury department even existed, laws were enacted establishing customs duties and providing for their collection (Kimmel 1959, p. 8). In his reports on public credit in 1790 and 1795, Hamilton argued the imperative importance of consolidating state debts, adding them to the national debt, and arranging to fund them with revenues provided for this purpose. This was hard for his agrarian, small-farmer, Jeffersonian opponents to swallow. For one thing, much of the debt had been severely discounted and was owned by speculators who stood to gain far more than the original holders. For another, there was no way to do even rough justice to states that had done the most for the confederation during the revolutionary period but that would not gain commensurately more from Hamilton's arrangement. Yet the idea of public faith and sound credit proved as difficult to resist as the related idea that funding the debt would help to balance the budget each year, thus encouraging each generation to pay its own costs (Kimmel 1959, p. 9). The difficulty Hamilton's arguments caused his agrarian opponents was well put—in the hyperbolical style of the age—by John Taylor of Carolina:

We moderns; we enlightened Americans; we who have abolished hierarchy and title; and we who are submitting to be taxed . . . without being deluded or terrified by the promise of heaven, the denunciation of hell . . . or superstition. A spell is put on our understandings by the words "public faith and national credit." [Forsythe 1977, p. 31]

Yet, as every schoolboy knows, there was more to this victory than a magic charm. In a classic case of bargaining, Hamilton arranged the transfer of the nation's capital from New York to Washington, D.C., which was nearer Virginia and the South, in exchange for enough votes to pass the bill providing for the assumption of debt (Forsythe 1977, pp. 28–29). Critical discussion of the subject usually ends here, but this is inappropriate. Without a general consensus on the virtue of a balanced budget, this political exchange would not have been feasible. Moreover, an integral part of this outcome—the successful attack of the Republican party on the powers of the executive branch—has been left out of consideration entirely. The agrarian, egalitarian Republicans feared a return to monarchy. They did not merely agree, albeit reluctantly, to an assumption of state and national debt. With the same skill as those who sought institutional safeguards through the Constitution, they filled the interstices of the bill with practices severely limiting the executive branch's use of whatever spending powers it gained through assumption. To a staunch Federalist like Representative Fisher Ames of Massachusetts, "our proceedings smell of anarchy. . . . The heads of departments are head clerks. Instead of being . . . the organs of the executive power . . . they are precluded of late even from communication with the House reports." Having ordained that ministers shall be dumb, Ames concluded, Congress had in effect forbidden them even "to explain themselves by signs" (White 1961, p. 94). Over a century was to elapse until, in 1921, the concept

of executive responsibility for budget preparation and execution was largely, though not entirely, accepted.

President Thomas Jefferson (1801–1808) promoted a
budgetary belief corresponding to his conviction that the soil
of liberty had to be nurtured with the blood of martyrs in every generation. Thinking it wrong for one generation to bind
the next by its debts, he believed that debts, when incurred,
should be paid within the same twenty years. Jefferson
favored the lowly style and the *lingua humis* popular among
Republicans, and he viewed economy and debt payment as
necessities of a moral life. "I place economy among the first
and most important of republican virtues," he wrote, "and
public debt as the greatest of the dangers to be feared."
Though he believed that "the earth belongs always to the living generation" and therefore favored rapid retirement of
the public debt, Jefferson would have preferred to cut spending rather than raise taxes. "I am for government rigorously
frugal and simple," Jefferson wrote, "applying all the possible savings of the public revenue to the discharge of the national debt" (Kimmel 1959, p. 14).

The War of 1812 upset budgetary expectations for two
reasons: it was expensive, and it disrupted commerce, thus
reducing income. Initially the war was to be financed strictly
by debt, but by 1813 millions in internal taxes were voted,
along with rate increases on tariffs. Still, the net result of the
war was a substantial increase in debt. Taxes were willingly
paid in view of the urgency and proximity of war, but there
was substantial misgiving about the debt incurred (Kimmel
1959, pp. 27–28; Forsythe 1977, p. 60). Following Jefferson's
lead, President James Madison (1809–1817) wanted his administration "to liberate the public resources by an hon-
orable discharge of the public debt." Similarly, James
Monroe (1817–1824) and John Quincy Adams (1825–1829)
wanted to reduce debt to free the customs revenues for all
manner of wonderful things (Kimmel 1959, pp. 16–17). The
ideal of a balanced budget took on increasingly moralistic

overtones; John Quincy Adams considered its achievement "among the maxims of political economy," and his secretary of the treasury called debt reduction "amongst the highest duties of a nation" since it showed that a government was a prompt payer (Kimmel 1959, pp. 17—18). Debt reduction was a good thing either in itself or as a prelude to incurring still more. It could mean both less or more spending.

How wonderful it was! By the time of President Andrew Jackson (1829—1836), debt reduction had become a patriotic duty. Realizing that the remaining debt might be retired during his administration, Jackson waxed lyrical: "We shall then exhibit the rare example of a great nation, abounding in all the means of happiness and security, altogether free from debt." American exceptionalism was publicly proclaimed when Secretary of the Treasury Levi Woodbury heralded the extinction of the debt as an "unprecedented spectacle . . . presented to the world" (Kimmel 1959, pp. 19—21).

Then, from within the wellsprings of abundance, the specter of a corresponding evil surfaced: "the unnecessary accumulation of public revenue," as Andrew Jackson called it, or more simply, a surplus. Why should this cornucopia be an embarrassment? Because, President Martin Van Buren (1837—1841) remarked, governments would be "constantly exposed to great deficiencies or excesses, with all their attended embarrassments." In his last annual message, Van Buren argued that the surplus "would foster national extravagance," and thus would encourage rapid accumulation of a larger and more onerous debt. His theory was that if a government did not have revenues, it could not spend them. Once a surplus existed, added spending would be too tempting to resist, and a vicious cycle of increasing expenditures would begin (Kimmel 1959, pp. 21—22).

American presidents did not believe government spending would further redistribution from the rich to the poor; on the contrary, "melancholy is the condition of that people," President Polk (1845—1849) wrote, "whose government can be sustained only by a system which periodically transfers large amounts from the labors of the many to the coffers of the few" (Kimmel 1959, p. 23). For these men, as for the citizens they governed, debt was equated with privilege.

Faith in the balanced budget ideal was strengthened by an economic theory that tied wages negatively to debt. As Secretary of the Treasury Robert J. Walker claimed in 1838: "Wages can only be increased in any nation, in the aggregate, by augmenting capital, the fund out of which wages are paid. . . . The destruction or diminution of capital, by destroying or reducing the fund from which labor is paid, must reduce wages." This wage-fund argument had the added value of suggesting that the wage earner would be hurt by any effort to go into debt to improve his lot (Kimmel 1959, pp. 24–25). It is essential to understand that the "progressive" opinion of the Jacksonian era believed that government took from—not gave to—the common man. The animus of the Jacksonians was reserved for government-sponsored privileges—banks, charters, monopolies. The economic liberty upon which political liberty depended was, in their view, best assured by eliminating the artificial privilege government introduced into the natural equality of men (Blau 1954).

During the recession of 1837 and 1838, when efforts were made to increase federal spending in order to alleviate suffering, President Van Buren invoked the sagacity of the Founding Fathers, who "wisely judged that the less government interferes with private pursuits the better for the general prosperity." The economy would improve through a reduction in the deficit, not through the construction of railroads or canals. President Buchanan blamed the financial panic and recession of 1857 and 1858 on "the habit of extravagant expenditures" (Kimmel 1959, pp. 25–26).

INTERNAL IMPROVEMENTS

Support for and opposition to internal improvements waxed and waned for the thirty years before the Civil War. The Jacksonians believed that interest payment on the national debt meant a redistribution of income from poorer to richer people, that the funds from which wages were drawn were depressed by such payments, and that the capital released from government spending into private hands would increase productivity and therefore wages. Consequently, in their view, disapproval of internal improvements went hand in hand with a public policy favoring the ordinary citizen. Favoring the common man, in those days, meant favoring individual and not governmental enterprise (Kimmel 1959, p. 19; White 1951, p. 483). President Polk, while vetoing a rivers and harbors bill, asked what would stop "a disreputable scramble for public money" if all that remained were congressional discretion as to the fitness of things. In Polk's view, internal improvements were "capable of indefinite enlargement and sufficient to swallow up as many millions annually as could be extracted from the foreign commerce of the country." Allied with a protective tariff that brought in ever-larger sums, Polk believed that "the operation and necessary effect of the whole system would encourage large and extravagant expenditures, and thereby . . . increase the public patronage, and maintain a rich and splendid government at the expense of a taxed and impoverished people" (Kimmel 1959, pp. 31–32).

If it was money that mattered to Polk, it was public morality that presidents Pierce and Buchanan cared about. They rejected internal improvements on constitutional grounds because they usurped state functions. The two presidents saw internal improvement as a means by which the general government would aggrandize itself at the expense of states (Kimmel 1959, pp. 34–35). Congressional advocates like

Henry Clay produced one bill after another to expand internal improvements. For other leading men of the day, however, from Daniel Webster to John Calhoun and President Millard Fillmore, the great issue was the growth of the nation. They believed that, while the work might be done locally, it had a general or national importance.

For the federal government, the era before the Civil War remained a time of tiny government. Between 1800 and 1860, as table 1 shows, federal expenditures rose from near $11 to $63 million in total. More than half were military expenditures. The general category of "Civil and miscellaneous" included a substantial amount for the postal deficit, thus covering everything except defense, pensions, Indians, and interest on the debt. Kimmel (1959, p. 57) is correct in his conclusion: "Federal expenditures made little or no contribution to the level of living. Only a minor portion of Civil and miscellaneous expenditures were for developmental purposes."

Table 1
Federal Expenditures, Fiscal Years 1800, 1825, 1850, and 1860
(in millions of dollars)

	1800	1825	1850	1860
Civil and miscellaneous	1.3	2.7	14.9	28.0*
War Department	2.6	3.7	9.4	16.4
Navy Department	3.4	3.1	7.9	11.5
Indians	—	0.7	1.6	2.9
Pensions	0.1	1.3	1.9	1.1
Interest	3.4	4.4	3.8	3.2
Total	$10.8	$15.9	$39.5	$63.1*

Source: *Annual Report of the Secretary of the Treasury on the State of the Finances for the Fiscal Year Ended June 30, 1934*, pp. 302–3.

*Includes postal deficit of $9.9 million.

CHANGE IN CONSENSUS

The Civil War of 1860–1865 marked the first break in the consensus on debt reduction. Balanced budgets, to be sure, remained the norm, but the growth of presidential discretion and the rise of industrial expansion left the role of debt open to argument. Abraham Lincoln (1860–1865) thought that citizens "cannot be much oppressed by a debt which they owe to themselves." His idea, followed by President Rutherford B. Hayes a decade later (1877–1881), was to secure a wider distribution of the debt among citizens. Considering that the debt might be paid over time, President Ulysses S. Grant (1869–1877), usually not considered a father of supply-side economics, asserted that the capacity to pay grew with the wealth of the nation. Rather than raise taxes to pay the debt in a shorter time, he would cut taxes to increase wealth and hence provide greater subsequent revenues (Kimmel 1959, pp. 65–69). During a time of expansion, the desire for internal improvements seemed compatible with fiscal prudence.

As a consequence of these developments, the government grew from tiny to small. It promoted the interests of businessmen and farmers, sometimes aiding railroads and other times intervening to regulate railroads in the interests of farmers. Beginning with the Morrill Act of 1862, which gave huge land grants to states for the purpose of establishing agricultural and mechanical universities, various measures were adopted to aid education. In general, presidents of the post–Civil War era, like Thomas Jefferson before them, regarded education as an exception to whatever strictures they laid upon unnecessary expenditures. And as the nation was settled and the frontier neared its end, the beginnings of a movement to set aside land for conservation purposes appeared. But it is not in these modest departures from the strict doctrine of the minimum state that one can find the sources of budgetary conflict or the seeds of future spending.

Money may or may not be the root of all evil. But the availability of substantial surpluses in the post—Civil War period
proved a greater temptation than most private interests and
public officials were able to withstand. No one can say
whether it was the change in national opinion attendant on
the swift pace of the industrial revolution, or whether it was
the huge revenues generated by the growing protective tariff
or the attendant changes in the process of budgeting that
mattered most. Suffice it to say that soon enough even the
$3 billion Civil War debt became readily manageable and
higher tariffs still produced substantial surpluses.

Despite the considerable increase in population and
wealth, President Andrew Johnson (1865–1869) was
startled to learn that expenditures during his term would be
around $1.6 billion, only slightly less than the entire amount
for the seventy-year-plus period from 1789 to 1861. He
feared that per capita expenditure would reach nearly $10,
whereas before the war expenditure had been held to $2 per
person. He responded by urging retrenchment. Expressing
the prevailing sentiment, Grant's secretary of the treasury,
George S. Boutwell, claimed in 1870 that "a public debt is a
public evil," especially injurious to working people (Kimmel
1959, p. 68).

Grover Cleveland (1885–1889) believed that withdrawing
capital from the people and transferring it to government
imperiled their prosperity. His words were a last stand
against the spending boom that followed (Kimmel 1959, pp.
71–73):

When we consider that the theory of our institutions guarantees to
every citizen the full enjoyment of all the fruits of his industry and
enterprise, with only such deduction as may be his share toward
the careful and economical maintenance of the Government which
protects him, it is plain that the exaction of more than this is
indefensible extortion and a culpable betrayal of American fairness and justice. This wrong inflicted upon those who bear the
burden of national taxation, like other wrongs, multiplies a brood
of evil consequences. The public Treasury, which should only exist

as a conduit conveying the people's tribute to its legitimate objects of expenditure, becomes a hoarding place for money needlessly withdrawn from trade and the people's use, thus crippling our national energies.

Between 1870 and 1902 there was no growth in per capita expenditures in the federal government. Spending in absolute terms increased approximately 3.3 percent per year, but gross national product (GNP), adjusted for inflation, increased by more than 5 percent per year. Thus the federal sector of government was continuously growing smaller in regard to size of the economy (Borcherding 1977*b*, p. 20). Using 1902 as a benchmark, federal spending constituted 2.4 percent of GNP. By 1922 this had more than doubled, to 5.1 percent. Nonfederal spending had also grown, but not as quickly, from 4.4 to 7.5 percent of GNP.

Viewing debt as something a people owes itself (to be judged not as an inherent evil, but relative to a country's ability to pay) is not far from the idea that the size of the deficit matters less than the government's (and through it, the people's) return on monies expended. The presidents from 1898 to 1920 (McKinley, Roosevelt, Taft, and Wilson) were all opposed to unbalanced budgets—or so they said, because the number of deficits began to increase at a rapid rate. For this new breed of presidents, efficient organization, and "value for money" as the English say today, mattered more than parsimony (Kimmel 1959, pp. 84–85). The American people, Woodrow Wilson said, "are not jealous of the amount their Government costs if they are sure that they get what they need and desire for the outlay, that money is being spent for objects of which they approve, and that it is being applied with good business sense and management" (Kimmel 1959, pp. 87–88). Whether the idea was to do what was being done at less expense, or to do more, was left unclear.

Fiscal prudence, both against the growing debt and for a balanced budget, reasserted itself in the 1920s. World War I had largely been fought on borrowed money. From 1914 to 1918 the government's role in directing economic activity expanded enormously. In response, there was sudden public concern that the profligate habits of wartime would carry over into peacetime civilian life. The Victory Liberty Loan Act of 1919 established a sinking fund to reduce the debt, which was cut by a third, from $24 to $16 billion by the end of the decade. Wilson's secretary of the treasury, Carter Glass, pointed out the "grave danger that the extraordinary success of the Treasury in financing the stupendous war expenditures may lead to a riot of public expenditures after the war, the consequences of which could only be disastrous." His successor under President Harding (1921–1923), David F. Huston, similarly observed that "we have demobilized many groups, but we have not demobilized those whose gaze is concentrated on the Treasury" (Kimmel 1959, p. 88).

The Budget Act of 1921 was thought by its sponsors to be the reform to end all reforms. The executive budget—introduced by the president with the aid of his new Bureau of the Budget through which all agency requests had to go—would simultaneously introduce order, expertise, and economy. And for a time there was more of all of these good things. But not for long. Just as there was more volatility in the money supply after the creation of the Federal Reserve Bank than before (Friedman and Schwartz 1963, pp. 9–10), spending expanded much more rapidly after than before 1921. Those of us (present company included) enamored of structural solutions may say that the Budget Act of 1921 did not change basic political incentives, which is true enough, but the other truth is that life overwhelmed the expectations of the reformers. There was greater coherence, which was expected, but also far greater spending, which was not.

Then came the market crash of 1929 followed by the depression of the 1930s, the worst in U.S. history. The depression marked both an end to emphasis on the balanced budget and a beginning of an attempt to stabilize the economy through variable expenditure techniques. Under Keynesian doctrine, the unbalanced budget became a virtue, as automatic stabilizers adjusted the economy. Whatever merit it had as theory, the unbalanced budget had strong social implications as well. So long as economic growth was maintained, all doctrines would work. But if it slowed down, shares in the nation's income would still have to be allocated. The doctrine of budget balance served to restrain the struggle over shares. It legitimated a minimal role for government in income redistribution. But when the heirs of Jefferson and Jackson concluded that only a strong central government could tame the power of the corporation, the alliance that created American exceptionalism was broken. The alliance of political egalitarianism with economic individualism, reinforced by the belief that equality of opportunity would lead to equality of result, has come apart. It remains to be seen whether there will be a new alliance among social orders reflected in refurbishing the balanced budget norm or in replacing it entirely with another doctrine and practice.

3

GEORGE F. BREAK

Government Spending Trends in the Postwar Period

Measuring the expansion of government programs. The Sixteenth Amendment. The social security system. Postwar role changes. Intergovernmental involvements. Categoricals, block grants, revenue sharing. Tax subsidies; loan and regulatory programs.

The world's most powerful democracy has elected to its highest office a candidate who presented himself as a kind of St. George, set to do battle with the voracious dragon of Big Government. Even as that campaign was gaining momentum, economists struggling with the complex task of measuring the dimensions of that monster were adducing evidence that while its lineaments have greatly changed and mushroomed in size during the past fifty years, some of the most important of them have actually shrunk of late in proportion to the nation's total output while others have grown apace. Government is multidimensional: the diverse trends of its growth are too kaleidoscopic to fit into a single, coherent picture. Their intricate complexity has much to do with the "unexpected difficulties" the dragon-slaying administration has encountered in its efforts to bring the monster to bay. The labyrinth of government expenditure trends is hard enough to trace, let alone to control.

MEASURING GOVERNMENT EXPENDITURE

Anyone trying to make ends meet today on the same number of dollars as a decade ago knows the meaning of "real" income. Government budgets have been no better treated by inflation than private ones. Yet inflation is only one of many factors to be considered in measuring the government's growth, for it is not just price-adjusted government spending that is of primary interest, but rather the growth of government relative to the whole economy. Growth rates of the private and public sectors can readily be measured and compared in nominal dollar terms, and much can be learned simply by studying the ratios of different kinds of government spending to gross national product (GNP; see figure 1). However, if one wants to take the next logical step of comparing real output trends in the two sectors, or of relating total price-adjusted government expenditures to real GNP, serious difficulties are immediately encountered.

Quality differences (and therefore, true costs) are hard enough to measure in inanimate goods. How much more costly,

Figure 1
Federal Budget Outlays as a Percent of GNP[1]

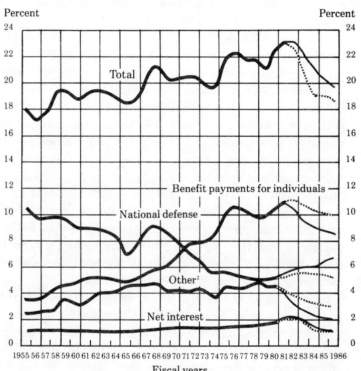

Source: Carlson 1981, pp. 31–39.

[1]Estimates for 1981–1986 are alternative projections: dashed lines are Congressional Budget Office baseline projections and solid lines are administration projections from *Mid-Session Review of the 1982 Budget* (July 1981).
[2]Other federal operations, plus grants to state and local governments other than benefit payments for individuals.

for example, is today's expensive but sophisticatedly computerized cash register, which performs multiple managerial functions, than yesterday's machine that did little more than add up and record receipts? Quality comparisons are still more elusive when it comes to human services. As government employees become more experienced and draw higher salaries, are they providing more effective and more valuable services? Or are they simply adding more subtle and complex dimensions to the paper shuffle? And can it be assumed that equivalent salaries yield equivalent services in the public and private sectors? These intractable questions make it hard to evaluate the rise in costs of that portion of government expenditure that buys goods and compensates government employees. But the difficulties of measuring the total increase in government's share of the economy are further compounded by the fact that a large and growing part of the budget is not spent to buy goods and services for government but goes directly into the pockets of private individuals in the form of retirement benefits, welfare payments, and the like. The purchasing power, and hence the real value, of these transfers is determined in the private—not the public—sector of the economy.

Economists wrestling with these complex problems are endeavoring to devise and refine a methodology for measuring government growth. While many simplistic assumptions are still necessary, different "deflators" are being devised for different types of expenditure. So-called "exhaustive" expenditures (purchases of goods and services) are differentiated from "transfers" (direct payments to people in the private sector), and separate adjustment factors are applied to employee compensation and purchases from private firms. The result is a weighted price index that not only makes for a clearer picture of government growth in the United States, but permits comparison with other industrialized countries (see Beck 1981).

When this kind of weighted price index is applied on a

step-by-step basis to the U.S. economy during the past half century, it appears that in real terms government more than doubled in relative size over the whole period. When analyzed more closely, however, the pattern of growth is seen to be neither stable nor steady. Different components changed at very different rates, and the combined size not only stopped getting bigger after 1969 (as measured in constant dollars), but actually decreased slightly. That, for advocates of reduced government, was the good news. The bad news was that the decline was in purchases of goods and services, which lend themselves comparatively readily to administrative control; in contrast, transfer payments, under entitlement programs such as social security, were rising at a rate that outstripped the growth of the economy as a whole (see figure 2). Moderating transfer outlays means involving the entire political system in some very difficult and painful decisions. Worse still, these difficulties were exacerbated by the postwar trend in national defense spending. Declining from 10 percent of GNP in 1958 to only 5 percent in 1979–1980, it permitted—and no doubt partially caused—a relatively painless expansion of federal transfer programs. This trend was all too easy to get used to, but in the nature of the case it could not continue indefinitely. By the end of the period international tensions were beginning to increase, and with the inauguration of the Reagan administration, national spending priorities were suddenly reversed.

THE GROWTH OF U.S. GOVERNMENT

The metamorphosis of that original government of "delegated and limited powers" into the behemoth of today dramatizes graphically the changing expectations of a developing nation's citizenry. It is true that the fiscal role of the federal government during the nineteenth century has been grossly underestimated in the standard perception of U.S. history, owing to the failure of many historians to understand the tremendous economic impact of federal land grants (which heavily and continuously subsidized such national interests as a transportation network and public education systems). Yet until the 1930s, government—outside the military and diplomatic arenas—was to most Americans largely identified with the housekeeping and basic service functions of state and local agencies. In retrospect, of course, a number of significant moves can be recognized as having prepared the way for the cataclysmic revolution in government responsibility that arose from the economic and social chaos of the Great Depression. Chief among these moves, insofar as it made the vast extension of federal government fiscally possible, was the adoption in 1913 of the Sixteenth Amendment to the Constitution, legalizing a federal tax on income. With the supply of public lands largely exhausted, Washington needed a new and major fiscal base. The ability to levy a direct tax on the incomes of individual citizens (a right explicitly denied by the original Constitution) not only provided the federal government with a rich source of revenue, but established a totally new and unprecedented personal link between that government and the people. Although the relatively high exemption level subjected only a small fraction of the population to the income tax for many years, it constituted a direct channel that opened vast fiscal possibilities for Washington and, conversely, led in time to widening expectations on the part of the citizenry.

This is not to say that Big Government followed quickly upon the heels of the Sixteenth Amendment. The bulge in federal spending for World War I subsided quickly in the 1920s, and the government that Franklin Roosevelt took charge of in 1933 was small in scale and cautious. Total federal expenditures in that year amounted to about $4 billion (just over 7 percent of GNP), while state and local govern-

Figure 2

Percentage Composition of Federal Budget Outlays[1]

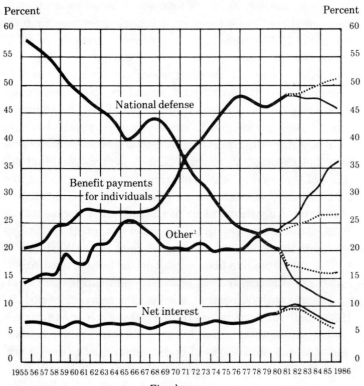

Source: Carlson 1981, pp. 31–39.

[1]Estimates for 1981–1986 are alternative projections: dashed lines are Congressional Budget Office baseline projections and solid lines are administration projections from *Mid-Session Review of the 1982 Budget* (July 1981).
[2]Other federal operations, plus grants to state and local governments other than benefit payments for individuals.

ments, shattered as their revenue bases were by the depression, were spending $6.7 billion (12 percent of GNP).*

By 1934 a federal government still wary of large-scale deficits was spending $6.4 billion, a total that almost matched the depression low of $6.5 billion spent by states and localities (all three levels together accounting for less than 20 percent of GNP). Although, except for a sizable dip in 1937, the dollar amounts edged upward during the next few depression years, government spending never reached 20 percent of GNP until 1941, at which time war costs skyrocketed it to more than 40 percent. With the return of peace, total government expenditures dropped back to approximately their prewar level, though the spending pattern had assumed an entirely new structure. Washington's share of the pie was dominant from that time on, accounting for two-thirds or more of total government expenditures.

The relatively modest size of the federal sector as late as 1939 should not obscure the enormity of the changes wrought during the depression decade. The Washington, D.C., of the 1920s had little impact on the lives of most Americans. Even though federal grants-in-aid to states and localities increased 400 percent during that ten-year period, by 1930 they still totaled less than $150 million, going mainly for highways, the National Guard, forestry, and conservation. And the entire federal budget amounted to only 3 percent of GNP. What happened between 1929 and 1939, though, caused a major revolution in fiscal federalism. The fact that the federal sector quadrupled as a percentage of GNP was the least remarkable of these changes. Of much greater significance was the general acquiescence in Washington's assumption of responsibilities far transcending the scope of federal powers as understood by most Americans since the establishment of the Union.

*These figures are from the national income and product accounts, which include grants-in-aid to state and local governments in the federal totals and exclude them from the recipients' totals. See *Facts and Figures on Government Finance*, 21st biennial edition (1981), p. 36.

The rapidity with which these changes took place was born of necessity. Skyrocketing unemployment and growing bread lines demonstrated the inadequacy of state and local public welfare services, which were still cast largely in the mold of the British Poor Law tradition. Within two years of the New Deal's inception, a network of programs had been enacted to relieve immediate need (such as general assistance and work relief), to revitalize the economy (such as farm subsidies and business loans), and to provide long-term safeguards against future economic collapse (such as insurance against bank failures, crop failures, and unemployment). The most significant innovation of all was the social security system, launched in 1935 as a rather conservative social insurance program but within four years redesigned to become the comprehensive and significantly redistributive income support program that is a major concern of budget-makers today.

From the beginning the social security system incorporated two different kinds of long-term protection against poverty. One was a set of categorical welfare programs to provide assistance for the needy aged, blind, and dependent children. The other was a retirement insurance program, financed by a payroll tax on wages that was split equally between workers and employers. Although benefits were from the outset scheduled on a progressive basis with proportionately more generous payouts for lower wage earners, there was a relatively strong relationship between contributions and entitlements, and coverage extended only to the workers themselves. Even before the trust fund had accumulated to the point at which the first payments were to be made, however, the amendments of 1939 restructured the benefit basis and added supplementary payments for workers' dependents. This general redirection has been greatly fortified by subsequent changes, extending coverage to include more people and more causes of income loss (e.g., disability coverage, added in 1956) and significantly raising benefit standards. As a result, income maintenance has been put far ahead of actuarial equity as the underlying principle.

The significance of the social security system, especially as redirected in 1939, is hard to overestimate. For the first time the federal government assumed responsibility not merely for providing public services and emergency protection against military and economic crises, but for overseeing and carrying out a broad-scale program of income redistribution. By a combination of progressive income tax and payroll taxes that redistributed income from high- to low-wage workers, large sectors of the population were guaranteed protection against income loss from a constantly expanding range of foreseeable contingencies. The constitutional injunction to "provide for the general welfare" had assumed totally new connotations with the birth of the welfare state.

Although World War II propelled the nation's economy back to full productivity, the restoration of peace brought no return to the days of small-scale, decentralized government. Like a trumpet call announcing the advent of a new era, the Full Employment Act of 1946 proclaimed the formal departure of U.S. government policy from the concept that Washington's job was to balance its budget and let business run the economy. For better or for worse, the federal government was now to become a full partner in the management of the economy, gearing tax and expenditure decisions to needs determined by the business cycle. Stabilizing the economy so as to "promote maximum employment, production, and purchasing power" ("a dollar of stable value" was added to this list in 1953) was declared the new national goal. This pronouncement far transcended the Monroe Doctrine as a momentous statement of U.S. government policy.

Postwar federal spending

Just as the Great Depression demonstrated the incapacity of the private sector to cope satisfactorily with severe business gyrations, World War II showed that government spending can not only achieve high levels of employment, but (given the right conditions) can run up substantial deficits without generating uncontrollable inflationary pressures. With the United States emerging from the war as the richest and most productive nation on earth, the partnership forged in wartime between business and government continued for an extended period to return big dividends. War-devastated Europe and Japan, plus continents full of nonindustrialized nations eager to develop their economies, created an immense market that the U.S. government was happy to supply with capital and that U.S. business was happy to supply with goods and services. If the distinction between public and private sectors was often blurred, few people minded as long as both were prospering.

The Eisenhower administration came into office with the stated intention of untangling the complex intergovernmental and regulatory relationships that muddled lines of authority and responsibility among government levels and between government and business. Ironically, it succeeded only in entangling itself even further in partnership arrangements. Prodded by the postwar boom in babies and automobiles, Washington poured out capital to finance construction of housing, schools, and highways. Shocked by Sputnik, the government showered money upon schools to enrich their instructional programs. Even its sustained attempt to make a clear separation between state and federal functions and revenue sources made little progress.

The Kennedy administration had very different goals in mind. Dreams of active federal participation in the maintenance of a full employment economy were revived, and the young but still fiscally conservative president was persuaded by his brain trust of liberal economists to make vigorous use of fiscal policy. In the face of a lagging economy, they won his somewhat reluctant consent to push through a tax cut in order to stimulate private spending; and with the success of that move they formulated a bold new plan of tax sharing that they hoped would permanently enable the federal government to give state governments greater fiscal strength and stability. The untimely death of President Kennedy turned this question of unrestricted general assistance grants (or "revenue sharing") over to Lyndon Johnson, who opted instead for a huge expansion of categorical grants to be targeted to designated national problems and administered from Washington.

The Great Society aimed at nothing less than the elimination of poverty. Its fiscal weaponry had all the precision of musket fire and cannonade. It was aimed, more or less simultaneously, at a wide spectrum of symptoms and presumed causes. The deterioration of cities, dramatized by riots and arson, was responded to by a doubling of financial aid (in real terms) to urban areas between 1964 and 1969. Categorical aid under the social security system was liberalized and made more accessible, with the result that Aid to Families with Dependent Children more than doubled between 1965 and 1969 and had doubled again by 1972. Medical assistance to the needy (Medicaid) climbed even faster, and the addition of Medicare to the system's Old Age, Survivors, and Disability Insurance program introduced entitlements that in the first decade (1966–1975) expanded from $1 billion to over $15 billion. This proliferation of income support programs and special assistance for the poor continued during the 1970s, with liberalization and extension of the food stamp program, addition of Supplemental Security Income (SSI) to the categorical aids section of social security, and increases in the duration of entitlements to unemployment insurance benefits.

Another area of government that burgeoned under targeted federal aid during the 1960s was education. The Kennedy administration hoped to get at the root causes of poverty and unemployment by funding broad-scale programs aimed at training disadvantaged young people. Those modest beginnings took a great leap forward under Johnson's Great Society with the 1965 passage of the Elementary and Secondary Education Act and the Higher Education Act. The battle for civil rights and the War on Poverty were merged, and the schools became a principal operational center. Aside from effecting changes in school curricula and social climate, the infusion of categorical federal grants into school budgets resulted in important alterations in their shape and form. For example, the typical urban school district greatly expanded its staff, both instructional and administrative, so as to cope with the new curricular and paperwork requirements. Under the tenure provisions of state education codes, many of the new teaching personnel (even those with skills limited to the needs of special categorical areas) became after two or three years permanent responsibilities of school districts. For ambitious administrators, this meant establishing strong lines to Washington, becoming adept at grantsmanship, and often playing nimble budgetary games to keep afloat between influxes of federal money. The typically conservative approach to school budgeting, which calls for underestimating expected revenues so as to assure a safe contingency fund, became too restrictive for many liberal districts. With federal money flowing freely into innovative projects, it became tempting to draw up budgets that assumed a generous influx of new grants.

Thus the Great Society not only broadened the areas of social responsibility, but also vastly complicated the entangled network of intergovernmental fiscal relationships. The veritable forest of vertical alliances that arose between Washington and nearly every kind of local government did not stop there but extended beyond, to thousands of subgovernmental and paragovernmental community groups set up to provide special services and to train previously inactive citizens in the mechanics and possibilities of the democratic process. By the time the Nixon administration took office, Washington's involvement with governing agencies at every level, and with citizens' groups eager to secure the blessings of liberty, was so complex that one of the first major calls of the incoming president was for a "new federalism."

As originally outlined, the Nixon program did not envisage any substantial reduction of governmental responsibility, but rather a restructuring and consolidating of programs that in categorical form were fragmented and frequently redundant. It also called for giving the states, which had often been bypassed, an important intermediary role in the distribution of federal funds. And it recommended the initiation of a program of general revenue sharing.

Developments in revenue sharing

Congress was far less interested than the president in sharing federal revenue with the states and giving up direct control over identifiable grants for which they could take credit and with which they could build solid constituencies. So after a long interval of inaction, President Nixon recast his proposal to recommend restructuring welfare and creating a dual system of revenue sharing that would provide some general purpose funds and some "special revenue sharing" or block grants to be allocated to broad but designated areas. After long debate, a program of general revenue sharing was enacted—though it had little resemblance to the plan envisaged nearly a decade before by Walter Heller, which would have made the states long-term partners in the federal income tax and allowed them maximum flexibility in the use of the funds. Various restrictive conditions were attached to the new program. It was approved for four years only, with no assurance of renewal. It apportioned money on the basis of a complex pair of formulas that made many jurisdictions feel shortchanged. Bureaucratic restrictions were attached that diminished the net value to the recipients. And Washington failed to make clear whether revenue sharing was expected to supplement categorical programs or replace them. So it fell far short of effecting the comprehensive rationalization of intergovernmental finance its originators had hoped for. When renewed in 1976, it was loaded with even more restrictions and mandates, and was given a fixed level of funding that shrank its value as inflation soared.

Meanwhile, block grants, as the direct descendents of "special" revenue sharing, were developing into a third major component of the federal grant system. The two main ones—the Comprehensive Employment and Training Act of 1973 (CETA), and community development block grants (CDBGs; 1974)—illustrate the seemingly insuperable difficulties of getting rid of established programs or even of reformulating them. They also demonstrate the strength of a kind of Gresham's law of politics—that short-run objectives drive out long-term ones. CETA was born of the hope that the maze of categorical, hard-core unemployment programs developed in response to the Watts and other riots of the 1960s could be consolidated and streamlined into a flexible and effective means of turning unemployed, underemployed, and disadvantaged members of society into productive citizens. Permanent employment in the private sector was the long-term goal. Unfortunately, the block grant concept was not sufficiently developed to overcome an inherent resistance to change reinforced by the immediate employment requirements of the recession of 1974–1975. As a result, training for permanent employment in the private sector became a decreasingly important feature of CETA, while the provision of short-term public service jobs became the major focus—largely accounting for the more than 500 percent increase in the program's budget during the Carter years. Community development block grants followed a somewhat similar course, with entrenched categorical recipients in the community development area protecting themselves, while vacillating direction from Washington made long-term planning all but impossible for many communities. Although not living up to the dreams that had spawned them, both block grant programs soon became major items in local budgets, thus contributing importantly to an increasing dependency upon Washington.

The postwar period, then, has witnessed major developments in intergovernmental fiscal relations. Whereas the federal government was the dominant provider of goods and services during the 1950s—12 percent of GNP in 1951, compared to the state and local sectors' 7 percent—these roles were reversed between 1967, when the GNP share of both sectors was 11 percent, and 1980, when the shares were 8 percent for the federal and 13 percent for state and local governments. While yielding place as a provider, the federal government increasingly became the country's great fiscal intermediary. As such, it collects money from taxpayers and redistributes it in transfer payments to other private individuals and in grants to state and local governments. These transfers and grants grew rapidly in size and complexity until they collided in the early 1980s with rising defense expenditures and falling federal income tax rates. It remains to be seen whether that collision will effect any major change in the configuration of fiscal federalism. Federal/local fiscal relations have become an important new element in the federal system, at the same time that the state/local fiscal nexus has tightened.

The transfer payments to individuals have had significant redistributive effects. Improvements have not come cheaply, as costs rose from $31.5 billion in 1965 to over $293 billion by 1981, or, as percentages of GNP, from 4.6 percent to 10 percent (see figure 3). Yet they have had an enormous effect on reducing the incidence of poverty. These transfers are of two kinds: cash and in-kind. Cash transfers alone (from programs such as social security, unemployment insurance, Workers' Compensation, Aid to Families with Dependent Children, Supplemental Security Income, and veterans' pensions) have had an important impact. In 1965 they kept 27 percent of the people who might have been below the poverty

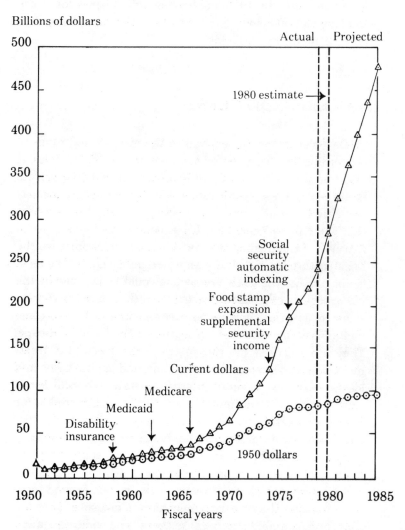

Figure 3
Outlays for Benefit Payments for Individuals
(fiscal years 1950–1985)

Billions of dollars

Actual   Projected

1980 estimate →

Social
security
automatic
indexing

Food stamp
expansion
supplemental
security
income

Current dollars

Medicare

Medicaid

Disability
insurance

1950 dollars

Fiscal years

Source: Congressional Budget Office 1980a. See Carlson 1981, pp. 15–24.

level out of that category; by 1978 the figure had risen to 44 percent. When in-kind transfers (from Medicare and Medicaid, food stamps, and housing assistance) are added to the cash payments, moreover, the results are far more impressive, producing a 78 percent reduction in the poverty-level population by 1980 and leaving only 4.1 percent of the total population below the poverty line (Danziger, Haveman, and Plotnick 1981, p. 1009).

TAX EXPENDITURES

While government was expanding the number and range of concerns being financed by tax revenue and debt issues, it was also increasing its fiscal involvement with the private sector along a less visible dimension. Numerous private sector activities and groups were being supported by a device that came to be known as "tax expenditures"—i.e., special features of the income tax law designed not to improve the tax structure but to achieve approved public goals. The term is apt because the goals in question could be pursued by the use of regular expenditure programs rather than tax concessions. Income tax loopholes, as everyone knows, have become an increasingly controversial feature of the fiscal landscape. They are a diverse lot, ranging from the special tax treatment accorded savings for retirement and capital gains and losses, to the exclusion of interest on state and local bonds from the taxable income of bondholders, to tax credits for business investment, to deductions—for charitable contributions, for interest paid on home mortgages and consumer credit, and for state/local income, sales, and property taxes paid by workers and investors.

As extensions of government activity, tax expenditures are anomalies that are extremely hard to measure. They are conceptually ambiguous because there is no wide agreement on what constitutes the best—i.e., most equitable and efficient—income tax base. One person's essential structural refinement is often another's unwarranted concession to special interests. Some, such as excess business depreciation, are hard to measure because there are no objective market-generated prices to measure "ordinary and necessary" depreciation. More important, the revenue losses caused by each of the 104 separate tax expenditures officially recognized in 1982 are estimated on the assumption that all other items remain part of the tax law. Since the presence (or absence) of one item frequently affects the revenue lost because of another, a meaningful revenue loss total cannot be derived simply by adding up each of the individual loss estimates, though popular discussions of tax expenditures tend to revolve around such apocryphal data.

The question of greatest public interest is how fast tax expenditures are growing. Official tabulations do indeed show rapid growth. From 50 items with estimated revenue losses totaling $36.5 billion in 1967, federal tax expenditures had by fiscal 1980 expanded to 92 items and $181.5 billion. That is a growth of 397 percent, as compared to only 260–270 percent for federal government receipts and expenditures and 230 percent for gross national product over the same period. These tabulations, and the separate estimates from which they are derived, are unfortunately not very useful to anyone interested in the size and growth of federal government. One cannot ignore them because some do have important economic effects, which could have been generated by standard spending programs that would be included in anyone's measure of government size. On the other hand, one cannot use them as they stand because of the conceptual ambiguities, measurement problems, and aggregation biases just noted. A more useful listing would give several alternative revenue loss estimates for each of the ambiguous tax expenditure items so that users could construct their own measures. For example, the official list now in-

cludes all features of the tax law that have some purpose
other than defining income in the particular way specified by
the government as the best attainable tax base. Two objec-
tions may be made to these procedures. Many users are likely
to find the government's optimal definition different from
their own. Others may object to the breadth of the official
concept of tax expenditures. Since most tax policies are
adopted for a variety of reasons, some structural and some
not, a good case can be made for restricting the concept of tax
expenditures to those features of the law whose nonstruc-
tural, incentive aspects are judged more important than
their structural aspects.

The full story of the economic role of federal tax expenditures has yet to be told. Moreover, the very nature of this
shadowy and elusive aspect of government activity may keep
it from ever being clearly understood. Taxing and spending
constitute a far easier equation to analyze than nontaxing
and surrogate spending.

FEDERAL CREDIT PROGRAMS

There is still another means by which the federal government
has a major economic impact on the private sector—credit
programs. Federal loan programs are extremely diverse and
take four different forms: direct loans, guaranteed loans, insured loans, and government-sponsored agency loans. All of
them add to the complexity of measuring the size and scope of
government and to the difficulty of making a clear distinction
between the public and the private sectors.

The Great Depression generated the first major cluster of
insured and guaranteed loan programs through the institution of the Commodity Credit Corporation, the Export-Import
Bank, the Reconstruction Finance Corporation, and the
Federal Housing Authority. These extremely active agencies,

which stimulate and subsidize important segments of the economy, impose relatively little out-of-pocket cost on the federal government (principally administrative expenses and payments of losses on defaulted loans), but the loans they guarantee are a major contingent governmental liability. Their initial impact can vary all the way from supplying some borrowers with funds that they could not otherwise have obtained at all, to providing other borrowers with credit on more lenient terms than they could have secured elsewhere.

Another important federal credit development was the creation of a number of off-budget direct lending programs in the 1970s. The activities of these agencies are by law excluded from the unified federal budget even though their impacts on domestic credit markets are exactly the same as those of any on-budget, direct-lending agency that obtains its funds by borrowing from the public. The most important of the off-budget agencies is the Federal Financing Bank (FFB), which began operations in May 1974. Created to eliminate the inefficiencies inherent in the separate and uncoordinated borrowing operations of many different federal credit programs, the FFB soon became a kind of fairy godmother to those agencies, supplying funds not subject to normal budgetary reviews or controls. Such efficiency did not fail to attract patronage. Net funds advanced under federal auspices, shown annually in *Special Analyses of the United States Budget,* rose from 11 percent of total funds supplied in U.S. credit markets in fiscal 1976 to 23 percent in 1980. In that same year the Carter administration reacted to this rapid, relatively uncontrolled growth by creating a separate Federal Credit Budget. It was designed to consolidate data on all federal credit programs—on- and off-budget, direct and guaranteed loans. The underlying purpose was to focus attention not on the net advances (loan disbursements minus principal repayments) stressed in the unified budget, but on new commitments of loan funds, since that is the control point at which federal lending operations may be either expanded or contracted. As fate would have it, this new budget instrument was put to its first use by the Reagan administration in the proposal to cut $20 billion from new federal credit guaranties in fiscal 1982.

GOVERNMENT REGULATION

Of all its many and varied activities, a government's regulatory programs are the hardest to quantify. Instead of inducing people to do something by offering them expenditure subsidies, transfer payments, or tax concessions, the government may simply pass a law requiring them to do it. In this way the costs of achieving a given national goal are largely shifted from the public to the private sector and in the process become hidden from general view. That government regulation in this country has increased greatly in recent decades is obvious. What is not at all clear, however, is the size of the total costs or total benefits it has mandated. Lacking such numbers, one must devise indirect methods of identifying changes in the growth rate of regulatory activity — i.e., by using observable transactions and measurable variables that appear to be highly correlated with that activity. Since the validity of these correlations can only be estimated in the absence of the (unattainable) information on costs and benefits, the whole exercise involves much inexactitude.

Economists have, of course, tried to quantify the costs of the network of regulatory programs. Budgeted outlays by the federal government, for example, amounted to $7.3 billion or 1.4 percent of the 1979 budget, and were projected in Carter estimates for 1982 at $9.6 billion or 1.3 percent of the budget. These outlays are, however, only the beginning of the story, as private costs are far greater. One well-known study carried out for the Joint Economic Committee of Congress put the total price tag for 1979 at more than $100 billion, while another one for the Commerce Department put it at $150 to $200 billion. Both estimates have been sharply attacked by some critics for being too high and by others for being too low. One reason quantification is so difficult is that there are at least three dimensions to the problem: direct costs to business of installing special equipment and otherwise adjusting to the physical requirements of regulatory mandates; paperwork costs involved in the complex process of demonstrating compliance; and the totally unmeasurable losses in productivity resulting from the diversion of business resources (including executive energies) to nonproductive activities required by compliance. The Reagan administration, committed as it is to a reversal in the growth of federal government regulation, will find the footing rather slippery as it tries to chart its progress toward that goal.

GOVERNMENT REVENUE SYSTEMS

The immense increase in the range of federal government responsibilities during the past half century, and particularly Washington's rapidly growing involvement with the economic well-being of individuals and businesses, has greatly affected the nation's trilevel revenue structure. The most striking change is the huge rise in social insurance contributions (and notably the social security payroll tax), which grew from 10 percent of total tax revenue in 1948 to 25 percent in 1978. Although in the "total tax" picture the proportion supplied by the individual income tax held fairly steady at about one-third, a different perspective is derived by comparing it with other "general" (nonearmarked) taxes. As a source of general revenue, the personal income tax grew from 36 percent to 46 percent during that thirty-year period, with much of that increase coming from the escalation in its use by state and local governments. Property taxes, in contrast, had already begun to fall in relative importance even before the spate of tax limitation measures spurred by Proposition 13. Less reliance, too, was being put on the corporate income tax and on excises, while general sales taxes were growing in importance.

When the different governing levels are looked at separately, it can be seen that the federal government's general fund has become almost a single tax system (87 percent from income taxes), while state and local revenue structures have become diversified. Between 1948 and 1978 states more than tripled their use of the individual income tax and also stepped up general sales taxes and user charges. The decrease in local government reliance on property taxes was also counterbalanced by relatively heavier use of income taxes, especially by cities. The most dramatic change for local governments, however, was their growing dependence on higher levels of government. In 1957, for example, all local governments drew 56 percent of their revenue from their own tax systems and only 30 percent from intergovernmental sources; by 1980 local taxes were supplying only 33 percent of local budgets while intergovernmental revenue accounted for 40 percent.

CONCLUSION

A brief survey of government spending may well indicate the large size and basic structure of the subject at hand, but it cannot reveal much about the many intricate and subtle details that are its true essence. Yet such an overview is worthwhile, both to expose the inexperienced observer to the magnitude and complexity of the issues and to tempt the venturesome into a closer exploration of their vastly intriguing ramifications.

4

MICHAEL J. BOSKIN

Assessing the Appropriate Role of Government in the Economy

Allocation in competitive markets. Public and private goods. Economic inequality. Redistribution issues and social security. The "intergenerational cycle of poverty." Community specialization. Fiscal federalism.

The large, growing, and rapidly changing roles of government in the economies of the world include establishing legal

procedures for engaging in economic activity; financing and
providing certain types of goods and services (e.g., highways
and defense); and attempting to redistribute income, to encourage or discourage specific activities, and to stabilize the
overall economy. Each of these goals is to a certain extent
controversial.

Government has not always been actively involved in
these areas: in the early part of this century, for example,
total U.S. government expenditures at all levels amounted to
less than 10 percent of total economic activity. Some major
reasons for the development of government economic activity are worth an inquiry.[1]

ATTEMPTING TO IMPROVE RESOURCE ALLOCATION AND EFFICIENCY

In our society, most decisions are left to firms or individuals,
and it is presumed that such decisions are usually correct and
do not require government intervention. However, the conditions under which a predominantly free-enterprise economy
produces efficient results are not always perfectly satisfied in
the real world. For example, some goods and services simply
cannot be produced by large numbers of private entre-
preneurs. It may be that large-scale activity is necessary to
achieve the minimum average cost of production, and this creates a natural monopoly. In the United States, as in many
other advanced economies, such natural monopolies are regulated—for example, by utilities commissions. In other cases,
monopolies or near monopolies may develop, and government
may intervene to improve or increase competition.

Even in a mostly competitive economy, however, there are
resource allocation problems that *may* make government intervention desirable. The first are called "external economies and diseconomies," or third-party effects. These result

when the behavior of an individual or firm affects the opportunities available to other individuals or firms. Since the actions of most individuals and firms are primarily motivated by the direct effects upon themselves, their decisions may indirectly benefit or harm others. An example is environmental pollution. When pollutants are dumped into a river upstream, it decreases the potential for use of clean water downstream.

In some cases, private incentives induce the offending parties to make mergers or side payments to ameliorate the problem. However, when many individuals or firms are involved, it is usually costly and difficult to coordinate their activities to decrease the level of the external cost. When this is the case, government increasingly has stepped in. There are many methods for doing so: rules, regulations, prohibitions, fines, taxes, and subsidies.

It is absolutely crucial to note that while private competitive markets may not insure the most desirable allocation of resources in such circumstances, it is by no means certain that direct government intervention will automatically do better. There is a case for government intervention only where its benefits exceed its costs. It would be foolish, for example, for society to spend half its national income regulating and policing the reduction of air pollution. A variety of anecdotal evidence suggests that government intervention does not always promote the general social good; sometimes it winds up promoting the self-interests of either those who are apparently being regulated or those who do the regulating. In short, it is certainly possible to substitute a government failure for an alleged market failure.

A second problem in resource allocation concerns goods that can only be simultaneously provided to many people. The most important example is national defense. The cost of an additional person to the group being defended is essentially zero, and it is very costly to restrict access to national defense. Protecting someone in New York generally implies protecting his or her cousin in California. Such commodities are generally labeled public or collective goods, since they must be provided collectively if at all.

If it were possible to determine the value placed by each individual on the provision of such goods, each person could be taxed according to the benefits he or she received, i.e., people would pay something similar to a user fee, relieving the general treasury from the burden of providing the service. Unfortunately, when we cannot exclude individuals from using the public good, a so-called "free-rider" problem is created; knowing they can add only an infinitesimally small amount to the quantity of the public good provided, individuals will have an incentive to underreport their true valuation of such goods. Thus it has long been argued that many goods are underprovided in a primarily market economy.

Once we get away from national defense, the list of candidates for "pure" public goods dwindles rapidly. While a variety of commodities may have some aspect of "publicness," many of these goods have substantial private characteristics as well. It is important—albeit extremely difficult—to determine where in the spectrum each good lies. Many public commodities are limited to residents of a small area, as opposed to the entire nation. An important example is police protection.

Attempting to determine demand for public goods in order to choose among alternative programs is perhaps the single most important quantitative task of general government budget policymaking. Since private markets are by definition not available to provide these marginal valuations and the free-rider problem makes it very difficult to estimate how much of these services individuals want and are willing to provide, there is enormous scope for unfairly benefiting particular groups in the population under the guise of providing genuine public goods.

While a variety of these difficulties occur in assessing the demand and cost of providing public or partially public goods, substantial improvements have been made in the criteria for evaluating spending programs. Social cost-benefit analysis is not dissimilar to decisions private firms make in considering alternative investment strategies. Having estimated costs and benefits and discounted them to the present, criteria may be employed to evaluate government projects that are very similar to the efficiency criteria economists use to analyze allocation efficiencies in the private sector.[2] These analyses of individual programs should form the basis for setting the aggregate level of the budget under normal economic conditions.

Although these criteria make systematic evaluations possible, substantial problems of measurement and interpretation remain. For example, many projects may have so-called spillover, secondary, or intangible benefits. These might include allowing a related activity (such as retailing in the area) to operate on a larger and more efficient scale, increasing the productivity of immobile resources, or providing increased diversity and pluralism. It may be even harder to quantify such benefits than to quantify the direct ones. Conceptually, by reducing the outcomes of government spending programs to a single substantive measure, it is easier to make comparisons, and thus decisions (hopefully) improve.

A thorny problem for social cost-benefit analysis, and one of increasing practical importance because of the enormous expansion of transfer payment programs and other government subsidies, concerns whether the government should weight benefits accruing to some members of the population (e.g., income groups) more heavily than others. In large measure, the practical answer depends on the extent to which concerns about inequality and poverty are taken care of elsewhere in the budget, and on the ways in which spending programs directly affect the overall well-being of different population groups.

Were it possible to estimate the benefits and costs of each

program precisely, cost-benefit analysis would give us an exact guide for budgetary policy in normal times: individual programs should be undertaken and/or expanded to maximize the difference between benefits and costs (forgone private sector opportunities). The total budget would then add the sum total of expenditures on all such programs. The problem is less with the conceptual apparatus, however, than with its implementation by fallible human beings with particular personal and bureaucratic incentives. An arms-length cost-benefit analysis done outside of agencies with particular responsibility for specific programs—for example, in the Office of Management and Budget (OMB) as opposed to the departments of agriculture or transportation or energy—is a useful way to monitor cost-benefit analyses prepared for Congress and the administration in the individual agencies.

Cost-benefit analysis thus is a potentially useful device for evaluating public goods–type programs. Sometimes the analysis can be stretched too far, and there are many examples of projects that turned out to have very different costs and benefits than originally projected. Something as simple as a minor change in the rate of discount can alter substantially the desirability of government investment projects, for example. In short, projecting substantial price increases into the distant future by analogy with experience in a recent short period can be very misleading.[3] The question is whether government estimates are systematically biased towards spending on particular programs or in the aggregate, and for the answer we must search the nature of incentives in the government budgeting process, a topic discussed in several of the chapters that follow.

A third resource allocation problem occurs even in well-developed, primarily free-enterprise economies. What if markets do not exist for some commodities? We just noted that they do not exist for public goods, since no firm could sell such goods because they would be available free of charge to everyone. Another important class of goods for which private markets are incomplete or lacking are those for goods to be bought or sold in the future. While some futures markets do exist, they are by no means complete. Further, risks and uncertainties associated with the future of the economy are not all insurable on private markets. Therefore, the government may be able to improve the allocation of resources by providing insurance that would be denied by profit-maximizing private insurers. Some of the justification for social insurance programs runs along these lines, although in practice these programs have also become vehicles for redistributing income.

GOVERNMENT AND THE DISTRIBUTION OF ECONOMIC WELL-BEING

Governments do many things to alter the distribution of economic well-being in society. In our country, programs such as welfare and food stamps give direct aid to the poor, while high income tax rates decrease the income of the rich. Also, many government policies have indirect effects, intended or not, on the distribution of economic well-being. Virtually every regulatory, tax, or expenditure decision on the part of any government affects income distribution. For example, tariffs may provide very little revenue and may not be seen as a vehicle for redistributing income, but they may nonetheless substantially increase the incomes of some groups—often those who are already well off. Worse yet, policies that are designed to help the poor may have the exact opposite effect. An example is the minimum wage, which probably worsens the lot of low-skilled workers, particularly minority teenagers.

If the distribution of economic well-being provided by the market is not desirable or even acceptable, how do we go about deciding what is? While partly a matter of ethics, inequality has increasingly been a target of government intervention. The government provides transfer payments to a growing percentage of persons in the lower end of the income distribution and has attempted—for example, via progressive taxes—to reduce the command over resources accruing to the rich.[4] As George Break and others in this volume note, the federal government of the United States now spends substantially more on transfer payments to individuals than it does on purchases of goods and services (almost $300 billion in 1981).

The issue of what government should do about economic inequality is not exclusively ethical. Economics has at least three important roles in analyzing the problem. First, it can help reveal the ultimate effects of particular policies. Second, it can help define which types of government intervention can affect which distribution of economic well-being. Third and very important, it can help identify the costs and benefits of various initiatives. For example, while many government transfer payments such as food stamps and housing subsidies directly aid the poor, they are financed by taxing the nonpoor population, and these taxes in turn may distort incentives to work, save, invest, and innovate that motivate the nonpoor. Thus programs that may help the poor in the short term may reduce *future* incomes and living standards. These costs must be revealed and accounted for.

There are four major issues in redistribution and government economic policy:

- Should the role of government be limited to amelioration of distress or should it focus on general income inequality?

- How efficient are alternative government programs in attempting to achieve their goals?

- Should government policies focus primarily on potential opportunities, ultimate outcomes, or some combination of the two?

- Is there a substantial concern about intergenerational transmission of poverty and/or wealth, and if so, what—if anything—should the government do about it?

Even in a world where everyone started out with the same earnings potential, a variety of factors would certainly lead to inequality in earnings outcomes. The distribution of ill health or other temporary impairments is bound to be very uneven, and the distribution of earnings-enhancing inputs to young children also is likely to vary substantially. Thus, a first question arises as to whether it is legitimate for a government to be concerned with altering outcomes as opposed to enhancing opportunities. Since it is impossible to purchase complete, actuarially fair insurance against all potential outcomes, there is a case for government action against particularly severe—and sometimes temporary—problems such as disability and ill health. Some of our social insurance programs at least partially serve this purpose.

It is also clear that individuals differ substantially in their potential earnings capacity, and that these differences are not wholly related to differences in education or early family life. However difficult to measure, numerous differentially distributed attributes are highly correlated with earnings ability. Given this potential inequality, a variety of attempts have been made to analyze the appropriate role of government in redistributing income.

One basic problem is that the further one pushes redistributive expenditures, the more revenue one has to attempt to raise. Eventually tax rates become prohibitive, and further increases lead to a decline in revenue. While it is doubtful that we are at that stage in the United States in general, we certainly have reached that prohibitive range—or revenue counterproductivity—with various features of our tax system historically. Critical factors are the degree of inequality, the degree of egalitarianism desired, and the limits of government's ability to redistribute in a decentralized society. There are also important philosophical issues con-

cerning the rights of individuals to retain the outcomes of
their efforts that might limit government redistribution
quite independently of how individual well-being is
measured. Simply put, there are substantial limits to
redistribution because of the importance of maintaining incentives in society (see Boskin 1980c).

The single largest theoretical and political concern is
whether it is legitimate for government to play a general role
in redistributing income, or whether the government's role
should be limited (at most) to alleviating poverty and mitigating the suffering from temporary unemployment or ill
health. While much popular rhetoric, the nominal rate structure of our personal income tax, etc., indicate that at least
some part of the population favors general redistribution, it
is my own opinion that in a society with an average income
level as high as ours the primary goal of government policy
ought to be—and an overwhelming bulk of citizens generally
support this—substantial relief for those at the lower end of
the income distribution. Simply put, there is no strong intellectual or ethical case for attempts to redistribute minor
amounts of the tax burden from the fifth to the fourth decile
of the income distribution.

An important concern is whether an intergenerational
cycle of poverty exists and whether the government could or
should do something about it. This cycle could occur, for example, because of differential parental inputs, partly based
on income level, in early childhood; it could also be buttressed
by differential educational opportunity and/or attainment.
As yet we know very little about "the cycle of poverty" (for
example, see Lillard and Willis 1979), but the very real
prospect of a permanent disenfranchised class in our society
lies behind my substantial concern with the growth of the
proportion of Americans heavily dependent on transfer payment income.

Next, substantial numbers of individuals express alarm
about intergenerational transmission of wealth inequality.

Usually referring to wealth as nonhuman wealth, which accounts for only one quarter of the total (the other three quarters being the capitalized value of earnings streams reflecting the knowledge and skill of the labor force), the distribution of wealth at any point in time is still less equal than the distribution of earnings. It also varies substantially with age, again because of the typical life-cycle pattern of wealth accumulation and dissipation. While some debate still remains, my own conclusion is that a very large fraction of accumulated wealth is due to the life-cycle savings of individuals and households rather than to inheritances. Despite the few obvious examples of substantial amounts of wealth passed intergenerationally, the ultimate effects of such bequests on the distribution of income and wealth are more complicated than might be supposed. For example, the wealth accumulated for bequests increases the pool of available capital and therefore the productivity of workers and hence, earnings. While we have a variety of policies from estate to gift to inheritance taxes, there is a concomitant variety of vehicles for avoiding them.

It is my opinion that the aggregate size of this transfer of wealth in any given year is quite modest; furthermore, that the overwhelming bulk of it is so concentrated in small bequests as to be virtually impossible to tax even if it were desirable to do so; and therefore, that little could be done to decrease inequality with steeply progressive estate taxes on modest estates. First, the primary result would be to increase the lifetime consumption of the wealthy potential donors rather than to dissipate the estate over several potential heirs and/or charitable organizations as well as the general public. Second, in my opinion public concern about the potential political power of large accumulations of wealth is substantially overstated. This potential has been significantly mitigated by election reform, the spread of the ownership of wealth, etc.

Yet myths about wealth distribution are hard to dispel. For

example, an increasing fraction of wealth has been accounted for by the capital owned on our collective behalf by the government,[5] as well as the capital owned by nonprofit institutions such as universities, hospitals, and foundations. That is, a decreasing fraction of total wealth is owned by individual households. Yet none of the studies of inequality attempts to account for this. In the extreme, one would come to the absurd conclusion that if government owned all the capital except for one machine, the distribution of wealth would be completely unequal: 100 percent of the privately held capital would be owned by one person.

Substantial concern remains over the ability of government to provide a minimally decent standard of living for the destitute. General welfare, social security, and a variety of other programs attest to the popular support for its attempts. Further, in recent years an enormous increase in commodity subsidization has occurred. There are a variety of explanations for this phenomenon, but perhaps the most compelling is the notion that the nondestitute population—the overwhelming portion of us—believes that it is worthwhile to transfer specific goods and services to the needy because they are "basic needs," whether food, shelter, education, or health services.

Thus far we have been talking conceptually about reasons for government intervention in the distribution of economic well-being. Before proceeding any further, it is important to point out a variety of potential inefficiencies or government failures in the attempt to provide particular income or commodities or services. Not only will the usual deadweight loss or inefficiency of the tax system in the allocation of resources occur (see Harberger 1971), but serious mistargeting of funds and substantial administrative costs may become the rule. Each of these problems makes the per-dollar equivalent received by a low-income individual substantially more costly than a dollar at the margin in large redistribution programs.

Many programs designed to provide basic commodities to low-income households, such as health care, food, etc., may, via the ingenuity of the recipients, merely redistribute cash equivalents. This occurs when programs with a marginal co-payment also have a cap or ceiling. For example, paying a certain amount per dollar of food stamps reduces the price of food by the fraction subsidized by the government. When the total amount of food purchases would have been less than the available amount of food stamps, the subsidy is effective at the margin. However, when total food purchases are greater, the food stamps no longer operate as a subsidy at the margin, and their cash equivalent value is quite similar in its potential impact to a general cash grant for the corresponding amount. For this and other reasons, integration of many overlapping income maintenance programs into a general cash assistance program is highly desirable.

Programmatic difficulties occur not just in the design of in-kind transfer payment programs, but because of the potential for private responses to a variety of incentives in cash payment programs. For example, many programs are designed to supplement income for certain periods of time, e.g., retirement, disability, and unemployment. However, features of the programs may induce some individuals to retire earlier than they otherwise would have, to remain unemployed longer than they otherwise would have, or to file for a marginal disability claim when they might have been able to find less demanding work and continue to earn an income. This is not to say that the overwhelming bulk of expenditures in these programs does not considerably aid those in economic distress; the development of such programs is one of the major reasons for the substantial reduction in the incidence of poverty in the United States over the last two decades—one of our greatest social achievements.

However, let us take a specific example of adverse incentives. It is now well documented that in some states the level of untaxed unemployment benefits is sufficiently high that individuals can get into situations where going back to work actually decreases their after-tax income.[6] Partly this occurs because some programs are administered on an individual basis, whereas others are administered on a family or household basis. In a two-earner family, for example, where each earner generates a substantial income, the taxes paid on the unemployed worker going back to work can account for the bulk—or even more—of the difference between earnings potential and unemployment compensation.

Our most important, and probably most successful, redistributive program is social security. It is important to clarify the extent to which social security both redistributes income and creates incentives that make the added income it provides the elderly much less than the total expenditures. First of all, social security is financed on a pay-as-you-go basis, and annually transfers almost $200 billion from the current generation of taxpayers to the current generation of retirees and disabled persons.[7] Its aggregate size swamps all of the other income maintenance programs combined. Since, historically, the elderly have on average been poorer than the general population, there is some justification for this type of program: the elderly are poor because their income sources decline late in life, because they have less time to adapt to rapidly changing economic conditions, and because of real income growth in the younger generations (at least, until recently).

However, social security also establishes a variety of deleterious incentives. For example, in some cases the program certainly replaces all or part of private intrafamily intergenerational income transfers. Many of us would feel more compelled to share our income in supporting our elderly parents and grandparents were it not for the presence of the social security system, which does this collectively through the tax system. Further, while the issue is much debated, it is my own opinion that social security and its promise of future benefits probably has had at least some negative effect on private saving for retirement, and elderly individuals thus have less accumulated savings to draw on late in life (although in that case they obviously consumed more earlier in life).[8] Finally, I and others have documented statistically a variety of other reasons why many features of social security are among the major contributors to the substantial decline in the labor force participation of the elderly population, and therefore to their continued earnings late in life (see Hurd and Boskin 1982). In short, social security, for many individuals and households, partly replaces continued earnings or accumulated savings from earlier in life, or private intra-family transfers. Thus, the fact that aggregate social security benefit payments, including disability and Medicare, are estimated to be $170 billion in fiscal year 1983 should not be interpreted as providing an additional $170 billion to the income of the recipients; while the number is much less, opinions differ dramatically on the extent of the substitution. It is certainly substantial, but I am dubious that it is anywhere near the dollar-for-dollar that some people have estimated; perhaps it is fair to say that maybe one-half to two-thirds of social security benefits really do supplement the net income, after accounting for these effects, of the elderly population.[9]

The fundamental dilemma in attempting to achieve cost-effective redistribution without impairing the incentives of the poor to participate in the market economy lies at the heart of the difficulties in integrating overlapping transfer payment programs into a single comprehensive negative income tax. This problem has led to the categorization of individuals rather than to a broad definition of eligibility based exclusively on income, categorization that attempts to separate those for whom market earnings are unlikely to be a tempting, desirable, or achievable alternative to transfer payments (e.g., the disabled, mothers with dependent children, etc.).

The inflation indexing of transfer payment programs or general redistribution or tax vehicles has become a major social issue in recent years. Given the complex design of many of our schemes—which often end up, ironically, redistributing from the not-so-well-off to the better-off—it is by no means clear that simple adjustment of existing features of these programs by an aggregate price index is desirable. Indeed, such an adjustment can be genuinely wasteful and cause a variety of practical problems in structural reform in the system. For example, general indexing of social security is justified on the grounds that a particular group in the population that may be differentially exposed to inflation ought to be prevented from bearing the potential losses involved in unanticipated inflation. Recent research suggests that the inflation rate for the elderly is no greater than for the general population (see Boskin and Hurd 1982), and that in the course of the 1970s real incomes for many groups within the population fell while most transfer payments were indexed to keep up with inflation. However, social security benefits were originally intended to provide the bulk of retirement income only for very poor and indigent elderly individuals and families. They were designed to be modest supplements for those of modest means, and only a marginal source of retirement income for wealthy individuals. Simple across-the-board inflation indexing may result in substantial income redistribution from current workers to many elderly retirees who are by no means poor. While the basic benefits for the needy and elderly should clearly be protected from the ravages of inflation, it is unclear that general across-the-board indexing is desirable in a society now suffering continued sustained lack of growth in real income. Should a large group in the population be insulated from sharing general societal income losses occasioned, for example, by the huge transfers of income to the Organization of Petroleum Exporting Countries due to oil price increases?

To return to the little-understood "intergenerational cycle of poverty," are the children of those on transfer payment programs much more likely candidates for transfer payments in the next generation? Concern with the growth of transfer payments and the fraction of the population who are net income beneficiaries is well documented in the chapter by Break. Indeed, a painful dilemma may occur between the potential for substantially increasing the level of well-being of future low-income households and the short-run pain and cost caused in disruption of households that have become relatively dependent on transfer payment income for some fraction of their support.

The debate over the appropriate governmental role in income distribution, income maintenance, income redistribution, and issues of intergenerational inequality will continue to rage for decades. It is clear that the attempt to focus on the absolute level of income on average must supplement any discussion of its distribution. At a time of generally sluggish economic growth, those who have not yet made it on the economic ladder face the most difficult task in improving their situations; and those who have not made it at all face a deterioration of political support for the growth of taxes to finance redistributive benefit payments.

Undoubtedly, the most substantial intellectual and empirical case can be made for those programs that provide a floor of support for the needy. While enormous implementation difficulties make these programs more costly than necessary, we should not forget that they have been among the major vehicles by which we have substantially reduced poverty in the United States. Our task is to ensure that needy individuals who are not now being helped will become covered, and also to make the expenditures much more target effective and cost conscious. There is a great need to eliminate overlapping programs with multiple cross-indexing and extensive, wasteful overhead. We should not delude ourselves that this will be an easy task, but it must be done.

There is much less consensus that, save for redressing the hardship of the needy, the degree of inequality in our society

is a cause for genuine social concern and government intervention. Certainly as a by-product of other aspects of government policy, such redistribution will occur. But a healthy
concern for preserving incentives to promote the growth of
income and wealth in society may be much more defensible
on economic, intellectual, and even ethical grounds.

Despite the periodic reference to an obvious large fortune,
the disappearance of general sloganeering with respect to
the intergenerational transmission of substantial wealth is a
healthy sign of both the spreading ownership of capital and a
growing popular sophistication concerning the importance of
capital accumulation in our society. Indeed, there appears to
be little resistance to the recent dramatic increase in the
exemption level in federal estate taxes, which would allow
the inheritance of modest-sized family businesses, for example. Such a change would have been vociferously opposed
by a segment of the population in the past.

In sum, the focus on redistributing income and opportunity
to the disadvantaged is now well established as a sensible
and desirable goal of government policy in our economy. We
have paid á very high price for learning the limits to cost-
effective redistribution and understanding disincentives
that the large growth of federal transfer payments has created. Fortunately, as discussed in other chapters in this
volume, increasing awareness of these difficulties is leading
to serious attempts at reform.

ECONOMIC STABILITY AND GROWTH

Active government intervention to promote stable growth is
historically recent. Only since the Full Employment Act of
1946 has the U.S. government assumed responsibility for
helping to steer the economy. In the economies of Western
Europe, governments have traditionally played more active
roles in this regard. Thus, tax increases or cuts have been

used to deal with the problems of inflation and unemployment respectively; in the United States the Federal Reserve has attempted to contract or expand the rate of monetary growth in an effort to curb inflation or spur real output. However, it is not always possible for the government to dampen the booms and busts of economic fluctuations.

Lags in recognizing the need for government intervention and administrative lags in implementing tax or spending changes may negate fiscal or monetary policy, for example, in smoothing out economic fluctuations.[10] For now, the jury is still out on the efficacy of monetary and fiscal policies, but enough historical experience has been generated to suggest that continued attempts to fine-tune the economy through discretionary monetary and fiscal policies are ill-advised and that their replacement by a clear set of rules for monetary growth and tax and spending programs has substantial advantages. On the other hand, lags, inflexibilities, and a variety of other factors may make activist monetary and fiscal policies desirable if and when an extreme deviation from the economy's approximately normal—if not perfectly stable—growth path occurs. We shall have more to say about the macroeconomic aspects of budgetary policy in chapter 6.

FISCAL FEDERALISM

Another important issue of government intervention in the economy refers not just to the types of goods the government ought to—and can—provide, but to what level of government should finance these goods or services or redistribution programs.

Economists have long touted the advantages of competition. If a variety of goods and services have public characteristics that are limited spatially, it would seem advantageous (following the analysis of Tiebout [1956]) to provide them in a system of competing local jurisdictions. With substantial mobility at relatively low cost over a span of time, individuals would tend to sort themselves into communities that provided, given their income, the level and composition of goods and services they desired, and they would have to pay local taxes commensurate with the provision of such services. For example, elderly retirees might wish to live in a community that provided numerous parks at public expense but did not provide extremely fine schools for children. If enough communities existed so that each of the goods and services could be provided at its minimum average cost, such local choice would be both natural and desirable. Local governments would have to provide public services as efficiently as possible and would be subject to a discipline similar to that of the marketplace: migration of taxpayers.

Clearly, different communities might have differential comparative advantages in the provision of alternative services. Some communities, located downwind from pollution sources, might find it very costly to provide clean air, whereas others might find it less expensive to do so. Communities, therefore, could specialize according to their comparative advantage (see Oates 1972) — although administrative complexity and the cost of an inordinate number of fiscal jurisdictions would naturally limit the amount of fiscal decentralization.

Many local public goods and services will have important spill-in and spill-out effects, i.e., externalities. For example, an upstream community that provides sewage treatment financed by taxing local residents is helping provide downstream communities with clean water; alternatively, failing to do so would mean that it was dumping some of its waste products into the river and increasing the costs to downstream communities for clean water. In such cases, the tax/subsidy schemes used to deal with external economies and diseconomies have a natural analog in an intergovernmental grant program. Simply put, a proportion of the costs of financing certain programs can be borne by residents out of the community to account for these spillover effects in grant arrangement between the governments involved. As a practical matter, such intercommunity spillovers are often dealt with at a higher level of government through the use of various intergovernmental grants-in-aid.

Intergovernmental grants-in-aid have become a substantial fraction of the federal budget of the United States, amounting to $90 billion in 1981. They contain a variety of features. Most important, they transfer revenues raised at the federal level to lower levels of government, whether state, county, city, or other. Some of these programs do so on a matching basis, either open- or closed-ended, whereas others do so on a purely general cash basis. The development of revenue sharing was primarily designed with the dubious notion of attempting to shift resources from "well-off" to "poor" communities. Clearly, grant programs that provide greater revenues on a per capita basis to a poor community do not necessarily redistribute public services to the poor residents of that community. When matching provisions occur, it is clear that local governments have a bargain sale on the items involved and may find it more desirable to match federal funds to provide services than they otherwise would have. If, however, the federal matching or state matching share is larger than the true spill-out, many communities will take advantage of these programs by building sewage treatment systems, etc., since they cost local residents only a small fraction per total dollar of expenditure.

The latter effect has led many people to suggest lumping categorical grants into block grants and allowing communities to spend them as they see fit. While certainly sensible on an interim basis, the block grant approach begs the question of why the local communities did not raise the revenues to provide these services themselves in the first place. If benefits to the local residents exceed the costs, one would expect

the local governments to be able to generate political support
for the necessary taxes; if not, it would seem undesirable for
the federal government to do so. If, on the other hand, it is
the externality or spillover effects that render the local
government unwilling to engage in such activities, appropriately chosen matching rates are most desirable.

Transfer payments for the poor pose a particularly
difficult problem for local governments, yet they also provide
an important opportunity to differentiate among individuals
and households in different locations with different standards of need. The problem occurs because, while each of us
might be willing to help care for the disadvantaged, we would
be even more happy to have our neighbors pay for them.
Thus each community may have an incentive to try to export
their poor people and reduce the tax burden of welfare-type
expenditures. If this is the case, the federal government may
be the most natural place for general income maintenance
programs to be financed. However, the variation in the cost
of living across communities, for example, may suggest that
a national uniform program may be much more costly and
less target effective than one disaggregated at lower levels of
government. Where the balance lies between these two conflicting forces is difficult to tell as a practical matter. Certainly our largest redistributive programs—social security,
Medicare, etc.—will continue to be financed at the federal
level. A key debate is now raging as to whether Aid to
Families with Dependent Children and other income maintenance programs for the nonelderly poor should be shifted
more to state and local governments or adopted entirely by
the federal government, and perhaps integrated into a general negative income tax or comprehensive income maintenance program. It would seem desirable, if the latter is
chosen, that it still be possible to differentiate by location; it
would also seem that administrative costs are increased as
more layers of government are added. This dilemma between
the incentives of each local government to try to have its

neighbors provide the bulk of welfare payments versus the efficiency advantages of decentralization will be at the center of debate over the new federalism in the years ahead.

The discussion above suggests that a concept of optimal fiscal area could be established. Systems of local government ought to provide site-specific local public goods. In areas where benefit or cost spillovers are easily established, a regional grant program can be set up, on an appropriate matching basis, to fund services with these spillovers. Further, income maintenance services probably need to be financed at a level beyond that of the local community. Also, the smaller and more economically open the fiscal area—for example, a local government as opposed to the entire nation—the less capable are fiscal policies of mitigating economic fluctuations.

Where in all this do state governments fit? State governments may provide a coordinating role among a variety of smaller fiscal units, internalize externalities, and provide a balance between full decentralization and economies of larger-scale operations. It may well be that natural economic forces will eventually shift some economic functions of state governments either to local or regional authorities on the one hand, or to the federal government on the other.

It is also worth mentioning that the optimum monetary area, given our economy, technology, and financial markets, is likely to coincide with at least the national economy as opposed to any given small community or state.

THE PROPER ROLE OF GOVERNMENT

We have traced a large number of criteria for judging government involvement in the economy to improve the allocation of resources, promote economic stability and growth, or maintain or redistribute income. This led to a dis-

cussion of procedures to be used in evaluating specific programs enacted at various levels of government and general
criteria for choosing the appropriate level for program financing. Much of the remainder of this volume concerns
specific programs and criteria for judging various features of
our federal budget. It is clear that, against a backdrop of a
very rapidly changing economy, the appropriate role of
government has changed dramatically. While on the one
hand the government has helped to reduce poverty and to
provide substantial infrastructure, it has also allowed programs to grow to serve many more individuals than those
originally targeted. It has developed programs that are not
very cost conscious, and it has also at times destabilized the
economy in its attempts to stabilize it. Government is now
such an important and pervasive part of virtually all economic decisions and all of our lives that the systematic
search for improved budget policy will in no small part influence not only the shape of our economy, but our view of
society's capability to provide economic opportunities as
well as insurance against the ravages of extreme economic distress.

II

Conflicting Pressures in Federal Budgeting

5

RUDOLPH G. PENNER*

Forecasting Budget Totals: Why Can't We Get It Right?

The understatement bias. New administrations and old budgets. Errors and discrepancies. Politics and the budget process—priorities. Befuddled voters. Improving the process. Forecasts and projections.

President Reagan promised a balanced budget in 1984 and gave us a plan to achieve it. Only a few months later, private and official estimates suggest that it will be extremely

---

*This chapter represents an elaboration on Penner 1981.

difficult to hold the 1984 deficit below $100 billion and that
something above $200 billion is quite possible without dra-
matic policy changes. Although President Reagan made one
of the most spectacular miscalculations in history, it is not
unusual for budget plans to go awry. Indeed, every president
in memory has promised us a balanced budget at one time or
another, but we have not seen one since President Nixon
delivered a small surplus in fiscal 1969. (That budget was
originally planned by President Johnson and then modified
slightly by President Nixon.)

In reviewing this dismal record, it is important first to
emphasize that a president's budget is not intended to provide the best possible forecast of final budget outcomes. It
represents a series of recommendations to Congress. A president is perfectly within his rights to recommend policy
changes, even though he himself and independent outside
observers may know that there is a high probability that
Congress will reject those proposals. Nevertheless, a president is entitled to leave a record of what he thinks is right,
and the budget is a statement of his position. He is also entitled to take bargaining positions advocating large spending
or tax increases or decreases, knowing that in the end he will
have to compromise. And there is, of course, no law against
his changing his mind as the year unfolds.

But even if we knew all future policy changes with cer-
tainty, it would not be easy to forecast future outlays and
receipts. The problem of forecasting budget totals with
known policies will be the focus of this chapter.

THE NATURE OF THE
ESTIMATION PROBLEM

Table 1 summarizes the differences between original estimates and actual outcomes over the period 1969–1981. Note

Table 1

Budget Outlays, Receipts, and Deficits: Totals as Estimated and Actual Outcomes
(billions of dollars)

Fiscal year	Outlays*			Receipts*			Deficit*		
	Original estimate	Actual	Percent error	Original estimate	Actual	Percent error	Original estimate	Actual	Percent error
1969	186.1	184.5	0.9	178.1	187.8	−5.4	8.0	− 3.3	141.3
1970	195.3	196.6	−0.7	198.7	193.7	2.5	− 3.4	2.9	−185.3
1971	200.8	211.4	−5.3	202.1	188.4	6.8	− 1.3	23.0	−186.9
1972	229.2	232.0	−1.2	217.6	208.6	4.1	11.6	23.4	−101.7
1973	247.3	247.1	0.1	220.8	232.2	−5.2	26.5	14.9	43.8
1974	270.2	269.6	0.2	256.0	264.9	−3.5	14.2	4.7	66.9
1975	305.7	326.2	−6.7	295.0	281.0	4.7	10.7	45.2	−322.4
1976	351.2	366.4	−4.3	297.5	300.0	−0.8	53.4	66.4	− 23.6
1977	394.3	402.7	−2.1	351.3	357.8	−1.9	43.0	44.9	− 4.4
1978	440.7	450.8	−2.3	393.0	402.0	−2.3	47.7	48.8	− 2.3
1979	501.0	493.6	1.5	439.6	465.9	−6.0	61.4	27.7	54.9
1980	531.5	579.6	−9.0	502.6	520.1	−3.5	28.9	59.5	−105.9
1981	615.7	660.5	−7.3	600.0	602.6	−0.4	15.7	57.9	−268.8

Source: Office of Management and Budget.

*The accounting definition of outlays and receipts differs from time to time. To the extent possible, outlays in this table have been made consistent with the latest definition; therefore, outlay and deficit numbers may not correspond to those found in other published sources. All changes, however, are quite minor.

that the original estimate is always taken from the January budget. Therefore, the discrepancies include the effects of policy changes undertaken whenever a new president has modified the budget bequeathed by his predecessor, though up until the Reagan revolution, which affects mainly the 1982 budget, those changes have been relatively minor.

While the original budget does not always understate outlays, there is a strong bias in that direction and the bias seems to have grown since 1974. Receipts are also frequently understated. Late in the 1970s biases were, in large part, the result of a tendency to understate the inflation problem. The table clearly illustrates that relatively small percentage errors in forecasting either outlays or receipts can result in huge percentage errors in forecasting deficits. It also shows how difficult it would be to operate with a constitutional amendment that sought to require a balanced budget.

The budget is so complex that it is difficult to break down the discrepancy between the original and actual totals into components due to policy changes and those due to other estimating errors. The Congressional Budget Office (CBO; 1981) has done some work on receipts-forecasting errors, and has shown that for personal income taxes between 1963 and 1978, about two-thirds average absolute error was due to estimating problems and the rest to legislative changes. To my knowledge no comparable effort has been made on the outlay side. It is seldom in the interest of either the executive branch or Congress to look back and ask what went wrong. For the outsider, such an effort is virtually impossible because of the huge staff resources that would be required.

However, as table 1 indicates, the discrepancy for 1980 outlays was particularly dramatic, and the Office of Management and Budget has studied that year. President Carter originally recommended outlays of $531.5 billion, while the final outcome was $579.6 billion or $48 billion higher. Policy changes, both those initiated by Congress and those initiated by the president, accounted for $19 billion or 40 percent of the discrepancy. About $10 billion of this amount was in defense and related to the Iranian and Afghan crises. The other 60 percent, or $29 billion of the $48 billion error, was related to difficulties in estimating the cost of given policies. Of the $29 billion estimating error, about $20 billion was the result of erroneous economic forecasting while the remaining $9 billion resulted from other estimating errors.

Although a careful breakdown of past outlay estimating errors has not been done for all of the years in the period, it is fairly safe to conjecture that a very large portion—and probably the bulk of the error over time—is due to errors in economic forecasting. For a given set of policies, actual budget outlays are very sensitive to the economy, and that sensitivity has grown significantly over the period shown in table 1.

In 1969 payments to individuals for income security and other programs constituted about 30 percent of total outlays, and the largest program—social security—was not indexed to the cost of living. In 1981 payments to individuals had risen to almost 50 percent of the budget, and close to 90 percent of that total is indexed either explicitly to some price or wage index, or implicitly because a program promises a certain real service regardless of its price—e.g., Medicaid and Medicare.

Table 2 illustrates the effect of errors in forecasting inflation on explicitly indexed programs in 1982, while table 3 includes the effect on Medicaid and Medicare and the indirect effect on the interest bill or the debt. The latter can be expected to grow rapidly in 1983 and 1984 because of the huge deficits expected over that period. The dollar numbers in tables 2 and 3 can be compared with a July 1981 estimate of total 1982 outlays of $704.8 billion, receipts of $662.4 billion, and a deficit of $42.5 billion.

The demand for payments to individuals is, of course, sensitive to the unemployment rate. The effects on unemployment insurance and welfare are obvious, but empirical

Table 2
Sensitivity of FY 1982 Budget Outlays
to Economic Assumptions*
(billions of dollars)

	1982 outlays
Prices (effect on indexed programs only)	
1 percentage point increase in consumer price index level by:	
First quarter, calendar year 1981	1.9
Third quarter, calendar year 1981	0.7
First quarter, calendar year 1982	0.4
Interest rates	
1 percentage point increase in interest rates by:	
1 January 1981	4.2
1 July 1981	3.3
1 October 1981	2.6
1 January 1982	1.6
1 July 1982	0.3
Unemployment rate	
1 percentage point increase in average rate for fiscal year 1982:	
Unemployment benefits	5.5
Other	1.5
Civilian and military pay raises October 1981	
1 percentage point increase	0.7

Source: Office of Management and Budget.

*For changes in economic assumptions in the opposite direction, outlay decreases would be of similar magnitude with the opposite sign.

Table 3
Sensitivity of the Budget to Economic Assumptions
(billions of dollars)*

	FY 1981			FY 1982		
	Outlays	Receipts	Deficit	Outlays	Receipts	Deficit
Effect of 1 percentage point higher annual rate of inflation beginning:**						
January 1981	2	3	–1	6	11	–5
January 1982	–	–	–	2	3	–1
Effect of 1 percentage point lower annual rate of real growth beginning:						
January 1981	1	–3	4	4	–13	17
January 1982	–	–	–	1	–3	4

Source: Office of Management and Budget

*If the rate of inflation were lower or the rate of real growth higher by 1 percentage point, the changes in outlays and receipts would be of the opposite sign but of similar magnitude to the figures shown above.

**Includes the effect of higher inflation on indexed programs, interest outlays, Medicare, and Medicaid; excludes effects on discretionary programs.

research suggests that retirements also rise in the face of higher unemployment; consequently, outlays on social security and Medicare also expand.

Receipts are also highly sensitive to changes in real growth and inflation. The short-run sensitivity is shown in table 3. In the longer run, a 1 percentage point change in nominal income, whether due to inflation or real growth,* results in a 1.2 to 1.3 percent change in total receipts, in large part because bracket creep in the personal income tax changes receipts 1.6 percent for every percentage point change in nominal income growth.

Although errors in economic forecasting are typically responsible for a very large portion of the errors involved in forecasting budget totals, other estimating errors can also be highly significant. A correct forecast of unemployment and real income can provide a fairly accurate estimate of the proportion of the population that will be eligible for programs such as unemployment insurance and welfare, but only a portion of the eligible population actually claims benefits and that portion can vary unpredictably.

Other "acts of God" can significantly affect outlays. Natural disasters such as Mount St. Helens and hurricanes exert large claims on the budget, and crop yields have an important effect on agricultural subsidies and agricultural disaster payments. In other words, if crops are too large, the costs of price supports rise. If they are too small because of droughts or other factors, farmers are also eligible for assistance. They have to be just right to avoid creating a budget burden.

It is also difficult to predict spending in any one year out of a multiyear appropriation, or even whether a single-year appropriation will be fully spent. Actual spending usually falls

---

*Table 3 shows that receipts are slightly more sensitive to changes in real growth than to inflation, but the difference is small and not as large as might be expected theoretically. It is conceivable that the dramatic changes in tax law in 1982 may alter these estimates, but the matter has not yet been studied.

short of planned spending. That is because spending money is hard work. Bids have to be solicited from potential contractors; contracts have to be negotiated; and eventually bills have to be paid. Bureaucrats are often overoptimistic about the amount of this work that can be completed in any one year.

Occasionally, contractors deliver products early and spending rises above planned levels. This is common during periods of economic slack when businessmen substitute work on government projects for private work. For this and other reasons, defense outlays in 1982 may be as much as $6 billion higher than the administration expected originally. Defense creates an especially difficult problem, in that sophisticated weapons systems take years to produce and the time lag between spending and appropriations is so difficult to predict— a problem that will be very important during the current defense buildup.

THE EFFECTS OF ESTIMATING ERRORS ON POLITICAL DECISIONS

Politicians are constantly frustrated by the estimation problem. They work very hard on program details in order to achieve certain budget goals, only to see their efforts overwhelmed by unforeseen events.

In the past the discrepancy between forecasts and budget outcomes was less of a political issue. Battles were fought over appropriations and the design of entitlement programs and tax law, but there was no need to vote on actual outlays and receipts. Indeed, few—except for economists and bond traders—worried about how well it all came out in the end.

The enactment of a new congressional budget process in 1974 changed all that. For the first time, Congress had to vote on targets for actual outlays, receipts, and deficits.

There was a whole array of new issues to fight over. The political system has not responded well to this challenge. There is an enormous temptation to fudge the numbers.

The temptation arises because there is an important asymmetry between the political implications of changing a program in order to achieve an outlay target and changing economic or other assumptions. For example, one of the bigger political battles of 1981 was fought over the minimum benefit provided in social security. The president recommended that the minimum benefit be eliminated and Congress at first acceded to his request. However, a political firestorm ensued, and with much embarrassment both Congress and the president reversed positions and restored the benefit. This major battle was fought over a budget saving of only $1 billion. Yet it is impossible to cut the budget without successfully carrying on hundreds of battles of this type.

A glance at table 2 or 3 indicates, however, that a $1 billion error in forecasting budget totals is trivial. That much can be saved in fiscal 1982 by lowering the forecast of interest rates, starting 1 October 1981, by less than one-half of one percentage point. No one could honestly protest such a change because no one can forecast future interest rates with that degree of accuracy. Faced with the hard choice of changing a program or the easy choice of changing assumptions marginally, the latter looks very tempting. In fact, it is quite remarkable that budget assumptions are as accurate as they are.

I think it fair to say that the public, the press, and even some decision-makers are not fully sensitive to the crucial role of assumptions in affecting budget decisions. One of the accomplishments of the new congressional budget process is that it has increased awareness of the issue; but public education has a long way to go and politicians meanwhile can use public ignorance to obfuscate the issues.

Debates over policy issues get hopelessly entwined with debates over forecasting issues, and even budget experts often have trouble figuring out what is going on. An interesting example of such confusion occurred during the debate on the 1982 budget that occurred in the summer of 1981. The battle was between the Democrats on the House budget committee and the president, who was backed by a coalition of Republicans and southern Democrats. Under identical economic assumptions, the two proposals would have resulted in almost identical outlay totals, though spending priorities differed. But the budget committee made the crucial tactical error of basing its estimates on a less optimistic—but as things turned out, a more accurate—set of assumptions, and it appeared as though committee members wanted a higher spending total than the president. The latter was able to attack them as big spenders, and they were never able to explain successfully to the public that the difference was mainly one of assumptions. They might have lost the battle regardless of the tactical error of choosing less optimistic assumptions, but given the lack of public understanding of the role of assumptions, it was clear that they started the debate with a severe handicap.

Even if everyone worked on formulating the most honest assumptions possible and the crucial role of those assumptions were understood perfectly, errors would still be inevitable. Those errors can distort decision making in a variety of ways.

Under the chosen assumptions, program cut A may save much more than program cut B. But, after the fact, we may find that program cut B would have saved much more. For example, if it is assumed that wages will rise faster than prices in the future, it would be foolish to start a battle over whether we should continue to index social security benefits to prices or whether we should shift to indexing the lower of price or wage growth. Choosing the latter approach would not allow us to show any budget savings if wages are assumed to grow faster than prices. But if, in fact, wages grow more slowly than prices, the savings could be impressive.

The choice of assumptions also has a subtle effect on public commentary and criticism of particular budget proposals. For example, if an outside academic wants to comment on a particular tax proposal, he or she has little choice but to adopt the official economic assumptions. All of the estimates of the effects of the proposal in the budget will be based on those assumptions. Redoing those estimates for a different set of assumptions involves an enormous amount of work far beyond the capabilities of most individuals. Nevertheless, the effects of a particular tax proposal on the allocation of resources and the distribution of income may be quite different under a different set of assumptions, and that crucial fact often goes unnoticed.

The problems caused by making errors in assumptions grow exponentially as budget projections are extended into the future. Since the beginning of the new congressional budget process, both the administration and Congress have made five-year budget projections. Thus, President Carter's 1982 budget, which was proposed in January 1981, projected budget totals through fiscal 1986.

The budget projections made for the remainder of fiscal 1981 and 1982 are based on economic forecasts for calendar 1981 and 1982. For subsequent years, the budget totals are based on what is called an economic "projection." These projections always show us making steady progress toward lower inflation and unemployment.

For a long period of time economists and budget experts had argued that budget decisions should be made with a longer time horizon. In the days when we looked ahead only one fiscal year, some serious mistakes were made; program increases that cost little in the short run were often adopted without full knowledge of the rapidly expanding budget burden they would impose in the longer run.

However, because longer-run budget projections are now based on wildly optimistic economic projections in which everything gets steadily better every day and business cycles are absent, it is not clear that rationality has been enhanced. Indeed, the apparent step toward more rational decision making may in fact have been a backward step, since it gives politicians one more degree of freedom in befuddling the voters.

For example, using optimistic projections, President Carter was able to seem frugal by promising the voters that he would lower budget outlays to 21 percent of the gross national product (GNP). Obviously, that promise was never fulfilled and outlays ended up above 23 percent of the GNP by fiscal 1981. If longer-run budget projections had not existed, it is quite conceivable that Carter would have felt more pressure to be frugal from the beginning of his term.

Similarly, President Reagan was able to talk Congress into major defense spending increases and huge tax reductions by claiming that all of that was quite consistent with a balanced budget in 1984. That claim was, of course, based on wildly optimistic economic assumptions and was already abandoned less than a year after being made.

It is interesting to speculate on what would have happened if we still had been budgeting one year at a time. Reagan's policies and assumptions led to a $45 billion deficit in 1982, and that would have been all that was shown in budget documents. It is doubtful that the program would have been passed without long-run projections showing that a balanced budget was possible in 1984.

Obviously, the problem does not lie with the principle of making projections of the long-run implications of short-run budget projections. Such projections are essential if the world is to be at all rational. But a rational world requires rational projections, which we have not yet seen in budget documents. Making long-run decisions based on erroneous assumptions may actually represent a backward step in our quest for rationality.

IMPROVING THE PROCESS

While the problems created by current estimating procedures
are apparent, solutions are more elusive. We are not good at
forecasting future events and are unlikely to get better very
soon. Yet since budget decisions are made for the future, they
must be based on some concept of future conditions.

In theory, it sounds appealing to investigate the implications of different spending and tax proposals under a great
variety of future scenarios. But this is not practical. It would
require enormous staff resources at a time when we are cutting rather than expanding the bureaucracy. Moreover, the
results would be too complicated for current congressional
decision processes and would be very confusing to the public
and the press.

Consequently, it is necessary to be more modest in seeking
improvements. I believe that a major step forward would occur if, in debating issues, we could clearly separate disputes
over policies from disputes over assumptions. Currently, it is
not unusual for the House, Senate, and administration to
enter the budget debate, each proposing different programs
and using different assumptions to evaluate them. Occasionally, the Congressional Budget Office comes up with a
fourth set of assumptions, but—mercifully—the CBO
assumptions are frequently adopted by either the House, the
Senate, or both.

Nevertheless, budget debates tend to be hopelessly confusing because no one, however expert, can easily separate the
effects of policy proposals from the effects of the differing
assumptions. I believe that all of the different policy
packages should at some point be evaluated using a common
set of assumptions that could be worked out before pre-
sentation of the president's January budget. Those assumptions could also be used as a basis for the First Budget

Resolution done in May. None of the contending parties would have to believe the common set of assumptions to be the best possible forecast, but one would expect that the forecast economic variables would be close to a consensus of private forecasters. With such a common set of assumptions, the policy differences among contending parties would be much clearer.

All of the parties would be free to concoct their own forecast if they thought that they could come up with a better one or if they believed that their program package would make the world a better place than would be implied by the common set of assumptions. If they chose a separate forecast, the public could clearly see the difference that different assumptions would make for the outlay, receipt, and deficit implications of that particular policy package. This would have the by-product of educating the public as to the importance of assumptions.

I would still call the common assumptions for the current year and the subsequent calendar year a forecast. For example, the January 1981 assumptions on which the 1982 budget is based should reflect the best thinking of private forecasters regarding the likely economic developments in calendar 1981 and 1982.

I say this because economic forecasts, despite their terrible reputation—even those made by various administrations— have not been too horrible in the short run. That can be seen in table 4's review of the forecasting record. The January forecasts were particularly good for the year in which they were made. (It must be admitted that forecast updates made in July often err more than the January forecasts.)

In the period 1975 through 1980, the largest error for the unemployment rate was 0.4 percentage points in the recession year 1975. Despite the strong temptation to be overly optimistic, the actual unemployment rate was very slightly overestimated on average. The real growth rate was missed by more than 1 full percentage point only once during the six

Table 4
Executive Branch Projections of the Economic Outlook 1975–1986*

Variable and forecast date	1975	1976	1977	1978	1979	1980	1981	1982	1983	1984	1985	1986
Nominal GNP growth[a]												
January 1975	7.2	12.6	12.4	12.0	10.8	10.8	–	–	–	–	–	–
January 1976	–	12.4	12.2	12.4	11.9	10.9	9.1	–	–	–	–	–
January 1977	–	–	11.0	11.3	11.6	10.5	7.9	6.4	–	–	–	–
January 1978	–	–	–	11.0	11.2	10.8	10.5	9.6	8.5	–	–	–
January 1979	–	–	–	–	11.3	9.5	10.1	9.4	7.9	6.3	–	–
January 1980	–	–	–	–	–	8.3	10.7	12.8	12.9	12.0	11.0	–
January 1981	–	–	–	–	–	–	11.4	13.1	12.3	11.8	11.0	10.2
March 1981	–	–	–	–	–	–	11.1	12.8	12.4	10.8	9.8	9.3
Actual	8.0	10.9	11.6	12.4	12.0	8.8	–	–	–	–	–	–
Real GNP growth[a]												
January 1975	–3.3	4.8	5.6	6.5	6.5	6.5	–	–	–	–	–	–
January 1976	–	6.2	5.7	5.9	6.5	6.5	4.9	–	–	–	–	–
January 1977	–	–	5.2	5.1	5.9	5.5	3.9	3.5	–	–	–	–
January 1978	–	–	–	4.7	4.8	4.8	5.0	4.7	4.2	–	–	–
January 1979	–	–	–	–	3.3	2.5	4.2	4.7	4.4	3.4	–	–
January 1980	–	–	–	–	–	–0.6	1.7	4.3	5.0	4.9	4.7	–
January 1981	–	–	–	–	–	–	0.9	3.5	3.5	3.7	3.7	3.7
March 1981	–	–	–	–	–	–	1.1	4.2	5.0	4.5	4.2	4.2
Actual	–1.1	5.4	5.5	4.8	3.2	–0.2	–	–	–	–	–	–

GNP deflator[a]

January 1975	10.8	7.5	6.5	5.1	4.1	4.0	—	—	—	—	—	—
January 1976	—	5.9	6.2	6.1	5.0	4.2	4.0	—	—	—	—	—
January 1977	—	—	5.6	5.9	5.4	4.7	3.8	2.8	—	—	—	—
January 1978	—	—	—	6.1	6.2	5.7	5.2	4.7	4.2	—	—	—
January 1979	—	—	—	—	7.7	6.8	5.7	4.5	3.4	2.8	—	—
January 1980	—	—	—	—	—	8.9	8.8	8.2	7.4	6.8	6.1	—
January 1981	—	—	—	—	—	—	10.5	9.3	8.5	7.8	7.0	6.3
March 1981	—	—	—	—	—	—	9.9	8.3	7.0	6.0	5.4	4.9
Actual	9.3	5.2	5.8	7.3	8.5	9.0	—	—	—	—	—	—

Unemployment rate[b]

January 1975	8.1	7.9	7.5	6.9	6.2	5.5	—	—	—	—	—	—
January 1976	—	7.7	6.9	6.4	5.8	5.2	4.9	—	—	—	—	—
January 1977	—	—	7.3	6.6	5.7	4.9	4.8	4.7	—	—	—	—
January 1978	—	—	—	6.3	5.9	5.4	5.0	4.5	4.1	—	—	—
January 1979	—	—	—	—	6.0	6.2	5.7	4.9	4.2	4.0	—	—
January 1980	—	—	—	—	—	7.0	7.4	6.8	5.9	5.1	4.3	—
January 1981	—	—	—	—	—	—	7.8	7.5	7.1	6.7	6.3	6.0
March 1981	—	—	—	—	—	—	7.8	7.2	6.6	6.4	6.0	5.6
Actual	8.5	7.7	7.0	6.0	5.8	7.1	—	—	—	—	—	—

Source: Office of Management and Budget.

a Percentage change, year over year.
b Total, annual average.

*Column headings are in calendar years.

years (again, in 1975), and in four of the six years the forecast was within 0.3 percentage points of being correct. The inflation rate was missed by more than 1 percentage point in two years (1975 and 1978), but the forecast was within 0.2 percentage points in two other years (1977 and 1978). Unfortunately, we have already seen that small errors of this type can still lead to significant errors in forecasting budget totals.

Needless to say, the forecast made in January for the following calendar year was considerably less accurate than that made for the current year. For the five years 1976 through 1980, however, the unemployment rate forecast was, on average, fairly accurate. Only in 1980 was there a severe error, when the forecast understated unemployment by 0.9 percentage points. The forecast for real economic growth understated the 1975–1976 recovery and failed to anticipate the recession of 1980 but was fairly accurate for the 1977–1979 period. After overestimating the inflation problem in 1975–1977, the most serious forecasting error involved underestimating the problem after 1977.

As already noted, it is quite remarkable how accurate these short-term forecasts are, given the strong temptation to be overly optimistic. Although there is much comment regarding the incompetence of the forecasting profession, table 4 suggests that politicians feel constrained not to wander too far from the consensus, which is not necessarily inaccurate. As an aside, it might be noted that much of the ridicule heaped on forecasters comes from politicians who would like an excuse to ignore them.

However, for the longer run, ridicule is appropriate to most forecasting efforts, and it is for the longer run that politicians have felt free to assume anything they want without much fear of challenge. The result has been sets of more or less arbitrary numbers, which table 4 shows to have been absurdly optimistic.

It is not easy to deal with this problem. I would suggest a

rather arbitrary approach. My desire for arbitrariness seeks to insulate the projections from political manipulation.

Specifically, I would recommend that projections of real growth and inflation be based on the average experience of the previous five years. That is to say, if this procedure had been in effect in the past, the budget assumptions made in January 1975 would have involved making a forecast for calendar 1975 and 1976 similar to that actually made, but the projections for the years 1977 through 1980 would have been based on the average real growth rate and inflation rate over the period 1970–1974. Since the real growth rate over any five-year period is not a bad approximation of the potential growth of the economy over the long run, it is reasonable to assume that the unemployment rate would remain constant over the projection period. In other words, in the above example, the unemployment rate for the period 1977 through 1980 would be assumed to remain constant at the level forecast for 1976.

Since interest rates are closely linked to inflation rates, and the proposed procedure would assume the same inflation rate in the 1977–1980 period as prevailed in 1970–1974, it is reasonable to assume that interest rates would also be identical in the two periods.

Table 5 shows the projections of several variables made for 1980 in the January budgets of 1975 through 1980, and compares them with the projections that would have been made if the suggested procedure had been in effect. (Past GNP data were revised several times over the period; the table ignores this problem and assumes that current GNP definitions were in use over the entire period.)

Table 5 shows that, except for the projection made in January 1976, the use of the proposed procedure would have been less accurate than actual budget procedures in projecting nominal 1980 GNP. The success of the budget in projecting nominal GNP was, however, the accidental result of two major offsetting errors. The official long-run budget esti-

Table 5

Comparison of Economic Forecasts Made for 1980 Using Past Budget Assumptions and the Proposed Alternatives

Variable and forecast date	Budget	Proposed alternative
Nominal GNP in 1980 (billions of dollars)		
January 1975	2,675.5	2,416.9
January 1976	2,725.2	2,551.1
January 1977	2,617.4	2,558.9
January 1978	2,623.1	2,606.5
January 1979	2,627.7	2,627.7
January 1980	2,614.3	2,614.3
Actual	2,626.5	2,626.5
Real GNP in 1980 (billions of dollars)		
January 1975	1,613.3	1,412.5
January 1976	1,663.7	1,496.0
January 1977	1,606.4	1,525.4
January 1978	1,577.4	1,550.3
January 1979	1,521.4	1,521.4
January 1980	1,474.1	1,474.1
Actual	1,480.9	1,480.9
GNP deflator in 1980 (1972 = 100.00)		
January 1975	165.87	171.51
January 1976	163.92	170.58
January 1977	163.04	167.88
January 1978	166.54	168.43
January 1979	172.59	172.59
January 1980	177.26	177.26
Actual	177.36	177.36
Unemployment in 1980 (percent)		
January 1975	5.5	7.9
January 1976	5.2	6.9
January 1977	4.9	6.6
January 1978	5.4	5.9
January 1979	6.2	6.2
January 1980	7.0	7.0
Actual	7.1	7.1

Source: The budget projections are based on data contained in table 3 and most recently revised GNP statistics. The proposed alternative is based on the author's own computations.

mates consistently underestimated inflation and over-estimated real growth. The proposed procedure would have been consistently more accurate over time than actual budgets in predicting real GNP, the GNP deflator, and unemployment for 1980. It would, therefore, have been much more accurate in projecting outlays even though receipts would have been underestimated.

Again, I would recommend that this arbitrary procedure be adopted by all parties in the budget debate, so that different policies could be evaluated using one common set of assumptions. Each could argue that their particular policies would bring about a future that was better than the past, and they could evaluate the implications of their policies using their own long-run economic assumptions based on their own favorite economic theory—Keynesian, supply-side, monetarist, etc. But the public would then be able to see clearly how important it is to swallow the proponents' theory along with their budget estimates.

The above discussion has focused on economic assumptions. It was noted earlier that a great variety of other assumptions regarding such matters as crop yields and natural disasters was necessary to put together a budget. To counter a tendency toward optimism in making such assumptions, I would strongly urge that an amount equal to 2 percent of the budget total be routinely added to the allowance for contingencies. This should be done in both the short and long run. It could be called the "Murphy's Law adjustment."

CONCLUSION

I would be the first to admit that my suggestions leave a lot of unsolved problems. My budget projections, like any others, would be sure to err in describing the future. The errors would result in many bad decisions. Moreover, I have not dealt with the problems posed by off-budget spending, credit programs, and mandated private spending. By forcing more realistic budget estimates, my proposals may induce Congress to rely more on nonbudget tools.

However, the goal is not perfection. The suggestions made above would heighten public understanding of the role of assumptions in formulating budgets, and would also create awareness of the nature of the future risks. At present the long-run risks are all on the down side because long-run assumptions are overly optimistic. Though arbitrary, my approach would present a less biased view of the future. Other arbitrary approaches may do better and I am not unalterably wedded to any particular technique. The main goal is to put restraints on the politicians. Currently, it is too easy for them to mislead us.

6

MICHAEL J. BOSKIN

Macroeconomic versus Microeconomic Issues in the Federal Budget

The budget process. Off-budget and mandated private activities, tax provisions, credit, and indeterminables. Variations in monetary and fiscal policies. Rational expectations. Deficits. Long-range planning and special interests.

The purpose of this chapter is to highlight some important interactions between the performance of the economy and its likely implications for the budget, and to offer some conjectures concerning the potential impact of the budget and/or

111

its components on the economy in turn. The latter is an exceptionally controversial issue on both analytical and empirical bases in economics, and we shall attempt to highlight some of the difficulties, although to do so fully would require a full treatise on macroeconomics.

When we speak of the federal government's budgetary process, we are talking mainly about the timing and character of budget recommendations, authorizations, appropriations, and spending. Almost a year before the beginning of the fiscal year, the Office of Management and Budget (OMB) prepares the current services' budget forecast. On the basis of forecasts about the economy, this budget provides estimates of spending necessary to maintain current services in the ensuing year. In January, still nine months before the start of the fiscal year, the president proposes his budget and presents it to Congress. Throughout the spring and summer Congress analyzes, debates, and approves the concurrent resolutions on the budget through its appropriations, tax, and budget committees. As the budget is finally approved, agencies are authorized to spend appropriated funds. An audit determines spending and revenue amounts in retrospect, following the end of the fiscal year.

In reviewing this process, it is important to understand the difficulty in forecasting actual outlays and revenues up to a year or more in advance. Penner notes that the government does not *directly* control outlays and revenues; a variety of stipulations in both tax laws and entitlement programs make actual revenues and outlays dependent on economic conditions. For example, a higher than forecasted inflation rate will drive people into higher tax brackets and raise revenues; a larger than anticipated unemployment rate will increase the number of new claims for unemployment insurance and other government assistance programs and increase outlays above projected levels—to name only two instances. In considering the effects of these phenomena on budget forecasting, it makes some sense to divide the post—

World War II period at the year 1968 (this was approximately the point at which inflation in the United States began to accelerate sharply). Note that the difference between projected and actual outlays and revenues in the federal budget was as likely to be positive as negative prior to 1968; since then, actual outlays have almost always exceeded projected outlays (although actual deviations have averaged only 3 to 4 percent). At the present time there is substantial debate about the accuracy of the current administration's forecasts and economic assumptions. Add to this the fact that the economic projections of private forecasters have also, on occasion, been far off the mark in recent years. In particular, attempts to estimate inflation in the 1970s almost universally underestimated the inflation rate.

So there are difficulties in budget revenue and outlay forecasts. Nonetheless, budgetary forecasts in the United States are heavily influenced by the course of economic fluctuations and the desire to counter cyclical fluctuations. The creation of new budget committees in Congress following the 1974 Budget Reform Act was widely heralded as a major vehicle for tying aggregate spending and aggregate taxation together. In principle, the budget committees were supposed to set spending limits and revenue minima within which the separate appropriations and tax committees were working. The aim was to delimit the overall level of the budget deficit that could be used in part to attempt to influence the aggregate performance of the economy. We discuss below the use of the deficit as a means of fiscal stimulus and the alleged relationships between deficits and a variety of key economic variables. In practice, it is unclear that much spending discipline percolated down from the budget committee to the appropriations committees. Last year's reconciliation package was perhaps the first real success in this effort.

Before proceeding to other issues, it is worth restating what the budget would be like in a world without economic fluctuations. Let us assume that budget policies, spending on goods and services, taxes, deficit financing, etc., were never to be used to attempt to counterbalance economic fluctuations, either because there were no fluctuations or because policymakers became convinced that it was counterproductive to act in this way. Under such circumstances, actual budget totals in principle would merely have to reflect the interplay of (1) cost-benefit analyses of particular programs for spending on goods and services—including government investments and research and development expenditures—and (2) judgments concerning the appropriate role of government in providing income security and/or general redistribution. Were there no economic fluctuations, the number of households eligible for unemployment insurance, for example, would change only slowly as demographic factors and attitudinal changes altered the entry, exit, and turnover behavior in the labor force. Thus it would be easier to forecast future revenues and outlays, since there would be much less uncertainty about the major macroeconomic variables that influence spending and revenues—inflation, unemployment, interest rates, etc. Unfortunately, since we do not live in a world free of economic fluctuations, actual expenditure and revenue figures reflect—and may also affect—economic performance. Therefore, conflicting criteria are often used in assessing the desirability of various spending programs and the methods of financing them.

THE FEDERAL BUDGET: DECREASING COMPREHENSIVENESS AND RELEVANCE?

For a variety of reasons, the federal budget is no longer a very comprehensive report, estimate, or forecast of government involvement in the economy. Neither the outlay and revenue totals nor the deficits are comprehensive. There are several causes for this. To begin with, substantial increases in outlays now occur in off-budget federal enterprises (although these are discussed in the budget, they are not included in the direct budget total). Further, federally sponsored agencies have substantial outlays and net deficits of their own. Three important categories that create major conceptual difficulties are tax expenditures, quasi-government spending in the form of mandated private activities, and net government investment or disinvestment.

One alternative to direct federal government spending with well-known economic impact is regulation requiring private individuals, households, or firms to adopt certain activities. For example, the cost of requirements for automobile pollution and safety equipment shows up in the accounts as part of gross private automobile sales. Nonetheless, from an economist's standpoint, it is conceptually quite similar to the government's levying a tax and turning the proceeds over to automobile companies to install the devices. The net outlays under such mandated private activity amount to perhaps another 10 to 20 percent relative to official outlay totals. Furthermore, potential major expansions of mandated private activities such as employer-paid national health insurance are waiting in the wings.

Other conceptual alternatives to direct spending are the so-called "tax expenditures," which (as defined by the Congressional Budget Office [CBO]) are revenue losses resulting from "special or selective tax relief to certain groups of taxpayers."[1] While there can be little doubt that special tax provisions can channel resources from one sector of the economy to another, the official definition of tax expenditures and especially their estimates and projections are open to serious question.[2] First, deciding on a tax expenditure implies a definition of an appropriate tax base, which is a generally debatable issue in economics; many items that are considered positive tax expenditures relative to, for example, a comprehensive income tax would be considered negative tax expenditures relative to a consumption tax. Since more and more economists and tax law specialists, as well as the public, seem to be leaning toward consumption as the desirable tax base relative to income, the official budget totals can be highly misleading (see Boskin 1980c). What is called "accelerated" depreciation may be "decelerated" depreciation relative to a consumption tax. Further, the estimates for individual budget items, and the totals, rely on a rather bizarre set of assumptions. The estimates basically assume that individuals are not responsive to the tax provisions in the allocation of their resources or in their factor supply. For example, the "tax expenditure" that puts a lower tax rate on capital gains assumes that all the income generated in capital gains could be taxed at ordinary rates were this "tax expenditure" removed. This assumption ignores the possibility that this income would find other nontaxable forms, or that capital formation and accumulation would decrease, thereby decreasing future tax revenues. Suffice it to say that such expenditures are much more difficult to estimate and identify than direct spending programs.

Further difficulties arise because of the astounding growth of the federal government's credit activity. Partly in connection with off-budget and federally sponsored agency programs, the federal government now subsidizes a substantial amount of direct loan activity and also guarantees approximately one-half trillion dollars in loans.[3] While we finally have developed a separate credit budget to document the growth and nature of the direct loan obligations and loan guarantee commitments, the federal government does not have a conceptually separate, complete capital account. This makes the deficit numbers exceptionally difficult to interpret. We do not yet have an accurate series for the real net worth of the federal government or the entire government sector of the American economy, although researchers are working on the subject (see Boskin 1982).

Consider, for example, the budget deficit, which—if all accounting were done appropriately—would merely be the difference between the government's revenues, R, and outlays, O:

$$D = R - O$$

Problems occur because it is difficult to measure both R and O. These problems include the discrepancies between classic accrual versus realization accounting; the difficulties posed by inflation accounting; the problem of developing appropriate price deflators for various categories; and the trouble involved in valuing services and goods that are not freely traded on well-defined markets (the public goods issue discussed in chapter 4). As with the private sector national income accounts, there are substantial problems in measuring capital gains and losses. Unfortunately, declines in the real value of outstanding government liabilities, the potential value implicit in contingent promises to provide cash or commodities under certain conditions, and similar indeterminables can swamp the official budget forecast or even the official totals in retrospect.

Because the federal government does not keep a separate capital account, official budget figures exclude the value of net investment and disinvestment. If we maintained a separate and conceptually correct current and capital account system for tangible capital investments, the deficit on the current account would be the true deficit. Any excess of expenditures over receipts on capital account does not change the net asset position of the government, since the new debt is matched by a new government asset. The current account of a divided budget would show smaller deficits than a unified budget when the capital outlays were increasing over time and a larger deficit when capital outlays were falling.

I have elsewhere estimated that in recent years the federal government has engaged in substantial disinvestment, which has not been included in the official deficit totals.[4] I have also estimated, as have others, that the decline in the real value of the previously issued national debt has at times been larger than the regular government deficit. In 1970, 1973, 1979, and 1981 the decline in the real value of the previously issued debt exceeded the deficit, and in fact the government ran a "real surplus." I shall return to this point below.

Government subsidy and loan guarantee commitments pose a conceptually more difficult problem. How should these be valued? What does one do for changes in the anticipated value of previously issued loan guarantee commitments? What fraction of these guarantees will ever have to be paid off? When? Under what terms? The deficit on a cash—as opposed to accrual—basis could balloon enormously in any given period if a substantial amount of loan guarantees were to become due. Should a reserve or contingency fund, based on some estimated percentage of loan guarantees that will have to be paid off, be established? What would be the appropriate rate? Would it closely resemble that commonly used as a bad debt reserve in the private sector?

I have also elsewhere estimated unfunded loan liabilities in social insurance programs. The social security system faces a long-term deficit substantially larger than the regular national debt. This will occur primarily because of the pending dramatic projected increase in the ratio of retirees to workers in our society when the post—World War II baby boom generation begins to retire early in the next century. My own estimate for the needs of the retirement part of the fund alone in real 1980 discounted dollars of the debt exceeds $1.1 trillion.[5] It is clear that the current rules and regulations of the social insurance program are not cemented into a unified capital account of the government, as might have been the case had we issued explicit long-term contractual debt obligations. When we think about the social insurance funds as government spending, and the implicit debt as a quasi debt, the accruing of deficits through time because of a variety of economic and demographic changes poses conceptual questions similar to those raised above.

The lack of a conceptually proper separate capital account leads to still further problems. Capital gains and losses on federal government land and mineral rights have not been properly valued. In a previous paper I estimated that at times the capital gains on land and mineral rights have exceeded the regular deficit in a given period (see Boskin 1982).

In summary, government economic activity and influence extends well beyond direct spending, taxation, and regular deficits. Off-budget and federally sponsored agency outlays and borrowings, loan guarantees, net investment or disinvestment, private activity mandated by government, and tax expenditures (however difficult to measure)—these have become the rule rather than the exception. When we discuss below the potential impact of the macroeconomy on the budget and the budget's impact on the macroeconomy, we will confine ourselves to brief discussions of the federal government's major activities: direct spending, taxation, and debt issue. However, it is important to bear in mind that the other activities just mentioned influence the economy if and when general fiscal policy does. If deficits matter, for example, it seems likely that total government borrowing, rather than just that reported in the official deficit estimate, is the appropriate variable to consider. Of the few available studies relating deficits to inflation, real activity, government spending, etc., most make only a few of the adjustments described above—so we are still in the early stages of understanding the complete role of the interactions of the macroeconomy and the budget.

INTERACTIONS OF THE BUDGET AND THE MACROECONOMY

The U.S. budget for fiscal year 1983 contains the following statement (Office of Management and Budget 1982*b*, p. 17):

"The economy and the budget are interrelated. Economic conditions affect the budget, and the budget, in turn, influences economic conditions." We have already discussed briefly the short-term potential impact of the performance of the economy on specific spending programs or tax revenues. The administration, through OMB and the Treasury, and Congress, through the CBO, have developed a variety of sensitivity analyses to trace the effect of changes in economic assumptions or forecasts on projections of revenues, outlays, and deficits. Chapter 5 by Penner discusses these in more detail. The important point is that changes in economic conditions in the short run, whether policy induced or not, can have substantial impacts on outlay, revenue, and deficit totals.[6] Indeed, a large fraction of the increase in deficits that typically occurs during recessions is relatively automatic and reflects the so-called automatic stabilizers in the economy — an increase in unemployment insurance payments, a decline in tax revenues, etc.

Still, there is a substantial confusion concerning the role of deficits in the economy. Aside from the demonstrable fact that deficits are potentially the results of a downturn in the economy, opinions concerning their relation to the economy differ markedly.

Unemployment and inflation have plagued virtually all societies at various points in time. Active government intervention to promote stable growth is a historically recent development. In the United States, since the Full Employment Act of 1946 the federal government has assumed responsibility for helping to steer the economy on a course of stable growth. In the economies of Western Europe, governments have traditionally played an even more active role. Thus tax increases or cuts have been used to attempt to deal with the problems of inflation and unemployment respectively; in the United States, the Federal Reserve has attempted to contract or expand the rate of monetary growth to curb inflation or spur real output. As with the case of providing public goods or ameliorating external economies or diseconomies, it is not always possible to improve the situation.

Lags in recognizing the need for government intervention and even administrative lags in implementing tax or spending changes may negate the potential usefulness of fiscal or monetary policy, for example, in smoothing out economic fluctuations.[7]

Aside from these practical difficulties in implementing Keynesianesque stabilization policies, there have in recent years been a variety of attacks on the analysis upon which traditional anti-recession and anti-inflation policies rest. Many economists used to believe that increases in government spending on purchases of goods and services, when financed by deficits, could substantially increase gross national product (GNP). Operating in the familiar "multiplier" fashion, the increased government spending would increase GNP by a multiple of the original spending increase. When the economy was well below full employment, spending programs were presumed to generate extra income and hence little pressure on prices. While most economists still believe that there are some recognition and administrative lags and some price inflexibilities and the like, which make some of the Keynesian analyses at least partially useful, academic analysis, quantitative study, and historical experience alike have cast considerable doubt on the extent to which changes in government spending or taxes can influence GNP, how rapidly they can do so, and whether the attempt to "fine-tune" the economy makes much sense.[8]

Historically, both monetary and fiscal policies have been widely variable. The growing interest in a specific monetary growth rule testifies to the deep concern about the potential influence monetary expansions have on inflation and about the tendency of the Federal Reserve to pursue erratic monetary policies, shifting from rapid short-term accelerations to substantial curtailments of money and credit. The most important critiques of the Keynesian analysis and its related activist fiscal and monetary policies place heavy reliance on the role of expectations and careful accounting of the national balance sheet. With respect to expectations, analytical and empirical studies have rendered most traditional Keynesian analyses at least suspect and perhaps obsolete.

According to rational expectations theory, macroeconometric estimates of fiscal and monetary policy interventions are highly unreliable because individuals—acting in their roles as intelligent consumers, savers, investors, and workers—make rational forecasts based on their available information. Since their forecasts anticipate the impacts of interventions by government monetary or fiscal policy, such investors and consumers will already have accounted for these, at least partially, in their private decisions to consume or invest. More (or less) government spending or saving will thus prompt a compensating private reduction (or increase) in spending or saving—with no net impact on the economy. In this view, only (or at least primarily) *unanticipated* monetary or fiscal policy will be effective. But if systematic Keynesian stabilization policies are followed, we should expect the private sector to learn to anticipate them, thereby rendering them impotent—or at least much less effective.

Potential weak links in this analysis do leave some limited scope for stabilizing the economy through discretionary fiscal policy. There may be better information available to the government than to the private sector, the private sector may learn only gradually of government policy "rules" while the structure of the economy changes, etc.

The empirical validity of rational expectations equilibrium models of the macroeconomy is a source of debate in the profession. The persistence of unemployment, for example, is quite difficult to explain in such models; they imply that deviations of the unemployment rate from its long-run "natural" level should be randomly distributed over time. While some ingenious arguments have been developed to explain the fact that we appear to go through a series of years with unemployment above and then below its natural rate, they are not yet convincing.

Perhaps a fair evaluation of the practical import of this line of reasoning is that it has cast very serious doubt on the efficacy of activist fiscal policy argued by Keynesians. And, as noted above, such efficacy has often been one of the arguments behind expensive programs whose benefits otherwise were unlikely to exceed their costs.

Another telling criticism of the traditional analysis has been rehabilitated by Barro who, relying on work going back to Ricardo (see Barro 1978 and Bailey 1971), argued that shifts in the finance method between taxes and debt for a given level of government spending do not alter perceived private wealth. The reason is that when the government borrows to pay for goods and services, the present value of future interest payments is assumed to equal that of present tax payments that would have been paid in the absence of borrowing. This analysis is particularly evident in the interconnection of families across generations. Since private wealth perceptions are not altered, real decisions about consumption and investment based on perceived wealth will not alter either, and substitution of debt for tax finance of a *given* level of government spending will not help stabilize the economy.

Another important feature of the more recent analyses suggests that it is important to draw a sharp distinction, as discussed above, between anticipated and unanticipated changes in monetary and fiscal policies. Anticipated changes tend to be incorporated in longer-term contractual decisions, and it is primarily unanticipated changes in monetary and/or fiscal policy that may quickly affect real output, the price level, etc.

On a more practical note, it has become clear that monetary and fiscal policy may not only fail separately to help stabilize the economy, but can often work at cross-purposes.

The notion of expectations formation and the substantial

role played by uncertainty in disrupting economic behavior suggest that fixed rules may have more of an appeal than purely discretionary activist policies, except in times of extreme emergency. Further, these fixed rules, such as that for relatively stable monetary growth within narrow targets or a clearly spelled-out course of future spending and taxing decisions, may not only decrease the costs associated with long-term investment decisions and hence raise the level of real activity on average, but may also mitigate the extent to which fiscal and monetary policies sometimes destabilize the economy.

The opportunity for deficit finance, however, may also increase the level or growth rate of government spending. This in turn can affect the level of real output, employment, and future living standards in a variety of ways, depending upon the nature of that spending. For example, debt-financed increases in government investment that are complementary to private economic activity may help increase productivity and expand output in the future.

The relationship between budget deficits—the usual means of economic stimulus—and other economic variables can work in a variety of ways. Simple correlations among deficits and the rate of growth of the money supply, the investment rate, the interest rate, the inflation rate, etc., are quite weak. There are a variety of conjectures concerning these relationships and a variety of studies have attempted to analyze the factors that influence the overall economy, including deficits and government spending. For example, Niskanen (1978) argues that federal deficits have increased the level of federal spending but have had no apparent effect on the rate of inflation. Barro (1978), in an important study, finds "surprisingly little support" for the conjecture that budget deficits, above and beyond the impact of spending, have an influence on money growth. Hamburger and Zwick (1978) find some evidence for the fact that increased federal government borrowing exacerbates inflationary pressures as the Federal Reserve is induced to expand the money supply to limit the rising interest rates. The deficit could increase prices through a wealth effect, a Federal Reserve monetization of the debt (thus increasing money growth and prices), or some combination of these phenomena. Several of these effects are virtually taken for granted in the general discussion of budget deficits, although empirical support for them is at best quite weak and possibly nonexistent. However, one should not conclude from available statistical studies based on historical data that budget deficits will not affect interest rates, investment, inflation, or money growth in the future.

This occurs because, once we are out of the current recession, the projected deficits—as a fraction of gross national product, or relative to the private saving rate, or just in real absolute dollars—are prospectively much larger than they ever have been in the postwar period. This increase in the size of the deficit can be explained primarily because often in the past, as noted above, the decline in the real value of the previously issued debt substantially offset the regular government deficit. Table 1 presents some Congressional Budget Office forecasts of future outlays, revenues, and deficits. As can be seen, even if one adopted the plausible first-order approximation that the decline in the real value of the previously issued debt was compensated by inflation premia in interest rates on government bonds and reinvested to maintain real principal in investment portfolios, the amount of deficit finance in prospect for fiscal year 1983 and beyond overwhelms the by now modest decline in real value of previously issued debt. However, the available studies all suffer from the problem of not having had substantial government balance sheets, with appropriate capital accounts worked out to provide data for actual government spending by type, disaggregated into investment and noninvestment, etc. Hopefully, these will be available in the near future.

It thus appears that (1) fiscal policy has some impact on

Table 1
Baseline Budget Projections, CBO
as of February 1982
($ billions, current)*

	1982	1983	1984	1985	1986	1987
Revenues	631	652	701	763	818	882
	(20.6)	(19.0)	(18.5)	(18.3)	(18.0)	(17.7)
Outlays	740	809	889	971	1,052	1,130
	(24.2)	(23.6)	(23.5)	(23.3)	(23.1)	(22.7)
Deficit	109	157	188	208	234	248
	(3.6)	(4.6)	(5.0)	(5.0)	(5.1)	(5.0)

*Numbers in parentheses are percentages of estimated GNP.

the overall performance of the economy—especially that concerning the level and growth rate of real government expenditure and its composition between investment and consumption; (2) the tax rates necessary to finance any level of government spending may influence (via the marginal rates and other features of the structure) resource allocation, including factor supply, and hence our ultimate standard of living; (3) the division of financing of a specified level of government spending between taxes and debt is probably less important than has previously been believed, up to modest amounts of new debt issue; (4) the efficacy of short-run fiscal policy in stabilizing the economy is certainly much less than was supposed in the Keynesian era. However, some limited scope probably does remain for discretionary fiscal policy. Further, the discussion above about the comprehensiveness of the outlay and revenue figures—and hence, the deficit—should make us wary about official deficit figures in the past, present, or future as an estimate of the potential stimulative or contractionary impact of the federal budget. And finally, recall the proviso that fiscal and monetary policies do not operate in isolation, but can complement or contradict one another.

MACRO STIMULUS AND SPENDING BIAS?

The short-run activist bias in Keynesian models of the economy—based on the assumption that increases in government spending are likely to increase real output and employment in the short run and increase prices only later on through a "Phillips curve–type"[9] trade-off—suggests that Keynesian analysis may lead to the adoption of more spending than is justified on individual cost-benefit analysis. This potential bias toward larger government than is justified on microeconomic grounds may also wind up feeding back to the macroeconomy in the way described above. Interesting historical examples of this are special countercyclical fiscal assistance to local governments and social security benefit indexing.

The official forecasts of the federal government are heavily influenced by many considerations, as discussed by Penner. But a particularly opprobrious feature is the legal requirement to make long-range assumptions that the economy is making consistent progress towards reducing unemployment, inflation, and interest rates in a relatively prescribed manner. This requirement makes long-range planning exceptionally difficult, because such assumptions are inconsistent with any reasonable model of the economy. Further specific problems may occur because of the particular bias built into the projection models used in the OMB, the CBO, the Treasury, or elsewhere for evaluating impacts of spending and tax changes on the overall economy or on specific elements in the cost-benefit analyses.

Continuous criticism of these models and the input they make into the decision-making process is a high priority in government decision making. Perhaps such criticism will not be able to overcome the enormous political biases encountered in making budget policy; nonetheless, improved estimates and evaluation are a necessary—if not sufficient—condition for improved policy. The vagaries of political pressure and the instability in the economy make the interaction of political pressure and economic forecasting difficulties hard to disentangle. But fortunately, on balance, the CBO, the Treasury, and the OMB have improved their forecasting capabilities and analyses over time. All three models still, however, substantially ignore long-term capital formation prospects and the resultant longer-term effects on tax revenue feedbacks, etc. The effect of this is to bias tax and spending policy away from capital formation toward current spending. In addition, they have very weak expectational responses built into them, which suggests that they are not fully capable of making accurate short-term forecasts of the effects that follow from dramatic announced changes in, for example, monetary policy. It is important to note that the models exist in the context of substantial disagreement among professional economists concerning the appropriate models and model parameters to employ in making such estimates.

If we are really to improve government decision making, it is not only necessary that aggregate forecasts and estimates be improved and sensible fiscal and monetary policies adopted; it is equally important that the individual cost-benefit analyses done at the agency level be done as accurately and as dispassionately as possible. Much is made of the incentive structure facing a Congress that is biased toward spending because the proponents of the spending programs can muster resources for specific spending proposals, whereas the beneficiaries of reduced taxes are diffused and hard to organize. It is equally important to realize that bureaucrats in individual agencies serve particular clienteles and have particular incentives themselves. They would prefer to have any reduction in spending growth come from the budgets of agencies other than their own, so the incentives to make existing programs more cost conscious and target effective come from the interplay of competing budgetary choices from above as often as they come from a careful reevaluation of existing programs from below. Improving the incentive structure to reevaluate from below would be the most desirable alternative. An important step in this direction might be the creation of a budgetary feedback rule that credited agency decision-makers with some fraction of the reduction in spending growth in their agencies, with the credit applied to development of new programs (this must be combined, however, with an effective overall spending limit reflecting the scarcity of resources).

Concern over government spending growth, the explosion of nominal deficits, and the shoddy performance of the U.S.

economy in terms of inflation, sluggish economic growth, and periodic substantial unemployment, continues unabated. While the potential culprits are many and are not limited to federal budget policy, it is clear that renewed efforts to make government spending more cost conscious and target effective are desirable. Aggregate fiscal policy should be more predictable and less susceptible to dramatic short-term changes intended to fine-tune the economy when such activity is likely to have little impact—or, worse yet, be counterproductive. While it is clear that Congress is attempting to move in the direction of greater budgetary control, it is also clear that the explosion of off-budget activity, tax expenditures, mandated private activity, loan guarantees, etc., combined with the failure to keep a conceptually separate capital account, leave the federal government's budgetary process difficult to interpret and somewhat in disarray as an accounting, control, and planning procedure. Indeed, the federal government's budgetary practices would not pass muster for a publicly traded corporation as required by the Securities and Exchange Commission. Improving the procedures will improve our ability to understand the impact of government's economic activity on the economy and vice versa. It will also provide us with a vehicle for trying to achieve our budgetary objectives more closely. We will be able to reduce the potential displacement of private economic activity with a more cost-conscious and target-effective government spending program. Also, when we wish to expand certain programs, we can be more confident that they will hit their target. The pressure for dramatic changes in government procedures is growing rapidly, as witness the various types of constitutional amendments proposed, debated, and working their way through various state legislatures—perhaps implying even an eventual constitutional convention to force a balanced budget and/or spending limitation. While more will be said about this in the conclusion, it is important to point out that improved comprehensiveness, accounting procedures, and understanding of the budgetary process may well be important first steps to improve federal budget policy and procedures. For example, merely imposing a balanced budget constraint would be extremely awkward without a conceptually proper capital account. On the other hand, doing so may well finally generate that separate accounting advancement.[10]

In summary, the activist Keynesianesque bias in short-term fiscal policy has probably led to a pro-spending bias and vice versa. While the extent of this is perhaps overstated, I too believe that the extent of its contribution to our inflation problem is only modest, since the nature of deficit financing has much to do with the potential economic impact. It is also clear that the generally available data to analyze the impact of spending, its composition, and its finance on everything from private spending to real output, monetary growth, inflation, interest rates, etc., are only just beginning to become available. Hopefully, in the not-too-distant future a greater consensus will be reached concerning the nature of these interactions. In this case the enormous hysteria and confusion that exist in the interaction of the macroeconomic impact of the federal budget and the micro decision-making process will find a happier resolution.

III

Current Budget Problems

7

ALAIN C. ENTHOVEN

Federal Health Care Spending and Subsidies

Medicare and Medicaid. Tax exclusion or tax subsidies. Cost controls and management economies. Insurance plans—incentives for choice. Coinsurance, HMOs, Medicare reform. Private insurance. Voluntary option programs.

Attention is now being focused on whether the share of federal revenues and spending in the gross national product (GNP) can be reduced or at least limited to present levels. It is thus appropriate to look at federal health spending and subsidies in terms of their growth in relation to the GNP.

HEALTH AND THE FEDERAL BUDGET

National expenditures on health care services and supplies, as well as medical research and facilities, increased from about $75 billion or 7.5 percent of GNP in 1970 to some $247 billion or 9.4 percent of GNP by 1980. The federal share went up from $17.7 billion or 24 percent of the total in 1970 to $70.9 billion or 29 percent of the total in 1980 (Gibson and Waldo 1981). And this does not include tax revenue the government loses because of the favorable tax treatment of health insurance.

Medicare

Medicare is the federal program of health insurance for social security beneficiaries. When first enacted in 1965, it covered retirees aged 65 and over. The 1972 amendments to the Social Security Act extended coverage to certain disabled persons, including those suffering from end-stage renal disease. The Medicare program is, in effect, an open-ended commitment by the government to pay for hospital and physician services, the former by cost reimbursement and the latter on a fee-for-service basis. Both methods of payment reward providers for supplying more—and more costly—care, and thus are inflationary. Medicare currently pays for inpatient hospital care for 60 days per spell of illness for each beneficiary after a deductible of $260; it also pays partially for up to 90 additional days, with increasing copayments by the beneficiary. Medicare's Hospital Insurance (HI) program is financed by proceeds from a payroll tax. Medicare also pays for physician and other health services provided by its Supplementary Medical Insurance (SMI) program. Enrollees pay a premium that was $11 per month as of July 1981, which increases in proportion to social security benefit payments. After the enrollee pays a $75 annual deductible, Medicare pays 80 percent of what it considers "reasonable costs" or "reasonable charges." Physicians are not required to accept Medicare's definition of "reasonable," and in the case of more than half the services and charges, they do not. As a result, beneficiaries pay out-of-pocket, or through supplemental private insurance (or Medicaid), about 38 percent of the costs of physicians' services they receive (Ferry et al. 1980). Beneficiaries' premium payments cover about 28 percent of the cost of Medicare's SMI; general revenues and interest from the trust fund pay for the rest.

Medicare outlays were about $14.8 billion in fiscal year (FY) 1975, and $35 billion in FY 1980. This was a growth rate of about 18 percent per year. Part of this, of course, can be attributed to general inflation and to growth in the number of beneficiaries. Over those years, the GNP deflator rose 7.2 percent per year and the number of beneficiaries grew about 2.6 percent per year. But this still leaves a real growth in outlays per capita of about 8 percent per year.

Put another way, in FY 1975 Medicare outlays were 1 percent of GNP. By FY 1981 Medicare outlays reached $42.3 billion, 1.48 percent of GNP. At this rate of growth, Medicare is doubling its share of GNP in about eleven years and will reach 2 percent of GNP in 1986.

The longer-term implications of this growth rate are staggering. In 1980 there were 0.194 persons aged 65 and over for each person aged 20 to 64; by the year 2000 there will be 0.215. In 1980 the cost of Medicare per person aged 20–64, the group paying for it, was about $264. If the 8 percent per year real growth rate were to continue, by the year 2000 the annual cost per person aged 20–64 to support Medicare would be $1,366 (in 1980 dollars). And the situation will worsen rapidly after 2010 as people born in the postwar baby boom reach retirement age. It seems inevitable that the government will have to do something quite fundamental to modify this trend.

Medicaid

Medicaid is a federal program of grants to states to help
them defray medical costs for welfare recipients and other
low-income people who do not quite qualify for cash assistance. The federal government contributes on the basis of
a complex cost-sharing formula that has, on average, paid
for about 55 percent of the costs of Medicaid. Medicaid
served about 17.6 million beneficiaries in FY 1972 and about
21.5 million—some 6 million of whom are also eligible for
Medicare—in FY 1979. Federal Medicaid outlays were about
$6.8 billion in 1975, about $14 billion in FY 1980. Relative to
GNP, federal Medicaid outlays are much smaller than Medicare and growing at a slower rate.

Legislation enacted in 1981 provides for small reductions
in federal Medicaid payments from what they otherwise
would have been, part of which can be forgiven in the case of
states that make certain cost reduction efforts. In and of itself, this provision does not reduce the cost of Medicaid; it
merely shifts the burden to the states. States in turn may respond by cutting back on eligibility and the scope of covered
services, thus shifting the burden of care for those who cannot pay for it onto local government and providers of care.
Unfortunately, such efforts at burden shifting have usually
appeared more attractive to all levels of government than a
concerted effort to reduce costs through improved efficiency
of the delivery system. The same legislation gives states
greater freedom to select cost-effective providers for Medicaid. If used effectively, this may reduce cost in the long run.

Revenue loss from tax exclusion

Employer contributions to employee health insurance are excluded from the incomes of employees subject to federal income and social security taxes and state income taxes. This

has provided a powerful incentive for employers and employees to agree that the employer will pay for comprehensive health benefits. The employer can pay with pretax dollars. If the employer paid the employee in cash and let the employee buy his own health benefits, the latter would have to pay out of net after-tax income. Since the average taxpayer is in roughly the 40 percent marginal tax bracket, counting federal income and payroll taxes, the federal government is, in effect, subsidizing about 40 percent of the cost of ever more comprehensive employer-paid health benefits.

Paul Ginsburg of the Congressional Budget Office (1981) estimated that the federal revenue loss in 1982 from this tax exclusion is about $23 billion.[1] In addition, the Treasury Department estimates about a $4 billion loss in revenue from itemized deductions of personal medical insurance premium contributions and expenses (Office of Management and Budget 1981*e*). We do not have good estimates of the rate at which this revenue loss is growing, but three factors have interacted to make it grow faster than the federal budget and the GNP. First, health care spending is growing faster than GNP. Second, inflation has been pushing us into higher marginal tax brackets, and social security payroll tax rates have been increasing. Third, there has been a considerable growth in the scope of covered benefits. For example, the number of persons with dental insurance (mostly employer paid) went up from 9 million in 1969 to 70 million in 1979.

From 1970 to 1980 personal health care expenditures financed by private third parties grew about 14 percent per year, compared to a 10 percent annual growth in GNP. It seems reasonable to assume that the employer's share has not been decreasing, so this source of revenue loss has been growing at least 4 percentage points per year faster than GNP, not counting the effects of "bracket creep" and increasing payroll taxes. Roughly eight-tenths of 1 percent of GNP in 1982, it is increasing its share of GNP by at least 50 percent every ten years.

Other

The federal government makes outlays for numerous other
health care—related programs, the largest of which are those
of the Veterans Administration (up from $3.5 billion in 1975
to $5.8 billion in 1980), the Defense Department (up from
$2.8 billion in 1975 to $4.2 billion in 1980), and health
research and education (up from $2.7 billion in 1975 to
$4.2 billion in 1980). Their combined total has grown at a
rate below that of GNP.

Collision course

The president's economic program seeks to reduce federal
outlays as a percentage of GNP from nearly 23 percent in
1981 to around 19 percent, which was typical of the early
1960s. The Economic Recovery Tax Act of 1981 provides for
three successive reductions in personal income tax rates intended roughly to offset the effect of inflation in raising real
tax revenues, followed by indexation of the tax brackets (i.e.,
annual adjustment for inflation) starting in 1985. This will
eliminate bracket creep as a source of increase in the federal
share of GNP. It will mean a large step toward fixing the
share of GNP taken by the federal government. These policies are on a collision course with Medicare and the tax subsidies to health insurance, whose combined share of GNP is
now about 2.4 percent and growing at a rate that would bring
their total to more than 4 percent in another ten years.

THE FAILURE OF THE PRICE
CONTROL STRATEGY

The main direction of public policy regarding health care
costs in the 1970s was to attempt to impose direct controls on

medical care is of significant benefit to patients and is being delivered efficiently, then we are faced with a very hard choice in attempts to limit public spending. Cutting cost in that case will mean cutting the quality of care and/or people's access to it. If, on the other hand, a great deal of care is delivered inefficiently and produces an insignificant marginal benefit to the patients, then we have substantial opportunities for cutting cost without cutting quality or access. I have written on this subject elsewhere and will not repeat the analysis here (Enthoven 1980; also idem 1978). However, I have reached the conclusion that the latter view fits the facts far better than the former.

Briefly, we now have a great deal of evidence, based on the experience of millions of people over decades, that efficient organization and rational economic incentives can produce substantial reductions in the cost of care, compared to that delivered in the dominant, uncontrolled, fee-for-service solo practice sector, with no apparent reductions in overall quality. A review of many comparison studies found that prepaid, group practice, health maintenance organizations (HMOs) deliver comprehensive health care services for from 10 to 40 percent less in total per capita cost than the cost for similar people, usually in the same employment group, cared for under traditional, insured, fee for service (Luft 1978). The biggest source of economy is reduced hospital use, which is important because hospital care accounts for about 40 percent of total health care services. These economical patterns of care are not limited to health maintenance organizations. Recent studies have found that such distinguished organizations as the Mayo Clinic and the Palo Alto Medical Clinic have hospital use patterns similar to those of the leading prepaid, group practice HMOs, roughly 30 to 40 percent below the national average after appropriate demographic adjustments (Nobrega et al. 1980; Scitorsky and McCall 1980).

The essence of this idea is not in the acronym "HMO." Some HMOs are not efficient. The point is that there are *organized systems* with built-in incentives to control cost and quality, and experience shows that some of these do a very good job. The problem for public policy is how to create an overall environment in which such cost-effective organized systems would grow and eventually replace the unorganized fee-for-service sector.

Several techniques are used by such organized systems of care. They match resources, such as facilities and numbers of specialists, to the needs of the populations they serve. There are economies of scale and experience in the production of some specialized services; efficient systems either produce at an efficient scale or buy the services from efficient high-volume producers. Efficient systems also avoid long hospital stays where short ones will do as well. They organize appropriate care in less costly settings. For example, they organize home care and outpatient surgery as an alternative to more costly inpatient care. They are selective in the use of technology, confining its application to patients likely to benefit from it. They avoid the waste of duplicate diagnostic tests. Each of these may contribute only a few percentage points to cost reductions. But taken together, if systematically applied to the whole health care sector, I believe they could reduce the total costs of care by something on the order of 25 percent or more below what they otherwise would be.

PROPOSALS FOR INCENTIVES REFORM

If efficient delivery systems can provide comprehensive care for so much less cost, why have they not driven out the inefficient providers and taken over the market? Many factors are involved, one of the most important being that the market, as shaped by the tax and social security laws, has left consumers and providers with little or no incentive to make economical choices. Other factors include the opposition of organized medicine and the difficulties faced by newly organized systems in obtaining management and capital. Because employer contributions to employee health care or health insurance are tax-free compensation without limit, employers and employees have a powerful incentive to agree that the employer will pay for all employee health care costs. Most employers still do not offer employees a choice of health insurance plans, or if they do, they usually pay more on behalf of employees who choose the more costly alternative, especially if it is the traditional fee-for-service plan. Medicare and Medicaid beneficiaries who choose cost-effective providers do not profit from most of the savings. It is too easy for providers to survive in the marketplace without being cost conscious, so the growth of efficient delivery systems is inhibited.

Recognition of this fact has led to various proposals to reform the basic financial incentives of the health care system (for a more complete explanation, see Enthoven 1980).

1. Limit the exclusions of employer contributions and provide incentives for employers to offer a fair choice. These ideas form the basis for Senator David Durenberger's Health Incentives Reform Act, first introduced in 1979.[2] This bill would limit the amount of employer contribution in 1982 that would be tax free to the employee to $50 per month for an individual and $125 per month for a family, indexed thereafter by the medical care component of the Consumer Price Index. Also, as a condition for continued favorable tax treatment, employer health benefits plans would have to meet the following conditions: (a) any employer of more than 100 employees must offer at least three options, each by a separate carrier; (b) the employer's contribution must not depend on which option an employee chooses. (The bill also includes requirements for catastrophic expense protection and continuity of coverage.)

The limit on tax-free employer contributions would be applied to all contributions received by an individual taxpayer or family. There are several reasons for applying the limit to the taxpayer rather than to the employer. First, many people work for employers who are not liable for federal income taxes, including state and local government and nonprofit institutions. Second, tens of millions of people currently have duplicate coverage because many families are supported by more than one job. Such duplicate coverage adds administrative costs, can defeat the desired incentive effects of coinsurance, and may lead to duplicate payments to providers and patients. Applying the limit on tax-free employer contributions to the taxpayer would provide a disincentive to duplicate coverage.

Such a limit could serve as a basis for a number of equity-improving changes in the tax subsidies to health insurance. For one, the itemized personal deduction for health insurance premium payments could be included in the same limit. From the point of view of health insurance policy, there would appear to be no good reason for granting a larger subsidy to those who itemize than to those who do not. In the longer run, as funds become available, the limit could be applied to the sum of employer and employee contributions, thus giving the same tax break to people receiving low employer contributions as to people receiving high ones. Today, employer contributions to health insurance are positively related to wages and salaries. Thus today's tax exclusion makes the tax subsidy to health insurance positively related to income. The reform described here would move toward equalization of the tax subsidy across income classes. (An equal exclusion would still be worth more to people in higher marginal tax brackets. Complete equalization of the subsidy across income classes could be achieved by replacing the exclusion with a refundable tax credit.)

The Congressional Budget Office (1981) estimated that a limit of $120 per family per month in 1981 dollars, indexed, could raise federal income and payroll tax revenues by $2.6 billion in 1982, and by roughly $7 billion a year by 1986. While this proposal would help to balance the budget, its main purpose is to make consumers price sensitive in their choice of health plans—that is, to put health plans under market pressures to organize care efficiently. In other words, the rationale for the limit is that government should give people incentives to purchase good quality but efficient comprehensive health insurance or health care plans. People who make more costly choices should have to pay the extra costs themselves, out of their own net after-tax incomes.

Various issues have been raised concerning the limit on tax-free employer contributions. First, there is wide variation in per capita costs of health care among geographic regions. While regional variation in the limit might be one answer to this, one advantage of a uniform limit is that it provides the most powerful incentive effects where they are most needed—in the high-cost areas. Another consideration is that some employee groups pay high premiums because they constitute higher medical risks, not because they choose costly providers. The eventual solution to this problem probably lies in a universal requirement for rating by community rather than by employee group.

2. Require employers to offer choices including a "low option" with 25 percent coinsurance of hospital expenses, and give employees who choose the low option a tax-free rebate equal to the difference in premiums.

These ideas form the basis for Senator Richard Schweiker's Comprehensive Health Care Reform Act introduced in 1979 and reintroduced by Senator Orrin Hatch in 1981.[3] As a condition for favorable tax treatment of employer contributions, this bill would require employers to offer employees at least one choice of health insurance plan with 25 percent coinsurance of hospital services and a limit on a family's incurred out-of-pocket medical expenses equal to 20 percent of earned income. Employers of 200 or more would have to offer three choices of health plans. Employers would have to contribute the same amount whichever option the employee chose. The maximum employer contribution would be the premium of the most expensive health plan chosen by at least 10 percent of the employees. Employees choosing a plan with a premium below the employer's contribution level would receive the difference in cash, free of federal income tax. (The bill also includes requirements for catastrophic expense protection and continuity of coverage.)

The purpose of the tax-free rebate is to give employees an incentive, without increasing their taxes, to choose the less costly option. In Senator Durenberger's bill, employees would have to pay tax on excess employer contributions; thus they would have to pay out of their own after-tax incomes the difference between the premium of the health plan of their choice and the exclusion limit. The Schweiker-Hatch bill's provision of tax-free cash rebates for employees choosing less costly health plans improves its political palatability at the expense of reduced tax revenues. In the short run, the Schweiker-Hatch bill exchanges one form of tax-free compensation for another. It neither limits tax-free compensation nor helps to balance the budget.

There are also serious problems in the way the proposal is structured. It seems clear, in the Schweiker-Hatch scheme, that the better risks—that is, people not anticipating hospitalization this year—will be motivated to choose the "low option," with coinsurance and low premiums, and get the tax-free rebate. Those expecting to be hospitalized will choose the more comprehensive options. Those who choose the low options and later have elective surgery recommended or a chronic condition diagnosed as likely to require hospitalization will be motivated to switch to a comprehensive option at the next annual enrollment. This is sometimes characterized as a "free-rider" problem. Thus this scheme, as proposed, would tend to divide the risk pool and drive up the cost of comprehensive options. Low-risk employees would get a tax-free windfall at the expense of the employer and the government.

One purpose of the "competition strategy" is to put economic pressure on providers of care to organize services efficiently. As noted earlier, there is evidence that this can be done and can achieve substantial savings. However, one must design the system so that health insurance plans cannot evade the intent of the strategy by selecting good health risks. The Schweiker-Hatch proposal is based on a different idea: that by offering a low option, one can start a process of risk selection that ends in the demise of comprehensive plans and leaves the field to low-option ones. It is a proposal for the rollback of health insurance without a clear limit on how far the rollback will go.

It is important to recognize that the tax subsidy for health insurance performs a socially desirable function in encouraging low-risk people to buy health insurance and share the costs with high-risk people. If not carefully limited, the tax-free rebate idea could undo this beneficial effect and create a serious free-rider problem.

There are ways in which the Schweiker-Hatch proposal might be modified to mitigate these problems. For example, the amount of employer contribution that is tax free could be limited, as in the Durenberger bill. The tax-free rebate could also be limited. The rebates could be tied to risk-adjusted "whole group premiums" instead of to the actual premiums that reflect risk selection. However, complexity grows and intelligibility declines with each of these adjustments.

3. Increase the coinsurance that is paid by Medicare beneficiaries.

As noted earlier, Medicare beneficiaries must pay a $260 deductible upon entering the hospital, plus additional copayments after 60 days in the hospital. Their insurance for physicians' services is subject to a $75 deductible, after which Medicare pays 80 percent of what it deems "reasonable charges," which in practice average around 72 percent of actual charges (Ferry et al. 1980). So Medicare already includes substantial coinsurance and deductibles.

One proposal for reducing costs to the federal budget is to increase the coinsurance paid by Medicare beneficiaries — for example, by requiring a 10 percent or $26 per day copayment for every day in the hospital after the first day. Two reasons are offered for this proposal. The first is that such a charge would provide a disincentive to using services of low marginal value. The second is that, even in the absence of an incentive effect on service use, the proposal could reduce federal spending by more than $2 billion a year.

The evidence in favor of the first argument is very weak. Sick people are not likely to be good cost-conscious buyers of medical care. A recent Rand Corporation report on the National Health Insurance Experiment found that once people were hospitalized, coinsurance had no significant effect on hospital expenses (Newhouse et al. 1981). (However, because all patients were protected by a $1,000 limit on annual out-of-pocket expenses, one could argue that the experiment did not provide a fair test of more extensive coinsurance.) In any case, about 80 percent of Medicare beneficiaries have private or public (Medicaid) supplemental insurance that pays all or most of their hospital coinsurance, so these people would be unlikely to feel any disincentive at all (Congressional Budget Office 1979).

Thus increased coinsurance of hospital services for Medicare beneficiaries is likely to be nothing other than a shift of costs from the government to beneficiaries.

4.   Offer each Medicare beneficiary the option of joining an HMO or other private health insurance plan to which the federal government would make a premium contribution about equal to what similar persons cost the Medicare program.
The central idea is for the government to make payments in fixed periodic dollar amounts, as opposed to the open-ended

fee-for-service and cost-reimbursement characteristic of Medicare, so that beneficiaries who join cost-effective organized systems of care can realize for themselves the savings associated with that choice.

This idea formed the basis for a proposal by the Carter administration, introduced as a bill by Congressman Charles Rangel in 1979, under which Medicare would pay 95 percent of average per capita costs for each class of beneficiary (grouped by such factors as age, sex, location, and disability status) in the form of a fixed periodic payment to the health maintenance organization of the beneficiary's choice.[4] The HMO would agree in return to provide at least all the benefits covered under Medicare. The beneficiary would agree to obtain all his care from or through the HMO during the period of his enrollment. The HMO would agree to make a total charge equal to its "utilization-adjusted community rate"—that is, the basic community rate it charges adults not on Medicare, adjusted upward by the ratio of average use of services by Medicare beneficiaries to average use by non-Medicare beneficiaries. If this charge were less than the government's contribution, the HMO would pass the savings on to beneficiaries in the form of enhanced preventive services, reduced or eliminated coinsurance, and additional benefits.

This idea has also formed the basis for a more recent proposal by Congressmen Willis Gradison and Richard Gephardt called the "Voluntary Medicare Option Act."[5] In this proposal, fixed-dollar federal premium contributions would be available for a larger class of "qualified plans." Basically, any organization would be allowed to participate in the voluntary option program if it met the following criteria. First, it would have to agree to abide by the rules of an annual enrollment open to all Medicare beneficiaries in its service areas (with certain limited exceptions). Second, it would have to provide or pay for at least the benefits covered under Medicare, using a stated premium set in advance. Third, it would have to set a premium for beneficiaries in each actuarial category without regard to individual health status or utilization. And fourth, it would have to limit each beneficiary's out-of-pocket costs to an amount related to average coinsurance and deductible payments by Medicare beneficiaries.

The federal contribution in the initial years would be based on the average per capita cost to the government for people in each actuarial category in a base year, updated annually by the medical care component of the Consumer Price Index. In later years the federal contribution would be tied to a weighted average of the premiums for qualified plans in each area. Since beneficiaries would always have the option of switching back to regular Medicare at the next annual enrollment period, it seems unlikely that federal contributions under the voluntary program would fall far below average per capita costs under regular Medicare.

Each enrollee in the private plans would agree to pay a supplemental premium if necessary. If the premium of the plan of his choice were below the federal contribution, the enrollee could receive half the difference in cash or additional benefits, tax free, up to an annual limit of $500.

The strength of these proposals is that they open up the Medicare market to efficiency considerations, allowing beneficiaries to realize for themselves the savings generated by their decisions to join cost-effective health plans. Opening this market to a broader class of health plans than HMOs would appear desirable. But the voluntary option program is unlikely to attract the participation of many insurance companies or Blue Cross or Blue Shield plans because of their inability to control costs enough to compete with Medicare. So the participants are likely to be mostly HMOs that can control costs. However, the voluntary option may attract some hospitals and group practices to offer prepaid plans to Medicare beneficiaries. Debate on the merits of the proposals is likely to focus on the adequacy of safeguards for quality and financial solvency of the non-HMO alternatives.

The primary limitation of these proposals is that they leave the main costs of Medicare tied to open-ended fee for service and cost reimbursement. Thus they do little if anything to slow the growth of Medicare outlays. In fact, such a "voluntary option" approach might well increase the government's cost in the short run. One reason for this is extra administrative costs. Another is that cost-effective systems match the number of physicians and facilities to the needs of the populations they serve. As the HMOs grow and take an increasing number of patients away from the traditional medical market, they leave an increased number of physicians and facilities per capita in the open-ended fee-for-service system. And studies by Victor Fuchs (1972) and others show that more doctors per capita mean more doctoring and higher costs. If the government's contributions continue to be tied to the costs of the open-ended fee-for-service system, this effect may cause them to go up faster. Another potential problem is risk selection. It is possible that, even without any overt attempts to attract preferred risks, the private alternatives to Medicare might attract better-than-average risks within each actuarial category (Luft 1979). One reason this might happen is that people joining an HMO usually must change doctors, and people currently under the active care of a physician are less likely to do so than those who are not. In that case, the government might end up paying average costs for people who otherwise would have cost it less than the average. It is also possible that the more comprehensive private alternatives to Medicare might attract worse risks.

All this is not to say that the voluntary option idea is not a good one. Indeed, it is a necessary transitional step toward more comprehensive reform. If implemented successfully, the voluntary option proposals may attract many beneficiaries and thus help to demonstrate the feasibility and acceptability of a comprehensive reform of Medicare along the lines described in the next section. However, as long as the government's outlays are tied to costs in the open-ended fee-for-service system, we cannot expect voluntary options to slow the growth of Medicare outlays.

5. Comprehensive Medicare reform on a phased basis: create a new Medicare system for newly eligible beneficiaries based on fixed-dollar premium contributions by government and multiple choice of private comprehensive health care financing and delivery plans. Such a system would resemble the Federal Employees Health Benefits Program (FEHBP) and the Health Benefits Program of the California State Public Employees' Retirement System (PERS), which have operated successfully for twenty years.[6] These systems have shown that large-scale multiple choice is feasible and that the administrative costs are low.

Under such a system, existing beneficiaries could be given a choice of staying with the existing Medicare system or joining the new one. The federal government would contribute its average per capita cost for each class of beneficiary in the base year updated annually for inflation. Thus health plans would get paid proportionately more for caring for beneficiaries in higher-risk classes. Beneficiaries would contribute the additional price of the plan of their choice; it could be withheld from their social security checks just as Medicare Part B premiums are now. Participating plans would have to cover at least Medicare benefits plus place a limit on the out-of-pocket payments for covered benefits made by any beneficiary. They would have to accept all beneficiaries who choose them in the annual open enrollment (subject to certain limitations). They would have to set a price in advance, and charge the same price to all beneficiaries regardless of health status or utilization.

If such a system were implemented successfully and worked as intended, gradually all beneficiaries would find it in their interest to join cost-effective organized systems of care, and the costs of their medical care would be brought under the control of the marketplace. The government's real, age-specific, per capita costs would be stabilized.

Making the "fixed-contribution multiple choice" system mandatory for new beneficiaries would solve several key problems for the government. Most important, it would break the link between government outlays and the costs of the open-ended fee-for-service system, setting in motion a process that would lead to the eventual phaseout of the present basis of Medicare. Combined with a limit on tax-free employer contributions to health insurance, this would be a powerful signal that the end of the open-ended system were in sight, that future health care would be made up primarily of cost-effective systems. Moreover, this would solve the risk selection problem from the government's point of view: in such a system, the bad risks would fall somewhere, but not on the government. The government could concentrate its attention on seeing to it that the risks are distributed equitably or that health plans serving a disproportionate share of high-risk persons are compensated for doing so.

However, this proposal, which was considered by the Reagan administration in 1981, has its share of political problems (Enthoven 1981). First, it is caught in a "long-run v. short-run" dilemma. The government is under great pressure to achieve savings quickly, and this proposal would not work quickly. Even sixteen years after enactment, in fact, half the beneficiaries might still be in the open-ended system. (Additional incentives for existing beneficiaries to join the new system might be needed, and these would probably cost money in the short run.) On the other hand, the political costs of requiring new beneficiaries to switch to a new system with less government funding would be incurred at the outset. Politicians facing the imperatives of upcoming elections are under powerful pressure to produce benefits *now* in exchange for costs that will only become apparent later. This proposal would entail costs now for the sake of benefits achieved gradually in the future.

Another problem the proposal has encountered is that Blue Cross/Blue Shield and the insurance companies have indicated a reluctance to participate in such a system. They are concerned, first, that their costs would exceed Medicare costs for providing the same level of benefits because Medicare pays hospitals substantially less than the charges for private customers, because they anticipate higher administrative costs associated with marketing to individuals, and because they would need to build up reserves to support the expanded business (Blue Cross/Blue Shield Associations 1981). They fear that since the supplemental premiums they would have to charge would appear very high to beneficiaries, they would be blamed and attacked politically. Second, since one of the main ideas of the proposal is to slow the growth in the government's outlays, they fear that medical care costs would grow faster than federal contributions, so that their supplemental premiums would have to grow even faster.

One of the premises of the competition strategy has been that, given the appropriate market environment, a sufficient number of private insurers and Blue Cross/Blue Shield organizations would be willing to innovate with alternate delivery system arrangements with built-in cost controls, as some have already been doing. For the reformed system to work successfully, it is not necessary that a majority of private insurers participate and innovate with effective cost controls—only *enough* are needed to cover the enrolled population.

6. Enact a universal system of health insurance based on the principles of consumer choice, and fixed-dollar premium contributions by government toward the qualified health care financing and delivery plan of each person's choice.

This idea is embodied in the National Health Care Reform Act,[7] first introduced in 1980 by Congressmen Richard Gephardt and David Stockman, and in the Consumer Choice Health Plan proposal the present author developed for the Carter administration in 1977 (Enthoven 1980).

In the Gephardt-Stockman bill, every citizen or legal resident would be eligible to receive a federal contribution toward the premium of the health plan of his choice. This contribution would be related to the average premium for qualified health care plans in each person's actuarial category. It could be received in the form of a limited, tax-free employer contribution or an equivalent refundable tax credit. Medicare eligibles would be allowed to elect either a voucher or continuation with existing Medicare. The election of a voucher would be irrevocable. In the year after 50 percent of all Medicare eligibles had chosen the voucher, Medicare would be repealed and all eligibles would convert to vouchers. Following a transition period, the value of the voucher would equal the weighted average of the premiums of qualified plans selected by the aged and disabled. Those choosing plans with premiums below the voucher amount would be allowed to receive the excess as a credit toward out-of-pocket expenses or as a cash refund. At the election of each state, Medicaid would be replaced with a voucher system for low-income people. The federal premium contribution for people whose incomes are below the poverty line would equal the weighted average of the premiums of qualified plans in their actuarial category plus the average eligible out-of-pocket expenditures. This amount would be paid to the qualified plan of the beneficiary's choice, and the qualified plan would have to provide all covered services for that amount, without further out-of-pocket payment by the beneficiary. For low-income people above the poverty line, the voucher amount would be reduced on a sliding scale related to income.

Plans eligible for these federal contributions would have to comply with a number of conditions including participation in an annual open enrollment; setting premiums on the basis of community rating by actuarial category (i.e., charging the same premium for the same benefits to all beneficiaries in the same actuarial category, regardless of utilization or health status); a limitation on each person's out-of-pocket expenses for covered services, not to exceed $2,900 per year; and demonstration of financial solvency to the satisfaction of a newly created Health Benefits Assurance Corporation.

A frequent reaction to these proposals for a universal system is that they are too radical and far-reaching to be enacted all in one step. Congress works incrementally rather than in radical steps. If that is the case, these proposals for universal reform still serve a valuable purpose as descriptions of long-range goals for a series of incremental reforms.

RECOMMENDED NEXT STEPS

Of all these possibilities, which should be acted on next? In my view, the most important next step would be to limit, as in Senator Durenberger's Health Incentives Reform Act, the amount of employer contribution to health insurance that can be tax free to the employee. This limit should be adjusted annually for inflation and applied to the taxpayer rather than to the employer. Such a limit would put the burden of "price-sensitive consumer choice" on the best insured and best paid, and therefore on those most able to bear it. At the margin—that is, above the limit—the best-insured employees would have to pay the extra cost of more costly health insurance plans out of their own net after-tax incomes. They would be rewarded for choosing more efficient delivery systems.

One can only speculate on the response to such a change in incentives. But it seems likely that employees would be strongly inclined to switch to cost-effective organized systems in groups in which they are offered. In groups in which they are not offered, there would be an incentive to offer them. And an increasing number of employers would be likely to make equal fixed-dollar contributions at the limit and to increase the number of choices offered.

It would be desirable to couple this reform with an incentive to employers to offer employees a multiple choice. These employers generally confirm that once the system is set up and in operation, administrative costs are low. But there is an initial start-up cost associated with negotiating the contracts and informing employees. An appropriate incentive might be a one-time tax credit to offset start-up costs available to employers in the year in which they first offer multiple choice as defined in the law. The cost of the credit could be paid out of the revenue savings from the limit on tax-free contributions. Beyond the financial incentive, such a provision would have a desirable symbolic value as an indicator of the direction of public policy.

Admittedly, imposition of such a limit would work some hardship among groups with the highest costs today, such as the United Auto Workers. Generous transition rules would be appropriate, allowing such groups time to adapt. For example, existing dollar levels above the limit could be "grandfathered" until inflation caused the general limit to reach those levels.

The other most important step would be a "voluntary option" program for Medicare. Congress ought to open a genuine fair-choice option for beneficiaries to join HMOs and other organizations capable of providing good quality care on a cost-controlled basis. Reasonable standards need to be applied to participating organizations to ensure that the system is not plagued by financial failures and scandal. (In the early 1970s, the Medicaid program in California contracted indiscriminately with many newly created prepaid health plans that abused the system and underserved their subscribers. The political backlash set back by many years the cause of delivery system reform in California.)

The purposes of such legislation would be (a) to demonstrate the feasibility and effectiveness of this model, (b) to expand the capacity of cost-effective organized systems of care to serve the Medicare population, and (c) to stimulate the Health Care Financing Administration to develop the necessary management tools, including a satisfactory system of actuarially adjusted, per capita cost factors, so that in the future HCFA would be able to manage a price-sensitive consumer choice system for all beneficiaries. The 1972 amendments to the Social Security Act included an attempt to create an HMO option for Medicare beneficiaries. But the law and the regulations were so biased against HMOs that very few were interested, and the Social Security Administration and Health Care Financing Administration have not effectively implemented them. Legislation creating a voluntary option program for Medicare should include a strong congressional mandate for HCFA to implement it effectively and to make it a step towards comprehensive system reform.

As noted earlier, such a voluntary option program would do little or nothing to constrain costs to the government in the short run. That goal would have to be left to other means, if such efficacious means exist. Rather, the purpose would be to lay the foundations for a comprehensive Medicare reform a few years later.

8

LAURENCE S. SEIDMAN

A New Tax Expenditure for Health Insurance

Health insurance as deduction or credit. Inequities of the deduction. Medicare and Medicaid. Income-related assistance. The advantages of cost sharing. The regulatory approach and excess demand.

Perhaps the least recognized federal expenditure for health care assists Americans who are neither old nor poor. While the public is aware of federal expenditures for Medicare and Medicaid, it is often unaware that there is a federal tax expenditure for private health insurance. Yet the sums involved are huge; according to a recent report prepared by the Tax Analysis Division of the Congressional Budget Office (1980), the health insurance tax expenditure was $12.7 billion in fiscal year 1980, roughly one-fifth of the total direct federal expenditure on health care. Thus, this tax expenditure has an important impact on the federal budget. Moreover, as this chapter will emphasize, most economists believe that it is a central cause of health sector inefficiency and cost inflation.

Traditionally, criticism of a "tax expenditure" is followed by a proposal that it be converted into a direct government expenditure that appears explicitly in the expenditure column of the budget. Such a proposal, however, will not be offered here. In contrast, it will be argued that a tax expenditure *is* the appropriate tool for the federal government to utilize for health insurance policy. The problem is the open-ended design of the current tax expenditure, which both inflates its impact on the budget and generates health sector inefficiency. A new, closed-ended design, advocated in recent years by many economists, will therefore be proposed.

THE FEDERAL TAX EXPENDITURE FOR PRIVATE HEALTH INSURANCE

When an employer raises an employee's compensation by $500, the $500 is clearly income to the employee. Yet if it takes the form of an employer contribution to a health insurance premium, the $500 is excluded from the taxable income of the employee. While the employee's true income increases by $500, he is in effect given a $500 tax deduction, so that his taxable income is unaffected.

The value of the implicit deduction to the employee depends on his tax bracket. If he is in a 20 percent bracket, the tax deduction is worth $100; in a 40 percent bracket, it is worth $200. It would be hard to justify this insurance deduction by the claim that it results in a more accurate measure of the employee's true income. Instead, the insurance deduction should be regarded as a method by which the federal government makes an expenditure to help wage earners buy private health insurance. Conceptually, it is as though the government taxed the $500 at the employee's marginal tax rate—but then immediately made an equal expenditure to help the same employee buy health insurance.

Once it is conceded that the insurance deduction is in reality a disguised government expenditure, it is clear that the federal government does not limit its financial assistance for health care to the elderly and poor, as a focus on Medicare and Medicaid might suggest. In fact, it is more accurate to argue that federal assistance, prior to Medicare and Medicaid, was in fact limited to households that obtained private insurance—people who had little real need for the tax expenditure benefits.

Because it takes the form of an implicit deduction, the insurance tax expenditure has the questionable feature that the greater the employee's income, the more assistance it gives. As the previous example indicates, the employee in the 40 percent tax bracket receives twice the aid of the one in the 20 percent bracket. Many would prefer the pattern of assistance to be exactly the reverse; some would claim that aid should be equal for all employees; but very few would defend the pattern that currently exists.

Even if this inequity were somehow eliminated, one might well ask if it is a desirable policy for the federal government to use the tax system to help people buy private health insurance.

At one philosophical pole is the view that it should be up to each household to obtain adequate insurance on its own, without assistance. At the opposite pole is the belief that the government should assure every household of comprehensive insurance that makes all medical care free. Probably most people hold an intermediate or moderate view. They feel it desirable to assist households to protect themselves against medical bills that are large relative to their income, and to assure such "major-risk" (catastrophic) protection for households unable to afford it. At the same time, assistance should not be given for more comprehensive, "first-dollar," "shallow" insurance; that decision should be left to each household. This intermediate view will be adopted here.

How does the current insurance deduction correspond to this intermediate perspective? The crucial discrepancy is that the current deduction is open ended. It would be desirable to provide assistance for the first $X of insurance, so that the household is encouraged to obtain major-risk coverage. But it is undesirable from this perspective to allow all insurance expenditure, without limit, to be deductible. This encourages comprehensive, first-dollar insurance.

A HEALTH INSURANCE TAX CREDIT

If a deduction (the employer exclusion) is retained as the method of providing assistance, the intermediate view could be implemented by reforming the tax law to place a cap, or ceiling, on the deduction permitted per employee. For example, suppose it is estimated that $800 is sufficient to purchase major-risk insurance. Then the new tax law would permit up to $800 of an employer's contribution to be excluded from the taxable income of an employee. If the employer contributed $1,300 then $500 would appear on the employee's W−2 form as taxable income.

As we have seen, however, the greater the household's income, the more assistance the deduction would in effect provide. It would therefore be more equitable to completely eliminate the deduction and replace it with a new health insurance tax credit. Under this approach, the entire employer contribution would appear on the employee's W−2 form as part of his adjusted gross income. But each household would be eligible for a health insurance tax credit. The key feature of the tax credit is that, for a household with a given income, it would partially reimburse insurance expense only up to an amount sufficient to buy major-risk insurance. For example, for a household with $30,000 income, it might equal 30 percent of the first $800 of expense on a premium. If the household obtained $1,300 insurance, it would receive no assistance for the last $500.

Unlike the deduction, the lower the income of the household, the more generous the credit. For example, a $15,000 household might be eligible for a credit equal to 60 percent of the first $1,000 of expense on a premium. The amount of $1,000, rather than $800, might be required to provide adequate major-risk protection, because such a household can afford less out-of-pocket burden. Scaling the credit to income would be included in the 1040 income tax form.

As stated earlier, it has been estimated that eliminating the current tax expenditure for insurance would have saved the federal budget $12.7 billion in fiscal year (FY) 1980. While an estimate of the cost of the new tax credit is unavailable, it would be substantially less than $12.7 billion because of two built-in limitations. First, the credit would apply only to the purchase of major-risk insurance, while today's deduction applies to high-premium comprehensive insurance.

Second, the credit would be scaled to ability to afford insurance. While it is true that low-income households would receive a somewhat greater subsidy than under the current deduction, middle- and upper-income households would receive substantially less, so a net saving would result. Because middle- and upper-income households can afford to buy major-risk insurance without assistance, only a small credit would be justified for these households.

Converting the current generous deduction into a limited credit would therefore reduce the subsidy received by the typical household; but it would also reduce the tax burden on that household. It may be asked: if the average household would experience both gains and losses from the change, why would it be desirable? The answer, to be developed in the next section, is that the shift to major-risk insurance with consumer cost sharing should significantly reduce the waste of resources in the health sector, and that should result in an important net gain for the average household.

Suppose the credit for which a household was eligible exceeded that household's tax liability (because its income was low). Since, in reality, the tax credit would be a device to implement an expenditure program in order to assure adequate insurance, clearly it should be "refundable." If the credit exceeded tax liability, the household then would receive a check from the Internal Revenue Service (IRS) equal to the difference.

Finally, despite the new credit, it is inevitable that a minority of households would continue to find themselves inadequately covered when catastrophic illness struck. They would vary in the degree of responsibility for their predicament. Some might have consciously refused to obtain coverage, though given the opportunity to do so at an affordable price. Others, due to poor health history, low income, or self-employment, might have found it impossible to afford adequate coverage.

Rather than attempt to separate those who deserve help from those who do not, the government could simply provide an insurance-of-last-resort tax credit. For example, once a household itself had borne medical expenses equal, say, to 15 percent of its income, it would be entitled to a tax credit equal to 100 percent of the expense above 15 percent. Such a credit would assure universal major-risk protection.

If the health insurance and last-resort credits were enacted, Medicaid could be ended. Because the new credits would be refundable, they would apply to persons with income so low that they pay no tax. Unlike Medicaid, which does not apply to all the poor, the credits would be universal in coverage. A simplified tax return might be devised to ease application for credit, although a credit card system would still be necessary to handle the cash flow problem. Loan institutions under contract with the government would pay providers promptly on behalf of low-income patients and would later be reimbursed by the IRS through the tax credit.

The new tax credits, like the current insurance deduction, would be tax expenditures. Why continue to help households buy health insurance through the tax system rather than through a "direct" government expenditure program, as critics of tax expenditures often recommend?

The answer should be clear from the previous discussion. Assistance should be scaled to ability to pay in order to assure adequate protection for all households at minimum cost to the federal budget. The most effective way to relate assistance to incomes is through the federal personal income tax. While preserving confidentiality and using a mechanism familiar (for better or worse) to almost all households, a tax credit can correlate aid to ability to pay.

Whenever income relating is a key purpose, a tax expenditure should be utilized without apology. The personal income tax provides a strategic policy instrument, the historical significance of which has been generally unrecognized.

To appreciate this, it is instructive to recall that when the movement for "free medical care" gained momentum in the late nineteenth and early twentieth centuries, no mechanism existed for income-relating assistance. In the United States the income tax was not enacted until 1913, and was applied to a relatively small fraction of the population until after World War II. Only in the past few decades has the instrument existed to reimburse households according to income while preserving confidentiality.

This instrument enables certain social goals to be achieved at a far smaller budget cost, and therefore at far less burden to the general taxpayer. If income relating is impossible, it is necessary to make it universally free in order to assure that everyone can afford medical care. This calls for

100 percent financing by the government, at a huge tax and budget cost. If assistance can be income related, total aid can be greatly reduced. The tax credit, therefore, enables equity to be achieved while limiting the total tax and budget cost. It is an invention to be applauded, not apologized for, as in much of the literature that criticizes tax expenditures.

THE CONSEQUENCES OF A HEALTH INSURANCE TAX CREDIT

Many economists support transforming the current open-ended insurance deduction into a closed-ended deduction or credit because such a transformation should remove perhaps the central cause of health sector inefficiency and cost inflation: excessive first-dollar, shallow hospital insurance.

Today's open-ended deduction encourages employees to prefer—and employers and unions to choose—high-premium comprehensive insurance that makes hospital care virtually free to the average patient. Nearly 95 percent of all hospital revenue for patient care comes from insurers, private or public. The typical patient has no reason to care about the cost of his own hospital care because the bill will be paid by an insurer. (It should be noted, though, that the typical patient *does* have reason to care about the physician's bill, since it usually is not fully covered.)

The impact of widespread comprehensive hospital insurance can be understood through a familiar analogy: restaurant bill splitting. Suppose members of a large group agree, in advance, to split the restaurant bill evenly, regardless of what each person orders. In contrast to the situation with individual checks, each person obviously no longer has much incentive to limit the cost of his order. The size of his preassigned share of the group bill will be virtually unaffected by his own order; it will depend on what everyone else orders. He will therefore order as though food were free. In the end, of course, each person will pay an inflated amount, but no individual will be motivated to avoid this outcome.

Our hospital system is financed by bill splitting. In the end, of course, we all pay the inflated bill through insurance premiums and taxes to finance Medicare and Medicaid. But the typical patient has no incentive to limit his own "order," because his own use of service will have no effect on the financial burden he bears through a premium or tax.

Each physician today knows that his patient will not want him to weigh cost when making decisions concerning hospitalization. The patient will probably never even see the bill. Physicians, acting as decision-makers for their patients, thus convey this message to hospital administrators. A hospital will be faulted for lacking some facility or equipment, but never for providing high quality at excessive cost. Administrators respond rationally by acquiring facilities and equipment without great concern for cost. The bill, however inflated, will not deter physicians and patients; it will be paid by insurers.

The new health insurance tax credit would encourage a shift from high-premium, first-dollar, shallow insurance to moderate-premium, major-risk insurance. Such insurance would require moderate patient cost sharing (deductibles and co-insurance) for hospital bills.

Gradually, each physician would recognize that his typical patient now does care about cost. True, at the time of hospitalization, the patient would ordinarily be in no mood to worry about cost. Eventually, however, the recuperating patient would develop a great interest in his hospital bill because he would then realize that he would have to pay for some of it. He would not appreciate costs that appeared excessive and unnecessary.

To avoid complaints, the average physician would try to avoid unnecessary costs and be sure he could justify those that were incurred. Such behavior would be partly self-interested, since patient resentment can translate into fewer recommendations and a decline in the MD's income. It would also accord with the ideal of the trust relationship between doctor and patient, in which the doctor is expected to act in the patient's best interest.

If the average physician gradually became concerned about cost, a new message would be conveyed to hospital administrators. If hospital X continued to provide a given quality at a higher cost than hospital Y, it would then experience a decline in demand as physicians took their patients to Y instead of X. Hospital administrators, long sheltered from the consequences of inefficiency due to 100 percent insurance, would at last experience the penalty inefficient managers suffer in any other industry where consumers care about price. The new incentive for efficiency should gradually improve performance in the hospital sector, as it has in most other industries.

It should be emphasized that consumer cost sharing does not imply that physicians and patients would seek low prices at the expense of quality. For other goods and services, consumers are often willing to pay a higher price to obtain higher quality; this tendency should be especially strong for health care. Thus a dramatic decline in cost should not be expected—nor would it be desirable. High quality, costly care would continue to be demanded by both patients and physicians. Technological innovations and medical advances would assure rising quality and cost.

The difference, however, is that cost increases would have to be justified by associated quality increases, as perceived by physicians and patients. If hospital X were more costly than Y because it offered valuable services not available at Y, then its higher cost would not deter patients in need of those services. But if X were more costly because of wasteful management, it would lose patients and experience financial difficulty. Similarly, cost would not deter a patient from obtaining an emergency operation at a hospital. But the patient might leave the hospital on day seven if he had to pay for part of his expenses, while he might have stayed eight days under free care.

These savings would reduce inefficiency in the hospital sector. Efficiency is promoted when consumers continue to use services they value more highly than the associated cost, but refrain from use when the value, as they perceive it, is less than cost. The central shortcoming of free care, induced by the open-ended tax subsidy to insurance, is that it removes the incentive for physicians and patients to weigh benefit against cost.

THE INCENTIVE APPROACH VERSUS GOVERNMENT REGULATION

The approach to health sector policy described thus far is one of two alternative strategies that the nation might adopt. The other is to accept free care, and to use government regulation in an attempt to achieve efficiency.

Advocates of the regulatory approach sometimes cite the public utilities as an example of tolerable regulation, and assert that similar measures can work adequately in the health sector. It is seldom recognized that there is a fundamental difference between the proposed health sector regulation and traditional public utility regulation.

Public utility service is not free to the consumer. Each household pays according to its own use of electricity, water, telephone, or natural gas; each therefore has an incentive to conserve. The reason for regulation is not to curb excessive use of a free service, but to prevent exploitation by a monopoly. To appreciate that the problem confronting health regulators would not only be different but much more difficult, imagine that long-distance telephone calls were

made free to the caller. Obviously, the telephone utility commission would have a new and huge problem to face as the
costs accelerated.

It is instructive to consider how telephone regulators
might cope. First, despite inflated demand, they might limit
the expansion of capacity in the system. Such a limitation of
supply would control the cost escalation. But this alone would
leave consumers dissatisfied. Chronic excess demand for
telephone service would result. Callers would often be unable
to get through. Some with frivolous purpose—even in their
own eyes—might succeed in getting a line and then talk for
an hour. Others with urgent purpose would be crowded out.
Inequity and inefficiency would result.

The second step of regulators thus would be to set priorities among callers in order to filter out those with frivolous
purpose and assure that urgent callers promptly obtain a
line. But how could this be done? Clearly, few would admit
that their purpose was frivolous. Fortunately, such regulation has never been necessary in the telephone sector—
or in any other public utility. For most users, long-distance
calls are not free. Consumer cost sharing automatically
limits waste.

Consider how health sector regulators might proceed in
the face of free hospital care. First, despite inflated demand,
they might limit the expansion of hospital capacity and the
acquisition of new facilities and technology. Such a limitation can succeed in limiting cost inflation. In Great Britain,
for example, where the National Health Service (NHS) controls the supply of facilities and technology, health care costs
have been held near 5 percent of gross national product,
compared to 9 percent in the United States.

The by-product of such supply restrictions, however, is
chronic excess demand. In Britain, while emergencies are
treated promptly, nonemergencies often suffer significant
delays. Waiting lists are endemic to the NHS, and while the
very affluent sometimes obtain prompt care from a small pri-

vate sector, the majority must simply accept delays. Inevitably, there is inequity and inefficiency.

Pointing out the shortcoming of the NHS is not to deny that many British citizens appear proud of their health service and that no one is denied care due to indigence. It is also important not to exaggerate the shortcomings of supply-restricted, regulated health care systems. After all, such systems exist in most "mixed capitalist economies" and succeed in functioning without serious crisis. It should be recognized, nevertheless, that these systems developed before a mechanism existed to reconcile concern for efficiency incentives with concern for universal access to needed care. Without a personal income tax covering most of the population, these goals appeared incompatible, and most countries chose to make care free of cost, sacrificing incentives and resorting to regulation.

The legacy of this past conflict will undoubtedly continue to affect political prospects for the tax credit approach. The traditional liberal/labor coalition, through inertia, may continue to object to any proposal that advocates consumer cost sharing, without appreciating the fact that it is now possible to tailor cost sharing to ability to pay. Nevertheless, the severe budgetary climate—and criticism of excessive regulation—may cause at least some members of this coalition to reconsider. It may be possible to appeal simultaneously to the pro-incentive sentiments of conservatives and the pro—ability-to-pay sentiments of liberals.

The central point of this chapter is that a new policy instrument—the tax credit on the personal income tax—now permits reconciliation of these two goals. The question, therefore, is not whether a supply-restricted, regulated, free-care system can "work." It is whether it works as well as an unrestricted system in which a tax credit assures universal ability to pay while consumer cost sharing automatically limits inefficiency.

CONCLUSION

The current tax expenditure for private health insurance has the serious shortcoming of being open ended for each person. While there is justification for a policy that encourages households to obtain major-risk (catastrophic) insurance, a tax deduction for shallow, first-dollar insurance that makes hospital care free to the user is a mistake for three reasons.

First, such shallow insurance is a central cause of hospital sector cost inflation and inefficiency. Second, the subsidy for shallow insurance imposes a large cost on the budget, notwithstanding that it is implemented through the tax side of the budget rather than the expenditure side. It therefore raises the general tax burden, reduces other government expenditures, or both. Third, tax expenditure in the form of a deduction is inequitable because the higher a household's tax bracket, the more aid it receives.

The proper response, in this author's view, is neither to reject all tax expenditures for private insurance, nor to switch to a regulatory strategy for the health sector. Instead, the tax expenditure should be reformed in three ways. First, it should be made closed ended for each person, so that each is assisted only in the purchase of major-risk insurance. Second, to improve equity and reduce budgetary cost, a tax credit rather than deduction should be used, so that aid can be correlated to ability to pay. Third, the health insurance tax credit should be complemented by a tax credit that provides last-resort, major-risk insurance for persons whose insurance is inadequate, assuring that no one must bear an excessive financial burden relative to income.

Reconciliation of the health policy objectives of efficiency and equity is possible only in a nation that has developed a modern policy instrument applicable to most of the population: the personal income tax and the tax credit. Despite criticism of "tax expenditures" as such, a tax expenditure is exactly the policy tool required for health insurance policy. It should be used without apology.

9

MARCY E. AVRIN

Financing Retirement Income

Changes in support programs. Increase in retired populations. Funding problems. Social security inequities and inefficiencies. Saving and private pension systems. Government employee programs. Veterans and SSI. Proposed reforms.

Estimates by the Office of Management and Budget (OMB) show that 26.4 percent of the fiscal 1981 budget was committed to support programs for the 11 percent of the population aged 65 and older. This includes the 71 percent of social security outlays, 67 percent of federal civilian retirement outlays, and 15 percent of military retirement outlays, that benefited those older than 65.[1] The distribution of total ex-

Table 1
Federal Outlays Benefiting the Elderly and Total Retirement Program Outlays 1981
($ billions)

	Benefits for elderly*	Total program
Social security (OASDI)	97.1	137.97
Railroad employees' retirement	4.1	5.29
Federal civilian employees' retirement	11.6	17.30
Military retirement	2.0	13.73
Coal miners	1.2	1.77
Supplemental Security Income (SSI)	2.6	7.19
Veterans' pensions	3.7	3.75
Medicare	35.8	42.48
Medicaid	6.0	16.95
Food stamps	0.9	11.25
Subsidized public housing	2.3	6.94
Other**	6.0	–
Total dedicated elderly resources	173.3	
Percent total federal outlays	26.4%	

Source: Office of Management and Budget.

*"Elderly" refers to recipients aged 65 and over in most cases. These estimates are based on federal agency information—which may be administrative counts, samples, or less accurate estimates from federal, state, and program staff. Other federal programs that assist the elderly (e.g., consumer activities, Department of Agriculture extension services, National Park Services) have been excluded due to data limitation.

**Includes Administration on Aging, National Institute on Aging, ACTION, White House Conference on Aging, other federal health programs, other retired, disabled, and survivors' benefits, FHA and elderly housing loan programs, social services, energy assistance, unemployment, and other miscellaneous discretionary program outlays.

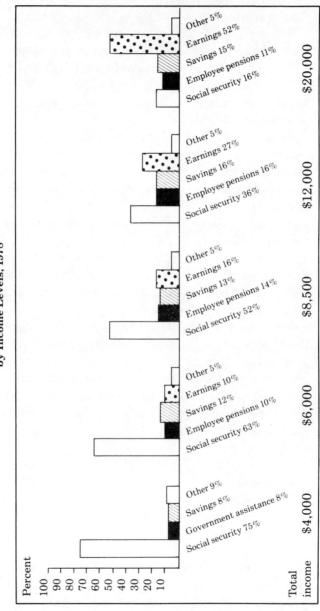

Figure 1

**Relative Contribution of Retirement Income Sources for
Individuals and Households, Head Age 65 and Over,
by Income Levels, 1978**

penditures among these and the various other programs involving the elderly is detailed in table 1.

Barbara Torrey (1981 b), a fiscal economist at OMB, estimates that if the total federal budget is constrained to be 20 percent of the gross national product (GNP) and if outlays for the aged increase as projected, outlays for other population groups must be decreased by 20.5 percent in 1990 and 40.6 percent in 2030.

Present and future federal budget deficits and the precarious financial situation of the social security system are forcing a reexamination of these programs. A growing consensus is developing that we can no longer afford them in their present configuration. This consensus is leading to attempts to restructure the retirement income support system to make it more cost efficient.

In considering the options for restructuring, one point becomes clear: the United States has no retirement income policy. Broad policymaking at the federal level has been impeded by the large numbers of departments, agencies, and congressional committees with partial jurisdiction over retirement issues. Responsibilities for income security are now scattered among ten of the twelve cabinet departments and more than twenty-five operating groups within them. The General Accounting Office estimates that 119 of the 306 congressional committees and subcommittees have policymaking, fiscal, or oversight responsibilities for income security programs.

The retired are supported in a variety of ways, most of which require government expenditures. Figure 1 shows the relative contribution of retirement income sources for individuals and households by income level.

Benefits from retirement systems provide over half of the income for all individuals except the wealthiest. In 1980, federal programs—including social security, railroad retirement, and federal employee plans—accounted for 78 percent of benefits paid, private plans accounted for 14 percent, and state and local plans, 8 percent (President's Commission on Pension Policy 1981, p. 12). Government welfare assistance also accounts for a substantial portion of the incomes of low-income individuals, aside from considerable in-kind benefits that are not included in the estimates.

REASONS FOR COST INCREASES

Current retirement income support programs developed in an ad hoc manner over the past fifty years to meet specific economic, social, and political needs. The past growth and prohibitively high projected future growth of the programs as a percentage of the federal budget have three main causes: demographic changes, financing methods, and economic factors.

Demographic changes

In the last half century, the numbers and proportion of the aged in the U.S. population have grown phenomenally. During that period the general population has doubled while the number of persons aged 65 and over has quadrupled. Between now and the year 2035, the Bureau of the Census estimates that the number of individuals 65 and over will increase 120 percent.[2] This presents a major problem for retirement income support programs, since the potential labor force from ages 18 to 64 that will have to support the retired is estimated to be only 6 percent larger in 2035 than it is today.[3]

The projected numbers of elderly largely result from past birthrates and changes in life expectancy. In 1800 an average of eight children were born to each woman who survived to the age of 44. By the early 1930s this had dropped to the replacement rate, which is approximately 2.1 children per woman. Immediately after World War II the birthrate rose rapidly to a peak in the late 1950s that was 60 percent higher than during the "baby bust" depression years. Since the late 1950s the fertility rate has been cut in half, creating another baby bust trough after the baby boom. The post–World War II baby boom produced a demographic tidal wave that will begin affecting retirement programs when the first members reach age 62 in 2009.

Because mortality rates have been declining fairly sharply since 1970, the baby boom generation will live longer than previous ones. Between 1965 and 1976 life expectancy for those 65 years old has increased 2.2 years and, for those 75 years old, 1.4 years.

Financing

The cost of supporting the increasing number of elderly individuals is prohibitive, largely because of financing arrangements that were established for the various retirement programs as they developed. The large federal pension systems and welfare programs are financed on a pay-as-you-go basis as government expenditures in the year they are paid. Current workers pay taxes that are then distributed to retirees. Thus, as the number of taxpayers decreases and the number of retirees increases, the burden on each taxpayer grows. To the extent that state and local pension plans are financed in this way, the situation with regard to state and local taxes is similar.

The cost to the federal government of the private employee plans is different from that of government plans, because the Employees' Retirement Income Security Act (ERISA) of 1974 mandated advance funding. Contributions are made to a trust fund on behalf of each worker to finance his retirement benefits. These contributions are tax deductible, and interest earnings on the fund are tax free until the pension is withdrawn. Thus, the federal government loses money in terms of forgone taxes.

Economic factors

Because of the indexed benefit structure of social security and other federal pension plans, high unemployment and inflation have significantly increased their burden on the federal budget. Benefits increase directly with the Consumer Price Index (CPI), whereas tax payments increase with wages. The CPI is currently increasing faster than wages, causing the rate of benefit increases to be greater than that of contributions. Also, the currently high unemployment rate means that fewer workers are paying taxes to finance the benefits.

COMPONENTS OF RETIREMENT INCOME

Since it is becoming increasingly clear that as a nation we can no longer afford the current mix of retirement income programs, changes are in order. Many changes have, in fact, been proposed. To understand these proposals, it is important to first examine each retirement income program in terms of its goals, financing, and benefit structure. The historical development of each program provides a key to determining the validity of its purpose and identifying inherent equity and efficiency problems. Is the program cost efficient? Is it target effective in terms of providing benefits to those most in need?

After examining the individual programs, it is also important to examine the total retirement income support system. How are programs integrated? What is the extent of coverage of the retired population? What is the degree of overlap? What types of incentives does the system provide for individuals to plan their own retirement support? How do the programs affect the economy?

Individual support programs

Social security. Social security has developed from a system of social insurance to one with a welfare or transfer as well as an insurance or annuity component. The Social Security Act of 1935 laid a foundation for the government to provide basic income protection to a majority of workers who became unable to work. In 1939 a major transfer component was added by basing benefits on average monthly wages rather than on cumulative wages. This allowed the earliest beneficiaries who paid taxes over the shortest period of time to receive the greatest windfall. Thus, income was transferred from the initial working population to the initial retirement generation.[4]

Over the years, benefits were expanded, including the addition of disability benefits in 1954 and health insurance for the elderly (Part A of Medicare) in 1965. Amendments added in 1972 and 1977 caused benefits to increase yearly with the CPI.[5] The original system was and still is self-contributory in that Old Age and Survivors' Insurance (OASI), Disability Insurance (DI), and Hospital Insurance (HI) are each financed with payroll taxes earmarked for three independently administered trust funds that accrue interest. A Supplementary Medical Insurance fund (SMI or Part B of Medicare) was added to pay for doctors' bills and other medical expenses. It is funded by premiums paid by eligible persons who are voluntarily enrolled and by contributions from general revenues. Since 1969 the operations of these funds have been part of the unified budget.

As Congress increased benefits over the years, it built an intragenerational transfer component into the system. Benefits in the evolving system became tilted in favor of the low-income worker, the worker with a short work history, the retiree with a spouse whose work history is not covered, and individuals with little retirement income. This redistribution is accomplished by such mechanisms as a progressive benefit formula, a minimum benefit, a uniform benefit for dependents, and an earnings test. Thus, every wage earner pays a social security tax on his or her income and receives a benefit at retirement. This system is far different from one in which each participant earns a common rate of return on his or her contribution to a given retirement fund.

Because Congress continually increased benefits without increasing tax rates, a pay-as-you-go financing concept evolved during the 1950s with the trust funds maintained at a minimum contingency level.

System difficulties. The most critical problem with the social security system is financial. Because the OASI trust fund was scheduled to run out of funds by the end of 1982, a law permitting interfund borrowing was recently enacted.[6] This short-term solution will not, however, solve the long-term problems evidenced by my projection of a $920 billion long-term deficit in the OASI fund adjusted for inflation and discounted to the present.[7]

With interfund borrowing and legislated tax increases that will take effect during 1985–1990, the financial projections of the trustees of the social security trust funds look favorable for OASDI until 2005.[8] For the period as a whole, the average annual income from OASDI taxes is estimated to exceed the average annual outgo. The HI system, however, shows a deficit under almost all assumptions. This deficit will be large enough to put the combined OASDHI system in difficulty during this period.[9]

From 2005 to 2030, OASDI tax rates are projected to become inadequate as expenditures increase due to a larger beneficiary population, while tax rates remain level under current law.[10] From 2030 to 2055, a substantial deficit is projected under all but the most optimistic economic and demographic assumptions (Social Security Administration 1981*a*, p. 67).

In 1981, 19.8 million retirees, 2.9 million disabled workers, and 13.2 million dependents and survivors were expected to receive income from social security. These beneficiaries would receive $138 billion in OASDI benefits and $42 billion in Medicare, and the programs would account for approximately 25 percent of federal outlays.[11]

Besides the critical financial situation of social security, the benefit structure of the system is plagued with problems of inequities and inefficiencies, including certain potentially undesirable income transfers. Many of these involve target inefficiencies, through which the higher-income individuals receive subsidies.

The first problem relates to intergenerational equity. Real social security benefits, measured by the average for all recipients, increased 52.7 percent from 1969 to 1980, whereas the real net average take-home pay, measured by the spendable earnings series of Data Resources, Inc., decreased 7.3 percent. Thus, the real value of social security benefits increased from 23.1 percent of real net average take-home pay to 38.2 percent over the 1970s.[12]

This situation has occurred for several reasons. Rising replacement rates in the early 1970s were increased further by a "double indexing" of benefits that mistakenly occurred in 1973 legislation. Although this error was corrected in 1977, the results are just now being worked out of the system.

Another reason for this increase is that social security benefits are not taxed. Benefit increases due to indexing are tax free, whereas inflation-related increases in the nominal wage are taxable. Also, "bracket creep" in the current progressive income tax structure reduces real net average take-home pay in inflationary times. Indexing of the tax system will eliminate bracket creep in 1985.

In considering intergenerational equity, it is important to note that our overall economic growth rate has slowed substantially. It is not clear that it will revert to the rate that existed from 1948 through 1973, which was about 2.5 percent real per capita income per year. Perhaps, even aside from the financing problems, from a normative point of view intergenerational transfers should decline in order to rectify the increased burden on the younger generation.

A second problem with the benefit structure results from a potential long-term indexing problem and involves the method by which the initial benefit is calculated. Calculation of the initial benefit at retirement, as opposed to subsequent changes in benefits, is based on a formula that relies on nominal wage growth as opposed to price increases. In the long run, with our return to sustained positive productivity growth, wages will increase more rapidly than prices and the system will result in rising real benefits—in addition to rising real relative benefits—since benefits are not taxed whereas wages are. Since the CPI will be the basis for indexing the income tax, the 1985 indexing reform will not alleviate this problem.

A third problem with the benefit structure arises because it is based on assumptions made about society in the 1930s that are now outmoded. Only 15 percent of households today fit the traditional stereotype of the male wage earner with a dependent housewife and children. As a result, the system discriminates against many groups in the population.[13]

Other inefficiencies in the benefit structure include the fact that the nontaxation of benefits is most advantageous to the high-income retiree. Also, benefits are not reduced for unearned income as they are for earned income.

Besides inequities, the system contains potentially adverse economic incentives. Since retirement earnings reduce benefits, retirees are less motivated to work. Also, by financing retirement, the system may encourage early retirement, reducing workers' productive years. Finally, an unfunded retirement system such as social security could cause individuals to save less than they would in the absence of the system, decreasing aggregate savings in the economy.[14]

Private employee pensions. While the purpose of social

security is to provide a minimum floor of retirement income, that of private employee pensions is to reduce the gap between this floor and an "adequate" retirement income. The federal government has encouraged employee pensions by allowing both employer contributions and earnings of the funds to be tax free until retirement. A significant growth in employee pension plans during the 1940s and 1950s was in part due to a combination of high corporate profits, taxes, and the tax advantages associated with establishing a pension plan. Pressure from labor organizations whose wage demands were restricted by World War II labor policies led to negotiations over pensions. Pensions became a fringe benefit regarded as a possible substitute for wage increases. Employers' personnel management objectives, such as employee recruitment, retention, and separation, also caused the growth of pension plans.

It is estimated that about half of the private work force currently participates in at least one of the half-million existing private plans.[15] In 1980, 9.1 million retirees and their survivors received benefits from these plans.

The cost of private plans in terms of tax expenditures has grown significantly. Plan contributions have increased from $2 billion in 1950 to $69 billion in 1980. The Treasury estimates that in fiscal 1981 it will forgo $23.6 billion of revenue because taxes on pension fund contributions and earnings are deferred until an employee retires.[16] This expenditure is expected to nearly double by fiscal 1985. Furthermore, tax expenditures for Keogh plans (established by individuals who are not covered by a private pension plan) and Individual Retirement Accounts (IRAs, currently available to all workers) will amount to about $2 to $3 billion in fiscal 1981. This amount is expected to increase to approximately $5.5 billion by fiscal 1985. The large increase is due to the 1981 tax law which extends the right to place $2,000 per year in an IRA account to all individuals, whether or not their earnings are covered by a private pension plan (Munnell 1982).

It is important to note that these estimates of tax expenditures are extremely sensitive to the assumed rate of return and tax rates. They are based on strong assumptions about economic behavior that are at best tenuous.

Also, a significant distinction between tax expenditures and actual expenditures should be emphasized. A tax expenditure of the type in effect in the private pension system actually encourages saving, thereby encouraging investment and capital formation. Direct government expenditures do not have this beneficial effect and, in fact, could actually decrease saving and investment. Thus, though a tax expenditure may increase the government deficit in the short run, it may have a positive offsetting long-term effect.

There are several problems with private employee pension plans. The major criticism is that the deferral of the tax on employer contributions and pension fund earnings makes pension coverage more beneficial to those in high income brackets.[17] A second problem is that the private pension system does not provide broad-based coverage. It has failed to extend benefits to lower-paid workers. Also, the number of qualifying individuals has been limited by ten-year vesting requirements, under which an individual is ineligible for benefits unless he holds a single job for ten years.

A third problem is that most plans provide a certain dollar benefit that is not indexed to inflation. In this period of high inflation, the real income from a fixed-dollar benefit received during retirement declines significantly over time.

Federal employee pension plans. The purposes of federal employee pension plans are significantly different from those of most private employee pension plans. Although 9.3 million federal workers participate in fifty-one different plans, the bulk of them participate in either the federal civil service or military retirement plans, each of which has 4.5 million members.

The military plan was established primarily as a personnel management tool rather than to provide retirement income.

As a model for plans for other hazardous duty occupations, it uses pension benefits as a mechanism for attracting and retaining younger workers and retiring older employees. Thus an individual is ineligible for the generous benefits unless he has twenty years of service. All personnel are covered by social security to provide retirement support to the majority of workers who do not enlist for twenty years. Benefits are completely protected against inflation.[18]

The military pension plan is financed on a pay-as-you-go basis, with government expenditures projected to increase from $12 billion in 1980 to $43.4 billion in 1999. Approximately 38 percent of total military compensation goes into benefits for the current population of military retirees. This expenditure is approximately 8 percent of the defense budget (Bassett 1981*a*, p. 644; President's Commission on Military Compensation 1978, pp. 8, 25).

According to the report of a commission established in 1978 to review military compensation, the system is inequitable and inefficient. In part, the system is unfair because it provides overly generous benefits relative to private sector plans.[19] Internal inequities exist as well. Those who serve for a number of years but leave before the full twenty years receive no military retirement benefits. Also, because retirement pay is based on the final basic pay rather than on the average basic pay over some number of years (as in most private employee plans), the system may provide widely varying benefits to retirees who have similar work experience.

The Civil Service Retirement System is intended to provide full retirement income because federal employees do not participate in social security. Until 1970, federal retirement benefits were considered a partial substitute for the higher wages earned by equivalent employees in the private sector. In that year, civil service pay was raised to levels comparable with those in the private sector—but the generous pension system remained.[20]

The system is partially funded. Approximately 31 percent

of payroll is set aside annually, while an actuarially funded system would require nearly 80 percent of payroll. In spite of a current unfunded actuarial liability of $304.8 billion, the fund and projected contributions will be large enough to pay benefits to current and future retirees over the next seventy-five years.

The Civil Service Retirement System cost the federal government $14.7 billion in fiscal 1980, a cost that is scheduled to increase to $57 billion or 34 percent of payroll in 1999 (Bassett 1981*a*, p. 644). Given the increasingly large burden on the federal budget, the system is being reevaluated from equity as well as efficiency points of view. The major criticism is that a significant number of workers retire from federal employment and work for the private sector under social security in order to qualify for a minimum benefit. This allows them to take advantage of the tilt in the benefit formula toward low-income individuals and become "double dippers."

State and local employee pension plans. State and local pension plans affect the federal budget only indirectly, to the extent that by burdening local budgets they necessitate federal subsidies in other areas. These programs were originally established for political reasons, to offset the fact that public employees received lower wages than their private sector counterparts. The situation of low wages and generous pensions allowed politicians to decrease current government expenditures by postponing contributions to the largely unfunded plans.

Though relative wages have increased, state and local plans provide more generous benefits than private employee plans, and like their private counterparts, these benefits are usually not indexed. Approximately 70 percent of the employees are also covered by social security.[21]

The maturing of state and local pension plans, along with the pressure to fund them over a reasonable number of years, have severely strained the budgets of states and cities.

A recent study by the Urban Institute (1981, part II), covering 95 percent of participants in state and local plans,
showed that only four of these plans were fully funded. If
contributions continue on schedule, however, about half of
them will be funded by 2024.

State and local plans paid $13 billion to individuals in
1980. Costs have increased from 7.2 percent of personal service cost in 1972 to 10.4 percent today (Bassett 1981*b*, p.
590). The major criticism of these plans is that, unlike those
in the private sector, benefits are not insured. Also, unlike
social security, benefits are not backed by the taxing authority of the federal government. Thus, with pressure on state
and local budgets, participants bear the risk of not receiving
pensions. Cities and states also face the possibility that they
could be forced to cut services in order to pay pension benefits. This came to pass in Oakland several years ago, as I
found in a study of their police and fire retirement system.
Given the new federalism proposed by President Reagan,
such situations will be receiving considerable attention in
the future.

Welfare programs for the elderly.   In terms of the federal budget, veterans' benefits are projected to grow faster
than any other program for the elderly. According to an estimate at OMB, there will be an unprecedented near-doubling
of federal outlays for older veterans between 1980 and 1986
as a result of the aging of the World War II generation (Torrey 1981*b*, p. 2). Veterans' compensation is paid to veterans
and their survivors for disabilities related to military service.
Veterans' pensions are also paid to those with no service-
connected disability if they are judged to be impoverished
and are either disabled or at least 65 years old. These payments were received by 2 million elderly beneficiaries in fiscal 1980, and amounted to $3.3 billion.

The major cash welfare program for the elderly is Supplemental Security Income (SSI). It is a means-tested program
for poor individuals who are blind, disabled, or age 65 and

older. The system replaced several federal/state welfare programs in 1974. Federally funded SSI payments were received by 1.9 million elderly in 1980 for a total cost of $2.3 billion.

Federal expenditures for the major in-kind benefits to the elderly are shown in table 1. They include housing, food stamps, social services, energy assistance, and various health programs such as Medicaid. These expenditures totalled approximately $12.2 billion in fiscal 1980.

Integration

As noted earlier, the various benefit packages and financing arrangements of our pension programs developed from a patchwork of laws, regulatory agencies, collective bargaining, and individual effort. The only significant program coordination is through the rules by which a majority of private pension plans and a small number of state and local plans are integrated with social security.[22]

This integration is based on the premise that public and private retirement programs should function as a unified system. Since social security benefits provide a higher proportion of pre-retirement earnings for low- and moderate-wage earners, these individuals will lose less income upon retirement, and consequently require less income to be replaced by employee pensions. Thus, current integration rules allow employee pension plans to pay proportionately higher benefits to higher-income workers.[23]

Integration is often criticized because current social security benefits are inadequate to meet the needs of many lower-income individuals. Under current integration rules, however, the lowest-paid employees, who are least likely to have other sources of income to supplement social security, may be excluded from receiving any employee pension benefits. Thus, all workers pay in terms of forgone taxes for a system that benefits only those with relatively high incomes.

A major concern about the current state of the retirement

income system is its potentially significant interaction with
the economy as a whole. Social security and other pension
benefits may well affect labor force participation, savings
and investment, wages, labor mobility, and labor/
management relations, all of which in turn affect the economy's performance. Current research as to these effects so
far is largely inconclusive, but study continues.[24]

Economic and demographic assumptions used for projections of the financial status of social security and various
retirement systems are treated as outside factors that act
upon the systems but are unaffected by them. Because of the
size and nature of OASDI and other retirement systems, this
perspective is probably invalid.

Another concern about our system of retirement programs
is its effect on the ownership and control of capital. Public
and private employee pension plans and OASDI have over
$650 billion of assets, or over 30 percent of the total net fi-
nancial assets of individuals in the United States. The assets
of private pension plans have grown from 3.3 percent of net
financial assets in 1950 to 17 percent today. Those of state
and local plans have grown from 1.3 percent to 8 percent during the same period (Barth et al. 1981). Continued fund expansion and federal policy affecting it will increase the
debate over the management of these funds from the
perspectives of public policy and economic productivity.

PROPOSALS FOR REFORM

The current budget problems and the realization that a significant amount of federal expenditure is used to support
the elderly have fostered numerous proposals for changes in
the retirement income system. These proposals are of three
types. The first concerns ways to change social security and
employee pension programs in order to make each one in-

dividually more cost efficient and target effective. The second suggests changes in the programs from the point of view of coordinating them into an effective system. The third involves changes in the entire structure of taxation and expenditures of the federal government.

Individual program changes

The three sets of problems plaguing the social security system—the long-term funding deficit, the apparent inequities, and the adverse incentives—have generated much interest in reforms. One of the most far-reaching proposals is to separate the system's transfer and annuity functions and fund them, respectively, out of general revenues and earmarked payroll taxes. This recommendation has been made for a number of reasons.

The current system is so complex that it obscures the relation between contributions and benefits. This situation makes it difficult for firms and employees to rationalize their total retirement support, including both private pensions and social security. Since many groups in the population are receiving a "bad deal" from social security compared to an actuarially fair system, separating the transfer and annuity goals would provide the same rate of return for all workers under social security's annuity program.[25] The inequities that undermine support of the system would be eliminated in this part of the program.

Financing transfers through general revenues would eliminate the incongruous situation of guaranteeing an income to the aged through a tax that bears heavily on the working poor. Also, general revenue financing would permit policymakers and the public openly to determine the value of transfers to the elderly in relation to other social priorities and to promote cost-effective implementation.

One of the more promising proposals for social security reform is slowly to increase retirement ages. The President's

Commission on Pension Policy recommended increasing the retirement age to 68 over a twelve-year period beginning in 1990. My own estimates show that this approach would go far toward solving the system's financial difficulties.

Finally, President Reagan recently proposed abolishing the special minimum benefit. He was, however, forced to drop the proposal due to its tremendous unpopularity.

The adverse public reaction to administration proposals suggests that it is easier to make drastic cuts in other government programs than to reform social security. This is especially true for reforms that are not phased in over time.

With the large projected deficits in Reagan's fiscal 1983 budget, however, attitudes may be changing. Senator Hollings, a Democrat, has recently proposed forgoing the July 1983 cost-of-living adjustment in both social security and government pensions and holding the adjustments in 1984 and 1985 to three percentage points below the rise in the Consumer Price Index. Such a policy, or a variant of it, is sensible in that a CPI based on purchasing patterns of the retired would increase at a slower rate than that constructed for the general population.

Another suggestion for alleviating short-term social security financing problems, which are expected to occur between 1985 and 1990, is to require Medicare patients to pay a modest share of their hospital charges in the same way that patients with private insurance do. Besides alleviating the system's financial problems, this change would help to stem the tremendous cost increases of health care.

Regarding the private pension system, reforms have been instituted recently in expanding the tax deferments for IRAs to individuals whose earnings are covered by pension plans. Such an expansion alleviates the portability problem—that is, how pension benefits can be transferred from job to job—inherent in the private system. Also, expanded coverage and earlier vesting have been proposed.

The major proposals with regard to federal employee pension plans involve reducing the cost-of-living increase. Reforms with regard to state and local plans involve mandating some sort of funding schedule.

Total system reform

Pressures to reform the entire retirement income system arise from several points of view: (1) a budget perspective in which individuals feel that government spending must be reduced; (2) an equity perspective in which uneven and unnecessary retirement income subsidies by the federal government are noted; (3) a welfare perspective that concentrates on the number of elderly individuals who are poor. To date, the President's Commission on Pension Policy, created in 1979, is the major public organization to consider all of these perspectives in making reform recommendations. The commission's recommendations cover employee pensions, including vesting, portability, integration, spouse benefits, retirement ages, ownership and control of capital; social security, including financing, universal coverage, tax treatment of contributions and benefits, the earnings test, spouse benefits, the special minimum benefit; individual effort, including saving and employment of older workers; state and local pensions; public assistance; and inflation protection for retirement income.

The commission's broader proposals are intended to eliminate the two-class retirement system in which only half of the work force participates in private employee pension plans. They are also intended to solve the social security financing problem and remove the adverse economic incentives present in the various retirement income programs.

One of the commission's more controversial recommendations is a Minimum Universal Pension System (MUPS) for all workers, funded by employer contributions of at least 3 percent of payroll. Vesting of benefits would be immediate and benefits would be portable. The system is intended as a minimum supplement to social security and therefore would not be integrated. Universal social security coverage would be mandatory.

In order to coordinate private and public plans with social security and avoid overlap, the commission recommended uniform retirement ages. It also recommended that contributions to—and benefits from—social security receive the same tax treatment as those of private retirement programs, taxing all benefits and allowing tax deductions for employee contributions. And it recommended that a special cost-of-living index be developed for the retired in order to more equitably index these benefits.

To strengthen the savings aspect of retirement income, the commission recommended favorable tax treatment of employee contributions to pension plans, including a refundable tax credit for low- and moderate-income individuals and a similar treatment for individual retirement savings. It also supported strengthening incentives for the elderly to earn some of their income, by removing the social security earnings test.[26]

The commission's recommendations are the most comprehensive to date. Both empirical and theoretical estimates have been made as to the effects of various proposals.[27]

Changes in the structure of public finance

The most far-reaching proposal for change actually involves the retirement system only indirectly. Many economists are proposing to abolish the income tax and replace it with a consumption or expenditure tax. The tax base would be an individual's income minus his savings. Such a system would provide an incentive to save and would therefore result in more savings for retirement.

Many versions of such a plan exist. The general idea is that if individuals are taxed on the money they spend rather than on the money they earn, they will tend to save a larger portion of their income. Under the current income tax system, the tax deduction of interest payments and the taxation of interest earnings provide incentives to borrow rather than to save.[28] The tax structure decreases borrowing costs and also decreases the after-tax rate of return on savings.[29]

It should be noted that the current tax treatment of private pensions is consistent with consumption taxation, which excludes savings from the tax base. However, while a consumption tax may indeed be preferable, income is currently the basis for taxation and ad hoc exclusions from a comprehensive income tax base result in serious inequities.

The provision in the 1981 tax law that extends the limits and eligibility for tax deductible savings on IRA accounts is also consistent with consumption taxation. Some economists, in fact, assert that this provision is a highly cost-effective way for the government to encourage saving. The increase in individuals' projected savings is significant relative to the projected government cost in forgone taxes.

Another far-reaching proposal that would cause major economic changes is a mandatory system in which defined contributions are tied directly to benefits. In establishing such a system, Congress would compel recipients of all income (including wages, dividends, and interest) to deposit a small fraction of it with a financial intermediary who would manage these funds until the individual retired. The fraction of compulsory savings would be changed from time to time in accordance with criteria of income adequacy and security established by law.

Because benefits are tied to contributions, this system would provide only minimal benefits to those who are unemployed during a significant fraction of their lifetime and, therefore, have only a small amount of contributions. Also, the protection against inflation in this system is provided only to the extent that there is a sufficiently high nominal rate of return on the portfolios managed by the trustees.

If it is considered desirable to provide a minimum income guarantee to the aged, the funding of this redistribution would come from general revenues, as is the case with other welfare benefits.[30]

CONCLUSION

Since the Great Depression our society has elected not to rely entirely upon a purely private mechanism of retirement income support in which each person saves as much for retirement as he believes individually optimal. Instead, we have developed both public and private pension systems that are heavily regulated and influenced by a variety of tax incentives. These systems were established in an ad hoc manner without any general plan or retirement income policy. Largely because of demographic changes, the projected increase in federal expenditures necessary to maintain them is prohibitive. The current and projected pressures on the federal budget have forced a reevaluation of the entire retirement income system.[31]

Because the various support programs did not develop within a general policy framework, they are costly and inefficient. Individuals with no need for additional retirement income are subsidized while those in need receive only minimal support. The system also creates adverse economic incentives.

In order to develop a cost-efficient and target-effective retirement income policy, we must first define its goals. Should a retirement income system assure a minimal or an adequate income for the retired? What, in fact, is an "adequate" income? Once these questions are answered, we must determine the extent to which inter- and intragenerational income transfers should be used and the extent to which individuals should be forced to save for their own retirement. Should employers defer income for their employees? Should individuals be forced to save on their own? Should a public system of taxes and benefits such as social security be used? What are the appropriate federal responsibilities for the older population?

Because of the ad hoc development of the system, changes will be difficult to implement. Each component was added for specific reasons, many of which are unrelated to the goal of retirement income support. Given the number of individuals involved in the various programs and the extent to which the economy is affected by the capital and economic incentives inherent in each, substantial controversy will surround any proposed reforms.

Large current and future federal budget deficits, however, are causing significant pressure for change. Because payments to the elderly constitute over a quarter of federal outlays, a relatively small change in retirement programs would have the same budgetary impact as large changes in several smaller programs. This is especially true with regard to social security, since these payments constitute approximately half of all benefits to the elderly. For example, forgoing the July 1983 cost-of-living adjustment in social security and government pensions would save $24 billion in fiscal 1983, which is over one-quarter of the deficit projected by OMB. In addition, holding the cost-of-living adjustment in 1984 and 1985 to three percentage points below the rise in the CPI would save $31 billion in fiscal 1984 and $35 billion in fiscal 1985. Because the potential budgetary impact of changes in social security and other federal retirement programs is both immediate and large, proposals for reform are gaining support. These proposals, however, address only a few of the many serious long-run problems of retirement income support in this country.

10

JAMES W. ABELLERA

ROGER P. LABRIE

Budgeting for Defense: The Original Reagan Five-Year Spending Program*

Outlays and TOA. Defense priorities in the Reagan budget. Obsolescence, and Soviet force expansion. System and nonsystem procurement. Military manpower costs, including civilian defense employees. Checking the long-term programs. Investment/O&M ratio. The lower cost of accelerated production.

*Adapted by the editors from James W. Abellera and Roger P. Labrie, "The FY 1982–1986 Defense Program: Issues and Trends," *AEI Foreign Policy and Defense Review* 3, 4/5 (1981). For complete documentation, the reader should consult the *Review.*

In February 1982 the Reagan administration announced its defense spending proposals for fiscal years (FY) 1983–1987. It is too early to make detailed judgments about this second Reagan spending plan, but it is clear that the administration has made adjustments to the budget assumptions and priorities that were evident in its first defense spending plan presented in March 1981. The FY 1983–1987 plan also contains the Reagan administration's first formal statement of military strategy. Critics as well as proponents of rising Pentagon budgets will have to examine the new strategy to determine whether clear connections exist between proposed spending and specific objectives for a force structure that will provide military capabilities essential to the nation's security.

By contrast, the Reagan administration's original defense budget proposals for FY 1982–1986, presented in March 1981, were not accompanied by a clear and comprehensive outline of U.S. military strategy for the years ahead. Without such an outline it is difficult to judge whether the proposed budgets would be just enough, too high, or even too low to make the nation secure militarily.

We examine in this article some of the details of the original Reagan spending proposals of March 1981. These proposals warrant attention for three reasons. First, they suggest how the course set by the Reagan administration in military affairs differs from the one proposed by the Carter administration for the same period. Second, it is necessary to chronicle what is known about the first Reagan plan so that ensuing changes in military spending priorities and assumptions may be identified and evaluated in future research. Third, a working knowledge of the financing associated with America's military buildup may assist the public to frame questions about other issues that are more basic to defense spending than its projected rate of growth or its contribution to the federal deficit: the forces it is supposed to buy and the new strategy guiding their use in protecting truly vital U.S. interests against foreseeable armed threats.

MEASURING THE DEFENSE BUDGET

The size of the defense budget can be measured in three ways: in obligational authority or outlays, in current or constant dollars, and in absolute or relative terms. Each of these measures provides different insights, but each is also often the source of confusion. We will define the three measures before comparing the Carter and Reagan defense programs.

Total obligational authority (TOA) is a measure of the funds requested in a particular year. Not all of these funds, however, will be spent in that year. The funds actually spent in a given fiscal year are called outlays, and the remainder is termed an unexpended balance of spending and authority. The outlays for one year are the sum of unspent authority granted in previous years and that portion of the authority requested for the current fiscal year that will be spent during the next twelve months. TOA thus directly influences the size of outlays in future years. In the Department of Defense (DOD) budget, about 30 percent of the outlays normally come from authority approved in previous years, whereas the other 70 percent come from the current year's TOA. Under the Reagan budget proposals, TOA for FY 1982 is set at $222.2 billion, and outlays will be $184.8 billion (Office of the Assistant Secretary of Defense [Public Affairs] 1981, p. 1).

Current dollars represent the value of TOA or outlays in the fiscal year in which the funds are authorized or spent. Thus TOA for FY 1982 is presented in FY 1982 dollars, whereas TOA for FY 1981 is presented in FY 1981 dollars. Constant dollars, on the other hand, show the impact of inflation by adjusting the cost of the defense program to reflect the purchasing power of the dollar in a given base year. The FY 1980, FY 1981, and FY 1982 budgets, for example, can be presented in terms of FY 1982 dollars. To illustrate the significance of the choice between current and constant dollars,

Table 1
Defense Budget Totals in Current and Constant Dollars, FY 1981–1986
(billions of dollars)

| | Fiscal year | | | | | | Total FY 1981–1986 | Average annual change 1981–1986 | |
	1981	1982	1983	1984	1985	1986		Amount	%
Current dollars									
TOA									
Carter	171.2	196.4	224.0	253.1	284.3	318.3	1,447.3	29.4	17.2
Reagan	178.0	222.2	254.8	289.2	326.5	367.5	1,638.2	37.9	21.3
Difference[a]									
Amount	6.8	25.8	30.8	36.1	42.2	49.2	190.9	–[b]	—
Percent	4.0	13.1	14.0	14.3	15.0	15.5	13.2	—	—
Outlays									
Carter	157.6	180.0	205.3	232.2	261.8	293.3	1,330.2	27.1	17.2
Reagan	158.6	184.8	221.1	249.8	297.3	336.0	1,447.6	35.5	22.4
Difference[a]									
Amount	1.0	4.8	15.8	17.6	35.5	42.7	117.4	—	—
Percent	0.6	2.7	7.7	7.6	13.6	14.6	8.8	—	—

Constant FY 1982 dollars

TOA									
Carter	186.5	196.4	206.2	216.5	227.4	238.7	1,271.7	10.4	5.6
Reagan	193.9	222.2	238.4	255.1	272.9	292.0	1,474.5	19.6	10.1
Difference[a]									
Amount	7.4	25.8	32.2	38.6	45.5	53.3	202.8	–	–
Percent	4.0	13.1	15.6	17.8	20.0	22.3	16.0	–	–
Outlays									
Carter	172.5	180.0	188.2	197.1	207.0	217.5	1,162.3	9.0	5.2
Reagan	174.0	184.8	205.6	218.1	245.3	263.3	1,291.1	17.9	10.3
Difference[a]									
Amount	1.5	4.8	17.4	21.0	38.3	45.8	128.8	–	–
Percent	0.9	2.7	9.2	10.7	18.5	21.1	11.1	–	–

Sources: Brown 1981, p. C-10; Office of the Assistant Secretary of Defense (Public Affairs) 1981, pp. 8, 9.
a Reagan less Carter.
b Dashes indicate data not computed.

we may compare the size of defense outlays for FY 1964 (the last pre-Vietnam budget) with FY 1982 (the current budget). In current dollars, the FY 1964 outlays amounted to $49.5 billion, whereas those projected for FY 1982 are $184.8 billion, a difference of $135.3 billion, or 273.3 percent. In constant FY 1982 dollars, the FY 1964 outlays are $172.1 billion, or only $12.7 billion less than the proposed FY 1982 outlays.

The defense budget may also be presented in relative rather than absolute terms. Outlays for a given year are usually related in percentage terms to the gross national product (GNP) and to the entire federal budget. These relative measures show the impact of defense spending on the national economy and the priority given to defense and other federal programs.

COMPARING THE CARTER AND REAGAN BUDGETS

Table 1 presents the TOA and outlay projections of the Carter and Reagan defense programs for the FY 1981–1986 period in both current and constant FY 1982 dollars. Both programs call for spending far more than $1 trillion on national defense during the next six years. In current dollars, President Carter proposed $1,447.3 billion in TOA and $1,330.2 billion in outlays during the FY 1981–1986 period. These sums represent an average annual increase in current dollars of $29.4 billion (17.2 percent) in TOA and $27.1 billion (17.2 percent) in outlays. In real terms, or constant FY 1982 dollars, the average annual increase during the same period would be $10.4 billion (5.6 percent) in TOA and $9.0 billion (5.2 percent) in outlays.

President Reagan's long-term spending proposals, presented to Congress in March 1981, call for substantial increases over those of his predecessor in both current dollars and real terms. The president has called for spending, in current dollars, of $1,638.2 billion in TOA and $1,447.6 billion in outlays during the period FY 1981–1986. Under the Reagan proposal, the defense budget would grow at an average annual rate of $37.9 billion (21.3 percent) in TOA and $35.5 billion (22.4 percent) in outlays. In real terms, the average annual increase would be $19.6 billion (10.1 percent) in TOA and $17.9 billion (10.3 percent) in outlays for the period FY 1981–1986.

Inflation estimates

Whether the Reagan administration will succeed in maintaining average real increases in defense spending of 10 percent a year during the FY 1981–1986 period will depend in part on the accuracy of its inflation forecasts. Both the Carter administration and the Reagan administration have assumed that their respective economic policies would succeed with time in bringing inflation under control. The new administration is more optimistic than its predecessor, forecasting an overall inflation rate of 4.9 percent in calendar year 1986, as compared with 6.3 percent anticipated by the previous administration (see Office of Management and Budget 1981*c*, p. 13; idem 1981*a*, pp. 3–5; Brown 1981, p. C–14; Office of the Assistant Secretary of Defense [Public Affairs] 1981, p. 9).

Relative priorities

Carter's projected defense outlays were estimated at 5.6 percent of GNP and 24.3 percent of the entire federal budget for FY 1982, growing to 5.9 percent of GNP and 27.9 percent of the federal budget in FY 1986.

The Reagan administration's projections show defense outlays amounting to 5.8 percent of GNP and 26.6 percent of

Table 2
Defense Authority (TOA) by Program, FY 1980–1982
(billions of current dollars)

Program	Fiscal year			Total FY 1981–1982	Difference (Reagan less Carter)		Increase FY 1980–1982	
	1980	1981	1982		Amount	%	Amount	%
Strategic								
Carter	11.1	12.6	15.0	27.6	3.0	10.9	3.9	35.1
Reagan	—*	13.2	17.4	30.6			6.3	56.8
General purpose								
Carter	52.4	65.4	73.5	138.9	19.4	14.0	21.1	40.3
Reagan	—	68.8	89.5	158.3			37.1	70.8
Intelligence and communications								
Carter	9.1	10.9	13.0	23.9	2.0	8.4	3.9	42.9
Reagan	—	11.4	14.5	25.9			5.4	59.3
Airlift and sealift								
Carter	2.1	2.8	3.5	6.3	1.1	17.5	1.4	66.7
Reagan	—	3.0	4.4	7.4			2.3	109.5
Guard and reserve								
Carter	7.9	9.4	10.3	19.7	1.5	7.6	2.4	30.4
Reagan	—	9.9	11.3	21.2			3.4	43.0

R&D							
Carter	11.8	13.8	17.3	31.1	1.6	5.5	46.6
Reagan	–	14.2	18.5	32.7	5.1	6.7	56.8
Central supply & maintenance							
Carter	15.3	17.5	19.5	37.0	0.8	4.2	27.5
Reagan	–	17.7	20.1	37.8	2.2	4.8	31.4
Training, medical, and other							
Carter	29.3	34.6	39.2	73.8	2.4	9.9	33.8
Reagan	–	35.2	41.0	76.2	3.3	11.7	39.9
Administration and support							
Carter	3.2	4.2	5.1	9.3	0.8	1.9	59.4
Reagan	–	4.6	5.5	10.1	8.6	2.3	71.9
Total							
Carter	142.2	171.2	196.4	367.6	32.6	54.2	38.1
Reagan	–	178.0	222.2	400.2	8.9	80.0	56.3

Sources: Derived from data in Brown 1981, p. C-4; Office of the Assistant Secretary of Defense (Public Affairs) 1981, p. 6.

*Dash = not applicable.

the federal budget in FY 1982. By FY 1986, outlays would account for 7.0 percent of GNP and 36.8 percent of the federal budget (see Department of Defense 1977*a*–1981*a,* passim; Office of Management and Budget 1977*a*–1981*a,* passim; Office of Management and Budget 1981*b,* p. 67).

The Reagan budget program accelerates the trends begun by President Carter in FY 1981 of increasing the priority of defense spending relative to social programs and of increasing the burden of defense on the economy. Under President Reagan's five-year program, the share of the federal budget devoted to national defense will substantially surpass the level that existed when President Carter took office. The renewed emphasis on defense in the Reagan budget projections will approach the levels in the pre-Vietnam period, when the DOD's budget consumed more than 8 percent of GNP and much more than 40 percent of the total federal budget (Office of the Assistant Secretary of Defense [Comptroller] 1980, p. 100).

Programs

The defense budget can be divided into nine major program categories reflecting the major mission and support activities of the Department of Defense. An examination of the distribution of budget dollars among these programs (table 2) provides another picture of spending priorities.

President Reagan has called for larger expenditures than his predecessor for FY 1981–1982 in all nine program categories. The programs receiving the largest percentage increases over the Carter figures include airlift and sealift (17.5 percent) and general-purpose forces (14.0 percent), accelerating the shift begun under the previous administration to an emphasis on improving the readiness and size of conventional forces and the means for their timely deployment to distant arenas of potential conflict, such as the Persian Gulf. During the period FY 1980–1982, President

Reagan more than doubled the funds (in current dollars) allocated to airlift and sealift in support of the rapid deployment force (RDF). Much of this increase will go to purchase pre-positioned ships, and some funds will finance the development of the CX transport aircraft, which will be either a new airplane or a derivative of an existing wide-body transport.

The Reagan administration's commitment to modernizing the intercontinental ballistic missile (ICBM) and bomber legs of the nuclear triad and to remedying their emerging vulnerabilities is evident in the 10.9 percent increase in funding for strategic forces over the level proposed by President Carter for FY 1981–1982. Included in the FY 1982 budget are development funds for the MX missile and procurement funds for a new strategic bomber, for air-launched cruise missiles (ALCMs) to be deployed on more than 150 existing B–52 bombers, and for one Trident missile submarine. It should be noted that the cost of developing and producing the nuclear warheads for these new weapons is assigned to the budget of the Department of Energy (DOE) and not to that of the DOD. For FY 1982, the DOE estimates the costs of its defense activities to be about $5 billion (Office of Management and Budget 1981*a*, p. 105).

Rearming America. Procurement is the budget title receiving the largest increase under the Reagan administration, rising 24 percent in current dollars and about 23 percent in constant dollars over the levels proposed by President Carter for FY 1981–1982. The Reagan budget adds $3.2 billion to the Carter procurement budget of $45 billion in FY 1981 and $19.7 billion to Carter's FY 1982 procurement budget of $49.1 billion.[1]

What will the additional funds in the Reagan budgets buy in the way of new weapons systems? As can be seen in table 3, the extra $3.2 billion in FY 1981 will allow purchases that include 7 additional fixed-wing aircraft, 1,315 extra missiles, and 309 more tanks and other combat vehicles. By adding $19.7 billion to the $49.1 billion recommended by President Carter for procurement in FY 1982, the Reagan administration will buy, among other things, 4 more combat ships, 115 additional fixed-wing aircraft, 4,432 more missiles, 287 more tanks and other combat vehicles, and 34 additional helicopters.

Several reasons can be cited to explain the substantial increases in the DOD's procurement budget during the past few years. First, the cost of replacing obsolete weapons systems is growing constantly. A new *Ohio*-class (Trident) submarine, for example, is more than five times as expensive as its predecessor, the Polaris. Other examples include the F−14 fighter (eight times as expensive as the F−4) and the M−1 tank (about three times the cost of the M−60). The escalating cost of new weapons reflects only in part the higher wages for skilled labor and the rising prices of materials; also adding to the rising cost of weapons are their greater sophistication and complexity as well as their enhanced capability, making today's new generation of weapons the most formidable of their kind ever devised.

Second, the Department of Defense is confronting the problem of bloc obsolescence in both its strategic and general-purpose forces. From the mid-1960s to the mid-1970s, funds that might have gone toward the modernization of our general-purpose forces were initially diverted to pay for the war in Vietnam and then went to meet rising personnel costs associated with the all-volunteer force (AVF) and operating costs connected with the rising price of oil. Consequently, the DOD will have to replace a great many of its conventional weapons with new ones during the next several years. In addition, the weapons in each of the three legs of the strategic triad are rapidly approaching the end of their useful lives. Most of the ICBMs and submarine-launched ballistic missiles (SLBMs) in the land and sea legs were deployed on a crash basis in the early to mid-1960s, whereas some of the B−52 bombers have been in service even longer.

Table 3

Aggregate Procurement of Major Weapons Systems FY 1981 and FY 1982

	Carter		Reagan		Difference (Reagan less Carter)		% change	
	FY 1981	FY 1982	FY 1981	FY 1982	FY 1981	FY 1982	FY 1981	FY 1982
Combat ships	16	9	16	13	0	4	0.0	44.4
Fixed-wing aircraft	385	220	392	335	7	115	1.8	52.3
Missiles	3,833	4,842	5,148	9,274	1,315	4,432	34.3	91.5
Tanks and combat vehicles	660	1,033	969	1,320	309	287	46.8	27.8
Helicopters	80	94	80	128	0	34	0.0	36.2

Source: Office of the Assistant Secretary of Defense (Comptroller) 1981a.

Third, while the United States was diverting funds from new procurement, the Soviet Union was steadily expanding the size of its general-purpose, theater nuclear, and strategic forces and was improving their quality as well. In some categories of weapons, the Soviets have expanded their inventories while those of the United States have declined or failed to keep pace with those of the Russians. Between 1970 and 1979, for example, the Soviets added to their arsenal approximately 700 SLBMs, 62 strategic bombers, 2 new aircraft/helicopter carrier ships, 11 cruisers, 55 frigates, 9,000 tanks, 8,000 artillery pieces, 29,500 armored personnel carriers, 1,000 fighter aircraft, and 750 helicopter gunships. By comparison, the American inventory of these weapons during this same period remained constant in SLBMs, declined by 93 in strategic bombers, declined by 2 in aircraft/helicopter carriers, remained the same for cruisers, increased by 14 in frigates, increased by 691 in tanks, declined by 2,730 in artillery pieces, increased by 2,777 in armored personnel carriers, increased by 102 in fighter aircraft, and increased by 242 in helicopter gunships. In addition, recent improvements in the accuracy of Soviet ICBMs and an increase in the number of their strategic submarines on station have raised concerns that two of our triad legs— ICBMs and bombers—are becoming increasingly vulnerable to attack, thereby reducing our retaliatory capability, which is the heart of effective deterrence. Both the Central Intelligence Agency and the Rand Corporation estimate that during the decade of the 1970s the Soviet Union outspent the United States in the investment area of military expenditures by 80 percent, or $100 billion (Alexander et al. 1979).

A recent report highlighting the findings of a Defense Intelligence Agency (DIA) analysis of U.S. and Soviet weapons production during the past five years supports these concerns. According to the DIA, the Soviets built four times as many tanks during the period as the United States, three times the number of armored vehicles, twice as many fighter aircraft, and twice as many battlefield ballistic missiles. Also, in 1980 alone the Soviets outproduced the United States in numbers of SLBMs, submarines (11 to 1), submarine-launched cruise missiles (700 to 0), bombers (30 to 0), and transport aircraft (350 to 0; O'Toole 1981; see also Department of Defense 1981 *b,* pp. 12–13).

Although continued improvement in U.S. conventional forces earmarked for the central front in Europe can be anticipated, both the Carter and the Reagan procurement programs for FY 1981 and FY 1982 call for major increases in funding as well for the "flexible forces" of the U.S. Marine Corps and the U.S. Navy that would be called upon to meet potential challenges in more remote parts of the world. Because of the lag between the initiation of a weapons program and its completion, however, substantial improvements in the capability of flexible forces may not become apparent until the latter half of the 1980s.

Procurement

The Department of Defense's procurement budget can be divided into two categories: system and nonsystem (routine) procurement. System procurement expenditures are made for new weapons systems and equipment, whereas non-system procurement funds cover the cost of such items as spare parts for already existing systems. About 75 percent of the total procurement budget normally goes for new systems acquisition.

Aggregate funding. Table 4 provides a breakdown of the Carter and Reagan procurement programs for FY 1981 and FY 1982; the FY 1980 program has been provided for comparison. Under both administrations' proposals, the navy would receive by far the largest share of the procurement budget, 44 percent in FY 1981 and 43 percent in FY 1982 under the Carter program, as compared with 42 percent for both fiscal years under Reagan. The largest portion of the

Table 4

Procurement Programs, FY 1980–1982

(TOA in millions of current dollars)

	FY 1980 Carter	FY 1981 Carter	FY 1981 Reagan	FY 1981 difference (Reagan less Carter) Amount	%	FY 1982 Carter
Army						
Aircraft	946.2	1,076.4	1,204.4	128.0	11.9	1,361.7
Missiles	1,150.3	1,519.8	1,546.8	27.0	1.8	1,650.5
Weapons and						
tracked vehicles	1,811.1	2,582.2	3,378.2	796.0	30.8	2,719.8
Ammunition	1,151.7	1,531.0	1,569.7	38.7	2.5	1,816.2
Other	1,483.0	2,259.7	2,956.3	696.6	30.8	2,325.7
Total	6,542.3	8,969.1	10,655.4	1,686.3	18.8	9,873.9
Navy						
Aircraft	4,331.7	6,110.7	6,254.3	143.6	2.3	6,960.3
Weapons	1,992.6	2,738.1	2,738.1	0.0	0.0	2,717.8
Ships and						
conversion	6,464.4	7,483.6	7,801.3	317.7	4.2	6,639.6
Other	2,586.0	3,037.7	3,037.7	0.0	0.0	3,459.7
Marine Corps	275.1	488.8	506.0	17.2	3.5	1,172.4
Total	15,649.8	19,858.9	20,337.4	478.5	2.4	20,949.8
Air Force						
Aircraft	8,017.6	9,674.1	10,390.8	716.7	7.4	9,469.9
Missiles	2,159.2	3,140.9	3,350.3	209.4	6.7	4,274.5
Other	2,654.8	3,003.4	3,142.1	138.7	4.6	4,013.2
Total	12,831.6	15,818.4	16,883.2	1,064.8	6.7	17,757.6
Defense agencies	288.7	305.0	322.5	17.5	5.7	483.7
Grand total	35,312.4	44,951.4	48,198.5	3,247.1	7.2	49,065.0

Sources: Office of the Assistant Secretary of Defense (Comptroller) 1981a.

*Dashes mean data are not computed.

FY 1982 Reagan	FY 1982 difference (Reagan less Carter)		FY 1982 less FY 1980, Carter		FY 1982 less FY 1980, Reagan	
	Amount	%	Amount	%	Amount	%
1,797.4	435.7	32.0	−*	−	−	−
2,842.5	1,192.0	72.2	−	−	−	−
4,142.7	1,422.9	52.3	−	−	−	−
2,444.5	628.3	34.6	−	−	−	−
3,869.6	1,543.9	66.4	−	−	−	−
15,096.7	5,222.8	52.9	3,331.6	50.9	8,554.4	130.8
9,352.5	2,392.2	34.4	−	−	−	−
3,271.8	554.0	20.4	−	−	−	−
10,290.1	3,650.5	55.0	−	−	−	−
3,865.0	405.3	11.7				
1,828.2	655.8	55.9	897.3	326.2	1,553.1	564.6
28,607.6	7,657.8	36.5	5,300.0	33.9	12,957.8	82.8
14,751.9	5,282.0	55.8	−	−	−	−
4,658.2	383.7	9.0	−	−	−	−
5,196.2	1,183.0	29.5	−	−	−	−
24,606.3	6,848.7	38.6	4,926.0	38.4	11,774.7	91.8
513.2	29.5	6.1	195.0	67.5	224.5	77.8
68,823.8	19,758.8	40.3	13,752.6	38.9	33,511.4	94.9

navy's procurement funds, $13.6 billion, or 65 percent, would go for purchasing new ships and aircraft under the Carter FY 1982 proposal, as compared with $19.6 billion, or 69 percent, under Reagan. The bulk of the air force procurement budget for FY 1982—53 percent under Carter and 60 percent under Reagan—is devoted to the acquisition of aircraft, as would be expected, whereas tracked vehicles, rockets, and artillery receive the largest single portion (about 27 percent under both Carter and Reagan) of the army's procurement funds.

Although most of the routine procurement items (such as spare parts for old weapons systems) are accounted for in the categories labeled "other" and "ammunition" in table 4, it should be noted that the procurement accounts for aircraft, missiles, tanks, and ships contain funds for the purchase of some spare parts for older weapons as well.

Cost of major weapons. Table 5 presents the nineteen most expensive weapons procurement programs funded in the Carter and Reagan budgets for FY 1982. (Total program costs for two other major weapons—the MX missile and the B–1 bomber—have yet to be determined; the FY 1982 budget contains no procurement funds for the MX and $1.9 billion in advance procurement for the long-range combat aircraft, or LRCA.) The first two columns show that the Reagan administration's estimates of total program costs for nine of these weapons are lower than the Carter administration's estimates, higher for eight systems, and the same for two. In the aggregate, the Carter administration estimated that these nineteen major weapons systems would cost $242.6 billion, whereas the Reagan administration revised the figure to $239.6 billion. The last two columns of the table show the dollars remaining to be authorized after January 1981, given the Carter and Reagan estimates for the total cost of each program. According to the Reagan estimates, $142.6 billion remains to be spent on these weapons systems.

Several points can be made with regard to table 5. For some of the weapons programs, the Reagan administration expects to buy more units than the Carter administration proposed in FY 1982, even though the total program costs of these weapons are assumed to decline. Examples include the F−18 aircraft (63 instead of Carter's 58), the F−16 aircraft (120 instead of 96), the CG−47 cruiser (3 instead of 2), the M−1 tank (720 instead of 569), the FVS fighting vehicle (600 instead of 464), the P−3C aircraft (12 instead of 6), and the AH−64 helicopter (14 instead of 8).[2]

There are a number of possible explanations for why the total program costs are estimated to decline for these seven weapons as well as for two other programs (Trident ballistic missile submarine and ALCM, unit purchases of which in FY 1982 are the same under the Carter and Reagan budgets). First, as was noted earlier, the Reagan administration is assuming lower inflation rates than its predecessor did for defense production and for the economy as a whole. Second, multiyear purchases are expected to contribute to a lowering of total program costs for some of these weapons, such as the F−16 (see Kyle 1981, pp. 12, 84). Third, economies of scale realized by larger unit buys should lead to lower costs. Foreign military sales of some weapons systems, such as the F−16, also contribute to lower costs by augmenting the unit purchase figures contained in the DOD budget. Fourth, the Reagan administration may plan to accelerate purchases to shorten the duration of production runs and thereby lower costs.

Improved readiness.   If one takes the entire FY 1982 procurement budgets of the Carter and Reagan administrations—$49.1 billion and $68.8 billion, respectively—only $18.5 billion (or 38 percent) of the Carter request and $27.9 billion (or 41 percent) of the Reagan procurement budget pays for the forty-nine major weapons programs funded in the new fiscal year. (These forty-nine weapons include those for which quarterly acquisition cost reports are re-

Table 5
FY 1982 Estimates of the Total Cost of Major Procurement Programs
(billions of dollars)

Program	Total program cost (Carter)	Total program cost (Reagan)	Authorized through FY 1981 (Carter)*	Remains to be spent (Carter)	Remains to be spent (Reagan)
F–18	37.9	35.3	5.2	32.7	30.1
Trident	31.7	29.9	15.8	15.9	14.1
CG–47	22.6	22.1	3.6	19.0	18.5
F–16	21.9	20.3	7.7	14.2	12.6
M–1	19.0	18.6	2.9	16.1	15.7
F–15	14.3	15.4	12.8	1.5	2.6
SSN–688	14.4	14.6	9.5	4.9	5.1
F–14A	12.0	12.1	9.7	2.3	2.4
FVS (MICV)	13.1	11.8	1.1	12.0	10.7

FFG–7	8.8	10.3	8.1	0.7	2.2
Patriot	8.3	8.5	2.9	5.4	5.6
P–3C	8.8	8.4	3.6	5.2	4.8
Black Hawk	6.6	7.3	2.0	4.6	5.3
AH–64	6.6	6.0	1.1	5.5	4.9
ALCM	6.1	5.9	2.2	3.9	3.7
A–10	4.7	5.4	4.7	0.0	0.7
Roland	1.4	3.3	1.2	0.2	2.1
CVN–71	2.6	2.6	2.5	0.1	0.1
Pershing	1.8	1.8	0.4	1.4	1.4
Total	242.6	239.6	97.0	145.6	142.6

Source: Office of the Assistant Secretary of Defense (Comptroller) 1980–1981.
*Includes funds in FY 1981 supplemental request.

quired by Congress and other major procurement programs.) The remaining $30.6 billion (or 62 percent) of the Carter procurement budget would pay for acquisition of other weapons, equipment, and spare parts; the comparable figures for the Reagan budget are $40.9 billion (or 59 percent).

An examination of procurement spending for "spares and repair parts" reveals that, for FY 1982, the Reagan administration has recommended that $1.6 billion be added to the amount contained in the Carter procurement budget for these items, resulting in a total of $7.5 billion (see Office of the Assistant Secretary of Defense [Comptroller] 1981a); this figure would amount to 3.4 percent of the entire DOD budget of $222.2 billion in TOA, or about 11 percent of the $68.8 billion devoted to procurement.

Personnel. The single largest element of Pentagon personnel costs includes the pay and allowances earned by active-duty and reserve members of the armed forces plus moving expenses, subsistence in kind, military clothing for enlisted personnel, and a number of miscellaneous costs, all adding up to $31.1 billion in FY 1980. Congressional approval of the Reagan administration's proposed 14.5 percent pay increase for military personnel on 1 October 1981 brings this figure to almost $44 billion in FY 1982.

Although most of the rise since FY 1980 in military personnel costs is explained by cost-of-living increases, military manpower levels have been rising as well. The Carter administration would have raised active-duty manning from 2.05 million members in FY 1980 to 2.094 million in FY 1982 (growth averaging about 1 percent per year) and to 2.1 million in FY 1983. In contrast, the Reagan administration proposes raising military strengths to 2.12 million in FY 1982, an increase of about 1.5 percent per year over the FY 1980 level (see Brown 1981, p. 267; Office of the Assistant Secretary of Defense [Public Affairs] 1981, p. 10). Plans have been reported for yearly increases of about the same magnitude that aim to add 160,000 to 200,000 personnel over the FY 1980 level, representing an overall expansion of about 8 to 10 percent by FY 1986. Secretary Caspar Weinberger has stressed that the additional military members will increase force readiness directly by raising combat unit manning and indirectly by bolstering maintenance and training staffs.

The Reagan budget also provides for 936,000 direct-hire civilian employees in FY 1982, up 21,000 from the FY 1980 level and 20,000 (or about 2 percent) above the Pentagon civilian work force contemplated by the Carter administration for FY 1982 (see Office of Management and Budget 1981*d,* pp. 390–97; Brown 1981, p. 269; Office of the Assistant Secretary of Defense [Public Affairs] 1981, p. 10). Foreign indirect-hire employees—that is, foreign nationals employed overseas under master labor contracts—will rise from 75,000 in FY 1980 to 89,000 in FY 1982, as compared with 79,000 in FY 1982 in the Carter budget. Secretary Weinberger has emphasized that these civilian additions are needed to allow military members now assigned to noncombat operations and support jobs to return to combat and combat-related positions and additionally to bolster maintenance depot, supply, and contract administration staffs.

The Carter administration planned no increases in direct-hire civilian employees during the FY 1981–1986 period, whereas the Reagan administration will require annual growth of about 1 percent per year in the civilian work force through FY 1982, no change in FY 1983, and a falloff in the last three years that almost completely reverses the original buildup. Thus there is little difference in the numbers of civilian direct-hire employees that will be needed by FY 1986, according to each administration's employment projections.

In FY 1980 about nine out of every ten civilian defense workers were engaged in operations and maintenance (O&M) activities, for about 45 percent of total O&M costs. Although temporary increases in direct-hire workers will add to those costs in the short term, subsequent civilian work-force drawdowns planned by the Reagan administration will help to restrain O&M spending increases in the longer term. Still, if more planes, ships, tanks, and other equipment appear after FY 1983 because of Reagan procurement programs, there is cause to wonder whether the force structure could be operated and maintained properly with a civilian work force that would return by FY 1986 to its approximate size in FY 1980.

Pay increases for military and civilian personnel are based in part on each administration's respective projections for economywide inflation. The Reagan increases are smaller than those planned by the Carter administration in all years after FY 1981 except one. The 14.3 percent increase in military pay slated for FY 1982 is well above the 9.1 percent jump that was planned by Carter.

On the civilian side, the Carter and Reagan boosts in FY 1982 are both quite low in relation to prevailing inflation of about 11 percent because each administration proposed a new method for maintaining comparability between compensation levels for federal and private sector workers. The Carter administration estimated that a 13.5 percent increase in FY 1982 for general-schedule federal workers would be indicated had there not been any change in the comparability calculation (see Office of Management and Budget 1981a, pp. 3–5; idem 1981c, p. 13).

Military retired pay is the third largest component of personnel costs. Together, military retired pay, military personnel costs, and civilian payroll constituted 87 percent of total defense personnel costs in FY 1980.[3]

Both administrations proposed changes in the military retired pay system in the FY 1982 budget. The Carter administration proposal provided for member vesting at ten (rather than twenty, as currently) years of active-duty service, deferral of retirement pay and benefits for many retiring members, one cost-of-living adjustment in FY 1981 and subsequent years instead of one every six months, and a host of other detailed changes. The Reagan administration also proposed one cost-of-living adjustment per year beginning in FY 1981 plus other unspecified changes that would take effect in FY 1983.

Annual differences between the Carter projections (with proposed changes) and the Reagan projections during the FY 1982–1986 period amount to $7.4 billion. Much of this difference in retired pay costs seems to be explained by the Reagan administration's expectations for lower inflation. Also, the administration's formal explanation of all proposed changes should be expected in the FY 1983–1987 spending plan.

THE FY 1982–1986 DEFENSE SPENDING PROGRAM

The five-year defense program normally presents long-term military spending for seven major budget titles, or appropriation categories, and for nine major program categories. By examining the spending "tracks" at this level of detail, the public and the Congress can judge whether the annual military budget under immediate consideration—the first in the five-year program—is part of a progression of sound financing steps leading to the force levels that the administration seeks five years hence. Thus descriptions of the full program provide a way of checking on the reasonableness of the annual budget under review and give a clearer idea of what subsequent budgets will require of the congressional committees that will authorize and appropriate funds for the various military spending categories.

To determine whether a long-term spending program is sound, we must know its specific goals and whether the major elements of the program fit together in a manner that will ensure their achievement. Although the Reagan administration's general aim of a stronger military establishment is well understood, the specific goals of its defense program will not be known until the administration presents a formal statement of its arms spending objectives, including a comprehensive description of the force structure it envisions.

Investment versus ownership

Comparison of the TOA tracks proposed by the two administrations, as estimated by the authors, sheds some light on the question of program balance. The Carter program in current dollars envisioned somewhat slower growth from FY 1981 to FY 1986 in military personnel costs than that projected by the Reagan program—about 55 percent as compared with 61 percent; also, the total five-year TOA value for this category is about $245 billion for Carter, as compared with $261 billion for Reagan (see table 6). These differences generally accord with the different active-duty military personnel strengths planned over the period by the two administrations, discussed earlier. In O&M funding, however, the Carter administration envisioned a larger percentage increase through FY 1986 than its successor—about 72 percent, as compared with about 66 percent—and the total TOA value of the Carter and Reagan O&M tracks are nearly the same in current dollars—about $388 billion for Carter and $389 billion for Reagan.

On the other hand, TOA funding for the investment categories in the Carter program is austere in comparison with that shown by the Reagan investment track. Carter procurement TOA in FY 1986 at $99 billion would have been about double the FY 1981 level, but Reagan procurement will almost triple in the same period. In the Reagan program, all investment categories combined exceed by more than $170 billion the Carter investment total of $542 billion for FY 1982–1986, in current dollars.

Clearly the spending programs are different in all appropriation categories except one, O&M, with the sharpest departures seen in the higher Reagan TOA levels for procurement and other investment categories. In contrast, there is little difference between the Reagan and Carter programs in the O&M area.

On the surface, it appears that the Reagan administration proposes to operate, maintain, and otherwise support increasing forces and facilities using approximately the same resources as those that the Carter program proposed for lower force levels. How is this possible? In addition to hoped-for economies to make O&M funds stretch further, differences in future inflation projections mean that the purchasing power of O&M money in the Reagan program is expected to be greater than current dollar comparisons with the Carter figures suggest. Thus, total Reagan O&M funding during the five years may buy a bit more despite the fact that its value in current dollars is about the same as the Carter total. Also, cutbacks after FY 1983 in the large civilian O&M work force will reduce civilian payroll costs and will thus make relatively more funds available for fuel, contract work, base and repair facility operations, and other O&M activities. It is possible as well that with rising military manpower strengths, some of the additional active-duty personnel will assume the duties of departed civilian O&M employees.

Nevertheless, if sharp increases in investment TOA cause weapons and equipment stocks to grow rapidly through FY 1986, ownership expenses are likely to increase as well. Thus comparison of the Carter and Reagan spending programs gives another indication that the new administration's original spending plan may have understated the O&M funding that will be required to support the force structure it envisions.

Table 6
Carter and Reagan Defense Spending by Appropriation Category
FY 1981–1986
(TOA in billions of current dollars)

	Fiscal year						FY 1982–1986 total	Difference (Reagan less Carter)	% change FY 1981–1986
	1981	1982	1983	1984	1985	1986			
Military personnel									
Carter	36.7	41.3	45.0	48.8	52.8	56.7	244.6	16.6	54.5
Reagan	37.4	43.8	48.1	52.4	56.6	60.3	261.2		61.2
Military retirement									
Carter	13.8	15.6	18.4	20.4	22.4	24.3	101.1	− 8.1	76.1
Reagan	13.8	15.4	17.1	18.7	20.2	21.6	93.0		56.5
O&M									
Carter	54.2	62.4	69.9	77.8	85.2	93.0	388.3	0.9	71.6
Reagan	56.0	64.1	70.7	77.2	84.4	92.8	389.2		65.7
Procurement									
Carter	45.0	49.1	59.7	71.5	84.4	99.0	363.7	146.3	120.0
Reagan	48.2	68.5	83.1	99.9	118.6	139.9	510.0		190.2

Other investment and family housing									
Carter	21.5	28.0	31.0	34.6	39.5	45.3	178.4 }	28.4	110.7
Reagan	22.6	30.4	35.8	41.0	46.7	52.9	206.8		134.1
Overall TOA									
Carter	171.2	196.4	224.0	253.1	284.3	318.3	1,276.1 }	184.1	85.9
Reagan	178.0	222.2	254.8	289.2	326.5	367.5	1,460.2		106.5

Sources: Office of Management and Budget 1981a, pp. 31, 105; Office of the Assistant Secretary of Defense (Public Affairs) 1981, p. 9; Kaiser 1981; and authors' estimates.

SUMMARY OF CARTER AND REAGAN DEFENSE PLAN DIFFERENCES

The Reagan administration's projected success in controlling economywide inflation during the FY 1982–1986 period accounts for a large share of the difference between the constant dollar values of the Reagan and Carter five-year defense plans. In one scenario of inflation higher than projected by the Reagan administration, outlays in current dollars would have to rise an average of $8 billion per year above those reported in the plan to preserve the buying power of funds spent over the FY 1982–1986 period.

Another difference between the two plans is the more ambitious Reagan target for growth in investment funding, especially for the procurement of weapons and equipment. Besides spending more money generally in this key area, the Reagan plan will accelerate weapons production rates beginning in FY 1982, causing unit costs to decline so rapidly that a number of weapons programs will yield more total units at lower overall costs than those that the Carter program would achieve. Also, as a direct consequence of reductions in the total costs of some weapons programs, a larger share of investment funds in the FY 1982–1986 period would then be made available for new and extremely costly activities such as MX production, B–1 bomber production, and expanded naval shipbuilding. The success of this strategy appears to depend heavily on multiyear purchases of weapons.

A comparative analysis of the unexpended balances (the cumulative difference between proposed annual TOA and outlay figures) implied by the Carter and Reagan plans shows that the latter will store up a much larger share of TOA granted from FY 1982 to FY 1986 for expenditure in outlays after FY 1986. The high rate of accumulation means that outlays during the five years of the Reagan plan will grow at a rapid but nevertheless controlled rate somewhat below the rate that would normally be implied by the TOA increases in the plan. One purpose may be to prevent still higher defense outlays during the period from adding to federal deficits, stimulating demand-pull inflation in the defense industry, and otherwise moving the national economy toward higher rates of inflation.

Of all the aspects of the Reagan program examined here, three stand out for their pivotal importance in making the program a reality. First, there must be early and continuing congressional support for multiyear procurement of weapons and like steps, for without greater deferral of outlays from new investment TOA, it is unlikely that unit costs of weapons can be reduced or that the Reagan total TOA and outlay tracks can be reconciled. There are understandable arguments against congressional appropriations far in advance of actual production; however, these must be weighed against the possibility that without a new legislative approach to investment funding, the Reagan defense program would founder because fewer weapons would be produced than had been planned, and (1) total TOA would fall below the prescribed track to preserve annual outlay objectives, or (2) outlays would rise above the prescribed track to preserve annual TOA objectives. In the second case, the broader Reagan economic program could be damaged as well, doing further harm to the defense program.

The Reagan TOA objectives for O&M purchases make up the second critical factor. Comparison with the Carter program suggests little difference in the funds planned by each administration for operating and maintaining the future force structure. Yet the Reagan force structure promises to be more extensive if that program succeeds. On the other hand, a shift of funds from investment to O&M to provide better balance between the two would make it even more difficult to reconcile the Reagan total TOA and outlay tracks through FY 1986. Further explanation from the administration on this subject would be helpful.

Finally, one cannot help but note the symmetry manifest in the Reagan five-year defense plan. The various parts may not fit together as might be expected, but they do fit together well in a budgetary sense—so well, in fact, that it appears that little tolerance has been allowed for deviation. Whether such a closely integrated plan is properly designed to endure even modest changes—those that Congress or the administration itself might wish to make—without breaking down in one or several critical respects may become clearer in coming years. There is little doubt, however, that if the March 1981 spending proposals were to be fulfilled, this would result by 1986 in a military establishment much expanded by comparison with that proposed by the Carter administration.

The Reagan administration's new spending proposals for FY 1983–1987 have already stirred strong reactions from supporters and opponents of rising Pentagon budgets. Some critics, underscoring military spending as a major cause of mounting federal deficits, argue for smaller budgets than proposed. Such views should, and perhaps do, proceed from a belief that whatever gains would result from a slower increase in defense spending would outweigh the costs. To understand the costs, one must examine the budget proposals closely to identify areas where reduced spending would have the smallest impact on current and future military needs of the nation. Whatever the outcome, a debate over defense spending that is informed by strategy as well as budgetary considerations is the best safeguard for the nation's future military security.

11

ROBERT D. REISCHAUER

The Federal Budget: Subsidies for the Rich

Transfer and subsidy programs. Cost to the federal budget. Direct and indirect beneficiaries. Program examination and reform.

Close to half of the federal budget is devoted to transfer programs, which provide direct support or subsidies for individuals, families, and households. For the most part, these programs are explicitly aimed at people with low incomes, the disabled and handicapped, and those who are not working because of retirement or unemployment. Transfer programs provide cash payments as in social security, in-kind benefits as in hospital care through Medicare, vouchers as in food stamps, or tax credits as in the earned income credit. Because the explicit objective of these programs is to raise a target group's standard of living, they are evaluated and analyzed in terms of their impact on the income and well-being of the recipients.

However, such programs are by no means the only ones through which the federal government significantly affects the incomes and well-being of a particular group. Virtually every federal program influences the nation's distribution of income and wealth. Some do so in subtle and virtually indiscernible ways; others represent as straightforward a subsidy to a particular group as a welfare check is to a family receiving Aid to Families with Dependent Children (AFDC). Yet the wealth or income distribution consequences of these other, nontransfer federal programs are rarely a focus of attention or concern. While much is made of the fact that some large, working families with incomes over $10,000 per year receive food stamps, no one questions the appropriateness of a farmer arriving in a Cadillac to pick up a payment from the commodity price support program.

The reason for this, of course, is that the primary objective of these programs is not to affect income distribution but to facilitate the attainment of some other worthwhile goal, such as the encouragement of home ownership, the preservation of the family farm, the support of state and local government borrowing for needed infrastructure, or the strengthening of the U.S. Merchant Marine. Because the distributional consequences are not important objectives, data concerning the income effects of nontransfer federal programs are generally unavailable. However, it is probably safe to assume that the preponderance of the benefits of many programs is garnered by profitable corporations and citizens in the top half of the nation's income distribution.

This chapter provides a brief introduction to the ways in

which federal programs that are not explicitly designed to affect income distribution do so by providing subsidies to one group or another. This treatment is by no means comprehensive, but rather is intended to illustrate the diversity of subsidy mechanisms and what is known about their distributional impacts. The final section describes some of the options available for reducing such subsidies, if it is determined that their budgetary costs and undesirable distributional implications exceed their benefits.

MECHANISMS AND TOOLS

Some federal government activities have no easily discernible impact on the distribution of income and wealth. This is the case with defense spending, federal employment, most government purchases of goods and services, and the grants given to states and localities for many governmental functions. While the composition and level of final demand are undoubtedly altered by such spending, it would be difficult to pinpoint particular groups that are disproportionately aided. Of course, defense contractors and their stockholders, workers, and suppliers benefit from government defense purchases, but some other groups of industrialists, stockholders, and laborers would benefit if the defense spending were redirected into other governmental programs or if the money used to support such spending were returned to the people in the form of lower taxes.

This is not the case with respect to the transfer programs or to a vast number of other federal programs that involve explicit subsidies to businesses and individuals. Some of the latter subsidies provide services benefiting a small group; others are designed to reward or encourage a specific type of behavior. The federal government traditionally has relied upon seven mechanisms or tools for providing such subsidies: direct subsidies, credit subsidies, purchase guarantees, tax expenditures, regulations, trade policy, and the provision of private goods and services free or at subsidized prices.

Direct subsidies. In addition to the transfer programs, the federal government provides individuals and corporations with direct payments or subsidies for engaging in certain types of activity. One example of such a program is the direct operating differential subsidy provided to a handful of companies that operate U.S. flag vessels in ocean-borne commerce. These subsidies average about $60,000 for each seagoing billet per year and cost the federal government an aggregate of $353 million in fiscal year 1981. The direct operating subsidies are intended to offset the higher costs U.S. shipping companies face when compared with those of foreign flag vessels. The rationale is to maintain a U.S. merchant shipping fleet that could be valuable in times of armed conflict.

Credit subsidies. Numerous federal programs provide individuals and corporations with credit, or the access to credit, at below-market terms. Some programs provide direct low-interest-rate loans, as is the case with the Export-Import Bank, which lends money to foreign purchasers of U.S. exports at subsidized rates.

In other programs the government may pay the lender the difference between the market interest rate and a lower rate that the lender has charged the borrower. This is the procedure in the guaranteed student loan (GSL) program, in which the federal government picks up the full cost of the loan while the borrower is attending school and part of the cost once the student has graduated.

A third credit subsidy mechanism is the federal loan guarantee. Such a guarantee allows a borrower to obtain credit at favorable rates, thus reducing borrowing costs, because the guarantee means that the lender is protected from the possibility of default. The most publicized example of this tool was the Chrysler Corporation loan guarantee, but similar guarantees are offered by the Small Business Administration, the Export-Import Bank, and a host of government-sponsored enterprises. In fiscal year 1981, $28 billion in net loan guarantees were issued by the federal agencies.

While direct loans and subsidized interest payments involve outlays by the federal government, loan guarantees involve an expenditure only if the borrower defaults. Loan guarantees do, however, cause a reallocation of resources, because they rearrange corporations and individuals in the queue of potential borrowers. Those receiving a guarantee suddenly become preferred borrowers and obtain credit at low interest rates; those less fortunate are pushed down the queue and must pay higher rates.

Purchase guarantees. A third tool used to subsidize certain corporations and individuals is the purchase guarantee, whereby the government stands ready to buy, at a fixed price, as much of a specific product as is produced. Many of the nation's agricultural subsidy programs rely on purchase guarantees. For example, from the dairy industry the government will purchase all surplus manufactured milk products at a price of $13.10 per hundredweight of milk. This purchase price guarantee is adjusted upward on a predetermined schedule.

Tax expenditures. Rather than providing benefits in the form of direct outlays, many subsidy programs operate through tax expenditure mechanisms. Tax expenditures are provisions of the tax code that provide preferential tax treatment (i.e., reduced taxes) in order to encourage certain types of behavior and to reward particular groups of taxpayers. Tax expenditures may take the form of special exclusions, deductions, credits, lower rates, or postponement of liability. The deductibility of mortgage interest on owner-occupied homes from taxable income is one example of a tax expenditure subsidy benefiting individuals.

Regulations. Many federal regulations restrict competitive market forces and thereby provide subsidies to favored businesses and individuals. For example, the federal government has restricted the acreage upon which peanuts may be grown as well as the right to market this crop. Only farmers participating in these restrictions are eligible to receive government-subsidized commodity loans and price supports. By restricting entry into the market, the federal government effectively reduces the crop's supply, thereby raising the price and benefiting certain farmers.

A similar situation exists in communications, where the federal government gives away a limited number of television and radio broadcast licenses. These monopoly rights can be worth millions of dollars to those fortunate enough to obtain them.

Trade policy. A related form of subsidy is found in the area of trade policy. By imposing tariffs or by negotiating agreements with foreign countries to restrict the quantities of cars, steel, television tubes, shoes, and sugar that are imported to the United States, the government holds up prices for these products. Domestic producers, their labor, and their suppliers benefit.

Private goods and services. A final mechanism through which the federal government may subsidize a specific group is the provision, for little or no charge, of goods and services for that group's particular benefit. For example, the federal government sells enriched uranium to utilities and foreign governments at a price that is roughly 30 percent below what a private firm would charge. The Bureau of Land Reclamation sells water for agricultural irrigation at approximately one-sixth full production cost. The Bureau of Land Management and the Forest Service charge between one-fifth and one-half of market value for grazing rights on federal lands (Congressional Budget Office 1982c). Recreational boaters benefit from the extensive system of navigational aids and rescue capabilities that the government maintains. Corporate and private aircraft operators benefit from the Federal Aviation Administration's (FAA's) navigational and landing facilities and vacationers benefit from the heavy subsidization of outdoor recreation areas.

Budgetary considerations

As budgetary problems have become more severe, much has been made of the rapid increase in the costs of the federal government's transfer programs. This increase has been traced to the uncontrollable nature of these programs. Most of the transfer programs are entitlements; that is, the government is obligated to provide benefits to all those who meet a set of predetermined eligibility criteria. Thus the government's financial exposure is open ended. Furthermore, the number of people meeting the eligibility criteria depends, more often than not, on demographic factors and the performance of the nation's economy—forces over which the government has little apparent control. When unemployment rises, the ranks of those eligible for unemployment compensation, food stamps, and AFDC swell, as does the number of people choosing to retire and receive social security and Medicare benefits. The costs of many of these transfer programs have also been pushed up because benefit levels are directly indexed, as is the case with social security, or indirectly linked to rising prices, as is the case with Medicare and Medicaid.

It is worth noting that many of the programs that provide subsidies to those with higher incomes share some of these budget-exceeding characteristics of the transfer programs. For example, all tax expenditures, like entitlements, involve an open-ended and uncontrollable cost to the federal government. Anyone meeting the requirements is free to take advantage of a specific tax expenditure in order to reduce his tax liability. While there are methodological and conceptual reasons why the total revenue lost from tax expenditures cannot be calculated with any degree of precision, it is clear that this loss has grown and will grow faster than federal direct spending.

As with a number of transfer programs, the costs to the federal government of some subsidies are determined by forces over which the government has little control. While federal Medicaid spending depends largely on state decisions in that the program is an open-ended matching grant, the amount of federal tax revenue lost because of the deductibility of state and local taxes is, in large part, determined by the taxing decisions of these governments. Like the transfer programs, the costs of many subsidy programs vary with economic conditions. When interest rates climb, the government's costs of providing direct loans or loan subsidies rise. Similarly, the costs of agricultural price guarantees depend not only on the guarantee level but also on market conditions. Weather, both in the United States and abroad, is often the most significant determinant of the commodity program costs.

While the benefits of social security, food stamps, and a host of other federal transfer programs are automatically and explicitly adjusted for increases in price level, this is not the case with other subsidies that are not tax expenditures. Some, such as the agricultural price guarantees, do involve legislated increases but lack permanent authorizations and therefore must be periodically reviewed. For example, under the Agriculture and Food Act of 1981, dairy price supports will rise in annual steps each October from $13.10 per hundredweight in 1981 to $14.60 in 1984. Tax expenditures, however, do incorporate an implicit form of indexation similar to that found in the Medicare and Medicaid programs. As prices rise, the value of tax deductions or exclusions increases automatically, reducing the federal government's revenues.

In short, many of the federal programs that benefit the

rich have costs that are as uncontrollable and rapidly growing as those of the more basic transfer programs.

WHO BENEFITS?

While the beneficiaries of transfer programs are fairly easy to identify, this is not always the case with other types of subsidy programs. To be sure, students and their parents benefit from guaranteed student loans, boat owners benefit from government subsidies for navigational aids, and home owners benefit from the deductibility of mortgage interest from taxable income. However, for subsidies that involve production of goods or services, or for some of those that involve state and local governments, identifying the beneficiaries is, at best, difficult and uncertain. The government subsidy could be captured by any of the factors of production or by the consumer. In some cases indirect benefits, not received by any direct participant of the program, may be as important as participants' more obvious direct benefits.

The federal farm commodity program offers one example of these complexities. Price supports raise wheat prices while evening out their fluctuations. In the short run, this benefits the farmer. In the long run, the persistence of wheat prices above competitive market levels will raise the rate of return and hence the price of the land on which the wheat is grown. An owner who sells his land may thus receive a capital gain attributable to the program. On the other hand, the farmer receiving payment from the current price support system may gain little of the real benefit if he bought his land at a price that was inflated because the benefits of the farm commodity program were capitalized into the land's value. To the extent that future benefits from such programs are capitalized into the price of farm land, those who own land at the time that benefits change reap the rewards. In some cases, they will be the farmers receiving this year's support payment; in others, they may be former owners who have nothing to do with farming today.

Maritime subsidies offer another example of how difficult it is to determine the true beneficiaries of many subsidy programs. Government payments are made to shipping companies and might therefore be viewed as aiding the management and stockholders of these corporations. However, this may not be the entire story. The existence of a strong and active union has ensured that some of the benefits have been captured by the seamen, whose wages have risen at a fairly good pace despite declining employment and business in the industry.

The subsidized loans offered by the Rural Electrification Administration for construction and operation of telephone and electrical utilities in rural areas offer an example of a different beneficiary—the customer. Because these loans are offered at subsidized interest rates of 2 to 5 percent, beneficiary utilities are able to charge rural electrical customers 3.3 to 9.9 percent lower rates than customers of other utilities (Office of Management and Budget 1982a, p. 201). In general, when a government subsidy is provided to producers who sell in competitive markets and who face competition for their labor and other inputs, most of the benefit is likely to be garnered by the consumers.

The exclusion of interest on state and local government bonds and notes from the federal income tax raises a different type of problem. Corporate and individual holders of these securities are the direct beneficiaries of this tax expenditure subsidy; most are in the top quarter of the nation's income distribution (Peterson 1976). However, the tax expenditure has allowed states and localities to borrow at roughly 60 to 70 percent of the rate of taxable issues. If they had to pay these higher interest rates, not only would their borrowing and capital spending be lower but, more important, their interest costs and the taxes needed to finance these costs would be higher. Since state and local taxes are, on balance, regressive, those who receive the indirect benefits of this subsidy are a very different group from those who receive the direct subsidy (Phares 1980).

In some instances, a subsidy to one group can have negative indirect impacts on others. For example, the federal subsidization of inland waterways represents roughly 30 percent of the costs of inland waterways shipping. While the shippers and their customers (primarily grain and soy bean farmers and utilities using coal) may benefit, competing modes of transportation that are less heavily subsidized lose business.[1] Similarly, provision of federally subsidized water for irrigation has encouraged farmers in the Southwest to grow cotton and rice, which would be uneconomical if the Bureau of Reclamation charged the full production cost of this water. Subsidized irrigation in the Southwest has undercut unsubsidized production elsewhere in the country, thereby reducing farm incomes and land values.

In summary, for transfer programs and for some subsidy programs, direct beneficiaries are easy to identify and indirect or secondary beneficiaries are relatively unimportant. For some other subsidy programs, direct beneficiaries are not easily pinpointed but are far more important than indirect beneficiaries. For still others, indirect beneficiaries may be as important as direct beneficiaries and equally difficult to isolate. Because of conceptual and data problems inherent in isolating the indirect beneficiaries, the following examples of the distributional consequences of a few selected subsidies for the rich describe only the apparent or direct beneficiaries.

Tax expenditure examples

There are 109 separate provisions of the tax code that are classified as tax expenditures (Committee on the Budget 1982; Joint Committee on Taxation 1982). Thirteen of these

provide subsidies to corporations, fifty-four benefit individuals, and forty-two provide aid to both corporations and
individuals. As was suggested, it is difficult to tell just who
benefits from subsidies directed at businesses. Much depends
on the nature of the markets in which the business sells its
products and buys its inputs. If all of the benefits were captured by the owners of corporations, it would be safe to
assume that the rich benefit the most from such tax expenditures. However, reliable data on the incomes of owners of
all corporations are not available. A crude picture of corporate ownership by income class can be surmised from the distribution of dividend income; data from tax returns indicate
that over half of all dividends are received by the richest 3
percent of all taxpayers (see table 1). However, even this can
offer little insight into who really might be the beneficiaries
of corporate tax subsidies, because many tax expenditures
are directed at specific types of firms and industries only—
for example, explorers or developers of oil and gas resources,
iron ore deposits, and stands of timber; investors in new
machinery; firms that sell products abroad; and firms that
offer employee stock option plans (ESOPs). Identifying the
benefiting firms and industries, let alone their owners, is impossible with available data.

Table 1
Distribution of Dividend Income by
Adjusted Gross Income Class 1980

	Adjusted gross income class			
	$0/ $9,999	$10/ $19,999	$20/ $49,999	Over $50,000
Percent of all reported dividend income	8.0%	12.2%	27.8%	52.0%
Percent of all tax returns	40.9	27.1	28.0	3.4

Source: Department of the Treasury 1981.

More, although not a great deal, is known about incomes of the beneficiaries of tax expenditures aimed solely at individuals. Some of these subsidies—the earned income credit, the elderly credit, extra personal exemptions for the blind and disabled, and the exclusion of disability pay and public assistance benefits from taxation—are directed disproportionately to those in the bottom half of the income distribution. Others provide benefits primarily to the wealthy (see table 2). These include:

The deductibility of charitable contributions. To encourage private giving, contributions made to charitable, religious, educational, cultural, scientific, and certain other types of nonprofit organizations may be deducted from taxable income by those who itemize deductions. The total revenue loss associated with this tax expenditure is estimated to be $9.7 billion in 1982. Over half of this benefit goes to taxpayers with incomes over $50,000.

The deductibility of home mortgage interest. Mortgage interest payments may be included among itemized deductions. This is intended to encourage home ownership by reducing its cost relative to renting. In 1982 federal revenues will be reduced by an estimated $23 billion from this tax expenditure. Almost three-quarters of the benefits are received by those with incomes over $30,000.

The deductibility of state and local taxes. Real estate, income, sales, and most other state and local government taxes can be deducted from taxable income by those who itemize their deductions. Federal revenues will be lowered by $30.4 billion in 1982 because of this provision of the tax code. Over four-fifths of the benefit from this deduction flows to those with incomes over $30,000.

Capital gains deduction. Only 40 percent of the gain realized on the sale of capital assets that have been held for more than a year is counted as taxable income for individuals. This preferential handling of gains has been ration-

Table 2
Percent Distribution of the Benefits of
Selected Tax Expenditures for Individuals
by Expanded Income Class 1981*

Tax expenditure	Expanded income class ($ thousands)			
	$0–$15	$15–$30	$30–$50	Over $50
Dividend exclusion	9.7	22.4	32.8	35.0
State and local tax deduction	2.8	16.3	35.6	45.3
Home mortgage interest deduction	2.8	22.7	43.7	30.8
Charitable contributions deduction	1.9	13.9	28.9	55.3
Capital gains deduction	5.5	11.6	19.6	63.4
Consumer interest expense deduction	1.4	23.6	42.2	32.9
Fraction of all taxable income**	20.5	36.9	25.8	16.8
Fraction of all tax liability**	10.3	30.6	28.0	31.1

Source: Joint Committee on Taxation 1981–1982.

*Expanded income is equal to adjusted gross income plus minimum tax preferences less investment interest expense to the extent of investment income.

**Based on 1980 adjusted gross income classes.

alized as appropriate treatment under a progressive tax system for gains that are accrued over a number of years, and as a proper reflection of the fact that some of the gain represents compensation for inflation rather than real return on investments. In 1982 federal individual income tax revenues will be reduced by some $18.3 billion from this tax expenditure. Roughly 63 percent of the benefit will accrue to those with incomes over $50,000.

Dividend exclusion. Individual taxpayers may exclude $100 in dividends (or $200 if filing a joint return when both spouses received at least $100 in qualifying dividends) from taxable income. The original rationale for this provision was to compensate for the "double taxation" of dividends through corporate and individual income taxes. An additional rationale has been to encourage stock ownership. In 1982 federal revenues will be reduced by an estimated $2.2 billion because of this provision. Approximately 68 percent of the benefits will accrue to taxpayers with incomes over $30,000.

Consumer interest expense deduction. Those itemizing deductions can subtract from their taxable income interest paid or accrued on nonbusiness debts. With the proliferation of credit cards, the cost of this subsidization of debt-financed purchases has grown substantially. In 1982 federal revenues will be reduced by $7.6 billion because of this provision of the tax code. Because higher-income taxpayers are more likely to itemize deductions, three-quarters of the benefit of this tax expenditure is received by those with incomes over $30,000.

Price guarantee example

Besides dairy price supports, the major farm subsidy programs are directed at producers of wheat, feed grains, cotton, and rice. Over the years a complex set of tools has been developed to stabilize the prices of these commodities and raise the incomes of the growers. These tools include deficiency payments, Commodity Credit Corporation (CCC) non-recourse loans, disaster payments, and various voluntary and mandatory land diversion policies.

Deficiency payments are direct payments to farmers. They are equal to the difference between the average market price for a commodity and a legislatively set target price or loan rate, multiplied by the farmer's normal yield, the number of acres planted, and an allocation factor.[2]

Farmers participating in the commodity programs may also obtain nonrecourse loans by placing their crops in approved storage facilities. The amount of the loans is equal to the legislatively set loan rate for the commodity multiplied by the quantity of the commodity put in storage. If the value of the stored commodity falls below the value of the loan plus the subsidized interest costs the farmer would have to pay before selling, he can fully satisfy the loan by transferring ownership of the stored commodity to the government. If the price rises above the loan rate, the farmer can pay off the loan and sell the commodity.

Disaster payments are made to farmers who cannot plant a crop or who suffer abnormally low yields because of adverse weather or other forces beyond their control. The amount of the disaster payment is determined by the short-fall in yield, the number of affected acres, and the crop's target price.

To participate in the various commodity support programs, farmers must agree to set aside a portion of their normal planted acreage if the secretary of agriculture decides that reduced production is in the national interest. In addition, various bonus payments are made to farmers who voluntarily set aside additional acres of land from production.

Not all farmers participate in the commodity support programs because there are costs associated with acreage diversion. Participation depends upon the farmer's assessment of future prices and of the risks associated with natural disasters. Participation rates fluctuate from year to year. In

1978 only 35 percent of all farmers, accounting for 53 percent of all eligible acres and 36 percent of all production, participated in these programs.[3]

The benefits of the farm programs accrue to nonparticipating as well as participating farmers. Nonparticipants benefit from the curtailment of production associated with acreage set-aside requirements, acreage allocations, and the storage programs, all of which reduce supplies and raise the prices available to all farmers. It is estimated that such supply limitations raised the price of wheat by 16 percent in 1978. Even farmers growing crops not eligible for direct price supports may reap benefits because higher prices for supported crops will increase the demand for substitute commodities. For example, controls on corn production were estimated to increase soy bean prices by 2 percent in 1978.

On the whole, the largest farms receive most of the benefits of the commodity programs. In 1978 over half of the net benefits went to the largest 10 percent of participating farms (see table 3). These net benefit estimates include the several forms of direct payments, indirect benefits arising from increased market prices, and the costs associated with removing land from production. To some extent, the concentration of benefits reflects the concentration of production on large farms. However, the largest farms do benefit disproportionately compared to their production.

In response to criticism about the farm programs' disproportionate benefits for large and wealthy landowners, Congress imposed limits on the size of payments from the deficiency and land diversion programs and the disaster programs. In 1981 these limits were $50,000 for the combined deficiency and land diversion programs and $100,000 for the disaster programs.

These limits, however, have had a minimal impact. In 1978 only 0.16 percent of the participants were affected and total outlays were reduced by less than 2 percent. The limits affected the largest farms the most, but even among these

Table 3

Distribution of the Net Benefit of Farm
Programs and Production 1978

	Percentile of farm size: smallest to largest					
	0–10%	10–30%	30–50%	50–70%	70–90%	90–100%
Percent of program's net benefit	0.8	2.6	5.1	9.5	26.5	55.5
Percent of commodity production	1.0	3.0	5.5	14.0	29.5	47.0

Source: Lin, Johnson, and Calvin 1981.

recipients the impact was small; the share of all direct benefits received by the largest 10 percent of all farms was reduced from 46.6 percent to 45.9 percent of the total. This small impact is explained by the relatively high level at which limits are set and by the fact that they are set on a "person," not a "farm," basis. Several "persons" or owners may be receiving payments for commodities produced on a single farm, and of course the limits create an incentive for people to organize themselves with that outcome in mind.

Credit subsidy example

The Higher Education Act of 1965 authorized a program of subsidized loans for students attending institutions of higher education. Under this guaranteed student loan (GSL) program, the federal government pays the full interest on the loan while the borrower is attending school, and it pays the amount by which the loan rate exceeds 7 percent after the borrower has left school. The loan rate paid to the banks offering these loans is set at 3.5 percentage points above the bond-equivalency rate on ninety-one-day Treasury bills. Thus the cost of the subsidy varies with the interest rate, and the lender has protection both from borrower default through the federal guarantee and from rising interest rates.

While the original program was limited to students of fairly modest means, the Middle Income Student Assistance Act of 1978 removed these restrictions and the loan volume more than tripled by 1981 (from $1.7 billion in 1978 to $6.3 billion in 1981). The elimination of the income restriction meant that many middle- and upper-income families with dependent students could benefit from this government-subsidized loan whether or not lack of affordable credit was important to their child's college attendance or choice of school. Only spotty data are available to show the incomes of those receiving GSLs. In Virginia some 39 percent of all borrowers in 1981 had incomes of over $30,000 per year; nationwide, the same fraction of dependent freshman borrowers came from families with incomes above that level (see table 4).

While the nation as a whole certainly derives some benefit from an educated work force and citizenry, those who obtain higher education unquestionably gain as well. Higher education is often the ticket to the top half of the income distribution. The role of education in enhancing future income prospects has led some to question the appropriateness of providing federal subsidies for students attending institutions of higher education during periods of budget restraint. In response to such arguments, Congress has moved to reduce these subsidies while expanding the availability of unsubsidized credit for those wishing to borrow to attend institutions of higher education.[4]

Examples of subsidized goods and services

Some of the goods and services provided by the government at little or no cost benefit the most affluent segments of the nation. Recreational boaters in coastal areas are particularly favored. Not only does the National Oceanic and Atmospheric Administration (NOAA) provide navigational charts at roughly one-third of cost to this group, but the Coast Guard provides over $200 million a year in other services. Almost three-quarters of this is the cost of search and rescue services for those who get into trouble in coastal waters. While data detailing the income distribution of these individuals are not available, more often than not they own boats worth tens of thousands of dollars.

Similarly, businesses and private individuals who own planes benefit from a wide range of government-subsidized goods and services including NOAA charts, aviation weather forecasts, and the Federal Aviation Administration air traffic control system and flight service stations. The Con-

Table 4
Distribution of Family Income for Guaranteed
Student Loan Borrowers

	Income ($ thousands)				
	Under $10	$10–$20	$20–$30	$30–$40	Over $40
Virginia (1981)*	24%	19%	18%	15%	24%
American freshmen (1980)**	9	23	29	20	19
	Under $12	$12–$21	$21–$30	Over $30	
Pennsylvania (1981)*	24%	26%	31%	19%	

Sources: Virginia Education Loan Authority data. Also Davis 1981; Astin, King, and Richardson 1981.

*Includes dependent and independent students.

**Dependent students only.

gressional Budget Office has estimated that such general aviation pays for about 5 percent of the costs of these services through fees and fuel taxes, while commercial aviation pays for roughly 82 percent of the services it receives.

While the only information available concerning the incomes of private plane owners is somewhat dated, it indicates that these individuals are far from poor (see table 5). In fact, the majority have incomes well over twice the national median.

Government subsidies of goods and services can also benefit upper-income groups in very indirect ways, as the example of the National Endowment for the Arts shows. The endowment provides roughly $140 million a year in grants for dance, music, opera, theater, museums, the visual arts, and other cultural endeavors. The objective of these grants is to nurture, sustain, and improve the cultural life of the nation. The most obvious direct beneficiaries of these grants are the performers and artists who, with the help of the endowment, are better able to pursue their chosen vocations.

However, there are indirect beneficiaries of the grants as well. Not only do the grants increase the availability of cultural performances, but they also allow companies to keep ticket prices from rising too rapidly. In fact, an explicit objective of the endowment is to ensure that the arts "may be experienced and enjoyed by the widest possible public" (National Endowment for the Arts 1978). Unfortunately, because of both taste and ticket prices, the audiences benefiting from reduced admission charges tend to be comprised of the most highly educated and financially secure people in the nation. While definitive national statistics are unavailable, data summarizing the results of numerous local studies of the educational, professional, and income characteristics of the audiences of the various art forms show this. For example, while 62 percent of those attending productions in the performing arts were college graduates, only 14 percent of the adult population were college graduates (see table 6). Similarly,

Table 5

Median Family Income of Individual Plane Owners by Size and Type of Plane 1974

| | All U.S. population | Single-engine piston | | Twin-engine piston | Turboprop | Turbojet |
		1–3 seats	4 and more seats			
Median family incomes	$12,836	$19,600	$26,100	$45,000	$80,000	$150,000
Percent of personal plane use 1976		24.9%	69.4%	5.5%	0.1%	0.1%

Source: Federal Aviation Administration, n.d.

over half of the audience tended to be professionals, while less than one worker in six was a professional in 1975. Although one analysis of the median family income of those attending the performing arts found it to be twice the median for all urban families, the survey of local audience studies found the gap to be somewhat lower (see table 6; Baumol and Bowen 1966a).

AVENUES TO REFORM

The rhetoric of recent years would suggest that the federal government does little besides provide for the national defense, give grants to state and local governments, and aid the aged, poor, and disabled through transfer programs. This chapter has drawn attention to a few of the large number of other activities in which the federal government is engaged. Its purpose has been to point out that many programs, while pursuing worthwhile objectives, provide substantial subsidies to profitable corporations and upper-income individuals.

As defense spending, the transfer programs, and grants-in-aid are being reexamined in an era of budgetary restraint, it is only proper that these other subsidies come under renewed scrutiny. Do these programs work? Do they achieve their objectives in a cost-effective manner? Are they equitable? During the past year, both the administration and Congress have shown increasing willingness to raise these difficult questions and institute changes.

Several avenues for further reform are available. Clearly, fees and charges can be raised for subsidized government goods and services. A relatively modest effort in this area could raise $5 to $7 billion a year. Both economic efficiency and equity would be served if the prices charged for government water, electricity, grazing rights, uranium enrichment, and nuclear waste disposal were raised to cover the full cost of production or to equal charges of private providers.

Table 6
Selected Characteristics of Audiences
Attending Various Art Forms*

| Art form | Median income (1976 dollars) | Educational attainment | |
		College graduate or more	High school graduate or less
Museums	$17,158	41.1%	27.6%
Performing arts	18,903	61.8**	17.0
Ballet and dance	20,082	65.0	12.9
Theater**	19,342	58.0	17.1
Orchestra	20,825	63.0	14.6
Opera	21,024	61.8	18.8
U.S. adult population		26.3	73.7
Families	14,960		
Families and unrelated individuals	11,920		

Source: National Endowment for the Arts 1978a, tables 3, 6.

*The figures represent medians of the values found in a large number of individual audience studies undertaken in recent years.

**Excludes outdoor drama.

Similarly, federal agencies such as the Federal Energy Regulatory Commission, the Commodity Futures Trading Commission, the Securities and Exchange Commission, the Federal Communications Commission, and the Patent and Trademark Office could charge fees that covered the full cost of licensing and regulatory services provided to the private sector. General aviation operators, recreational boaters, commercial users of the inland waterways, coastal harbors, and channels, and those using outdoor recreational areas could be asked to pay more of the cost of the services provided through government programs. Of course, fees and charges cannot be imposed for every good and service provided by the government. In some cases the costs of collecting the charge may outweigh the benefits. In others, charges may have undesirable distributional consequences or other ill effects.

With respect to credit programs, interest rates can be raised to reduce or eliminate subsidies. The level of federal subsidy in many credit programs has expanded dramatically over the years as interest rates have risen. For example, when the Rural Electrification Administration first established its direct loan rates of 2 to 5 percent, interest rates were only slightly above these levels. The availability of credit for a risky activity was the major benefit, not the low interest rates. With the prime rate over 15 percent, however, such loans now provide a huge subsidy. Credit programs could be restructured to tie the interest rate charged borrowers to the federal government's borrowing rate. For example, the Export-Import Bank's direct loans might carry an interest rate that was 90 percent of the federal borrowing rate or one percentage point below the ninety-one-day Treasury bill rate. Because such a change would affect only new loan commitments, a few years would pass before the full savings from reducing federal loan subsidies could be realized. A reasonable target for such savings in the short run would be $14 billion per year, an amount roughly equivalent to raising the average interest rate on new direct loans by 1 percent and to imposing a one-percentage-point fee on loans benefiting from a federal guarantee. These savings would more than double after several years.

Tax expenditure subsidies persist partly because large constituencies benefit from them and partly because there is no formal mechanism requiring that they be periodically reviewed and reauthorized. In this respect, they are similar to the basic entitlement programs. While no one would advocate a tax code that was continually subject to change and uncertainty, periodic review of the various tax expenditures, like that called for in some sunset legislation proposals, would be beneficial. With the lost revenue from tax expenditures currently amounting to over $250 billion a year, a goal of reducing these subsidies by $25 billion within several years is attainable.

In time, subsidies become built into the expectations and behavior of individuals and businesses. Anticipated benefits are capitalized into the price of land, houses, and other resources. Wages, infrastructure, industrial capacity, transportation modes, and business location patterns all come to reflect the operations of an economy with a certain pattern of subsidies. For this reason, rapid change or sudden elimination of major subsidies is likely to raise problems of fairness and to be fiercely resisted and economically disruptive. If subsidies are to be reduced, for both political and economic reasons the change should be gradual. For example, price supports for agriculture might be frozen at fixed levels while inflation reduced the real level of the benefits. Similarly, the interest rates charged on federally subsidized loans could be raised by a percentage point every year until the desired reduction in subsidy were achieved. A similar phase-in could apply to fees and charges. While reducing subsidies for the rich can contribute to an effort to balance the federal budget, even a major assault on such subsidies could not close half of the total gap between spending and revenues.

Finally, that a program appears to benefit profitable corporations or wealthy individuals should not be taken as prima facie evidence that it should be discontinued. Tax breaks, low interest loans, direct subsidies, and price guarantees may be the most efficient or least intrusive ways in which the federal government can intervene in private markets to achieve desired public objectives, but such assertions should be carefully reexamined on a periodic basis.

12

ROBERT W. HARTMAN*

Federal Employee Compensation and the Budget

Personnel costs, appropriations, and supplementals. Government work grades in comparison with the private sector. Distortions. Retirement benefits and double dipping. Demoralization at the top. The Civil Service Retirement System trust fund and taxpayer liability. Advocated reforms.

Pressures to hold down the federal budget in recent years have so dominated federal policy that employment, pay, and

*The views expressed are solely the author's and should not be attributed to the Brookings Institution. Allan Rivlin assisted in preparing this chapter.

fringes of the federal civilian work force have become vic-
tims of the short-run budget crunch.[1] So far, not much
money—if any—has been saved and the interplay of
budget-motivated policies and the existing personnel system
has exacerbated structural and managerial problems. Unless
and until the federal government deals with the fundamen-
tals of compensation policy, the situation will not improve.

THE FEDERAL BUDGET AND
PERSONNEL CUTS

About 2 million people work in white-collar occupations (excluding the postal service) for the federal government, earning an average salary of about $20,000 annually. Total com-
pensation, inclusive of benefits, has made up some 10 percent of the total obligations of the government in recent fiscal years. Contrary to popular opinion, employment has
grown very little in past decades (see table 1) and salaries
have fallen behind private sector workers in equivalent jobs
(see below). Nonetheless, 10 percent of the budget ain't hay,
and it ranks just below national defense (26 percent of
budget), social security (21 percent), and health care (10 percent) as an obvious target of attention for budget-cutters.

Personnel control

The problem is that there is no single line-item in the budget
that funds personnel costs. Appropriations are made for "salaries and expenses" in each agency to pay for personnel costs
(and to fund from the same appropriation such items as utility charges, office equipment, travel, computer and consultant services, and the like). In addition, since federal pay
raises are ordinarily determined in September (effective in
October), after the budget process is supposed to be com-

Table 1
Government Employment and Population
(selected years 1955–1983)

Fiscal year	Government employment				Population		
	Federal executive branch[a] (thousands)	State and local governments (thousands)	All governmental units (thousands)	Federal as % of all governmental units	Total United States (thousands)	Federal employment per 1,000 population	
1955	2,371	4,728	7,099	33.4	165,931	14.3	
1960[b]	2,371	6,073	8,444	28.1	180,671	13.1	
1965	2,496	7,683	10,179	24.5	194,303	12.8	
1970[b]	2,944	9,869	12,813	23.0	205,052	14.4	
1975	2,848	12,114	14,962	19.0	215,973	13.2	
1980[b]	2,821	13,557	16,378	17.2	228,297	12.4	
1981 (est.)	2,787[c]	13,281	16,068	17.4[d]	230,477[e]	12.1	
1982 (est.)	2,770	–	–	17.5[d]	232,474[e]	11.9	
1983 (est.)	2,740	–	–	17.7	234,645	11.7	

Source: *The Budget of the United States Government, Fiscal Year 1983*, Special Analysis, I, table I–4.

[a]Covers total end-of-year employment of full-time permanent, temporary, part-time, and intermittent employees in the executive branch, including the Postal Service; beginning in 1970, includes various disadvantaged youth and worker-trainee programs.

[b]Includes temporary employees for the decennial census.

[c]Reflects fractional counting of part-time permanent positions, pursuant to the provisions of Public Law 95–437.

[d]The percentages shown for these years are consistent with reasonable estimates based on recent trends in state and local government.

[e]U.S. population data for 1980–1983 are the latest available from the Census Bureau. Revised estimates, based on the 1980 census, were not available.

pleted, an additional round of appropriations ("supplementals") for salaries and expenses is introduced in January
with the president's budget, four months after the start of
the fiscal year.

In order to get some grip on personnel costs in recent
years, the executive and legislative branches have attempted
to use rather blunt instruments: curbs on hiring, personnel
ceilings, and cutbacks in annual pay increases. Ronald
Reagan's first action as president was to freeze the civil service by banning new hiring in most agencies. Throughout the
campaign he made the point, as he did in his inaugural, that
"it is time to check and reverse the growth of government
which shows signs of having grown beyond the consent of the
governed." The hiring freeze did not last very long, as differential rates of attrition (clerical workers, for example, have
very high turnover rates) began to create distortions in agency management. The freeze was succeeded by personnel ceilings for each agency. Administrations have long been limiting the size of the work force through agency personnel ceilings. This has probably contributed to the overall restraint
on employment noted previously. Congress joined the fight in
a clause of the Civil Service Reform Act of 1978 that restricted until 1981 the aggregate federal employment level.

Personnel ceilings cause two distortions leading away from
efficiency in agency management. When agency managers
are restricted from hiring but still have room in budget lines
for salaries and expenses, they will contract out essentially
inside work to private firms—jobs from floor waxing to legal
consultation to writing the annual agency report can be done
by nonfederal personnel often with a higher price tag. The
General Accounting Office (GAO) estimates the maximum
cost of this indirect labor force to have exceeded $68 billion
in fiscal year (FY) 1980 or 71 percent of the total direct personnel budget (these data include military as well as civilian
functions).

The other distortion caused by personnel ceilings affects

another component of total personnel costs: the distribution of workers among grades. The slot limit treats a $30,000 lawyer as equal to a $12,000 typist. As long as a manager can get more output (including prestige and justification for his own grade) out of the lawyer than the typist (and assuming that agency desk purchases or travel can be transferred within the salaries and expenses line), he hires the lawyer. This situation leads to top-heavy departments where junior lawyers must type some of their own memoranda.

The structures of agency work forces are not entirely unregulated. Each agency's grade structure is monitored by the Office of Management and Budget (OMB). Neither the grade structure nor the personnel ceilings are based on any sophisticated mission-based personnel requirement studies, but they are based on previous levels, agency requests, and general governmentwide practices. According to data over recent years, grade inflation has been significant (see table 2).

Timing problems

The poor fit of the timing of pay raises and the congressional budget process makes sensible personnel planning in federal agencies difficult; in fiscal year 1982 it has made planning impossible. When the president submits his budget in January, he guesses at what a survey of private sector jobs taken in March will indicate for the comparability of federal employees' pay; based on that guess, he tentatively estimates a pay raise for October. Congress, as it passes budget resolutions in the spring and appropriations during the summer, typically endorses the president's guesstimate and allows for expected supplemental appropriations funding pay raises to be submitted the following January. Unfortunately, there is therefore a great temptation for the president to underestimate the pay raise he will eventually recommend, and for Congress in its regular budget deliberations to go along with —or even to underallow for—the pay raise they know is

Table 2
Grade Inflation

GS grade	Number in grade		Change	Percent change
	1977	1980	1977–1980	
1	2,070	1,828	− 242	−11.7
2	24,271	20,602	− 3,669	−15.1
3	97,236	84,037	−13,199	−13.6
4	167,105	157,803	− 9,302	− 5.6
5	171,678	170,841	− 837	− 0.5
6	81,865	81,708	− 157	− 0.2
7	124,128	126,365	2,237	1.8
8	26,242	25,488	− 754	− 2.9
9	134,020	134,847	827	0.6
10	25,134	28,208	3,074	12.2
11	147,027	152,665	5,638	3.8
12	142,011	158,115	16,104	11.3
13	105,705	110,206	4,501	4.2
14	51,340	57,588	6,248	12.2
15	24,656	27,586	2,930	11.9

Source: U.S. Civil Service Commission, Bureau of Manpower Information Systems, March 1977 *PATCO Survey;* Office of Personnel Management, January 1980 *PATCO Report* totals, excluding "other and unspecified" category.

eventually coming. The safety valve in this system is "absorption."

The pay raise supplemental passed during the fiscal year typically funds only part of the pay raise granted; since agencies have to pay the statutory salary rates inclusive of the raise, they absorb the shortfall by leaving some slots vacant and cutting back on travel, the purchase of office equipment, consulting services, etc. In fiscal year 1979, for example, such agency absorption constituted about one-third of the full pay raise (see table 3). The amount of absorption needed is generally not known until well into a fiscal year, since the president's supplemental is not issued until a quarter of the year is over. Congress, moreover, usually turns the screws a little more to avoid busting its budget resolution (see table 3). In FY 1982 this situation was made even worse: in that year even the first round of appropriations for salaries and expenses was not known by the start of the fiscal year, since all agencies were funded on a stopgap continuing resolution. Thus in October 1981 an agency manager could only guess how much he would have available for salaries and expenses during the year. Some agencies react overcautiously to such uncertainty by freezing new hires, banning travel, not buying pencils, etc.—and will probably engage in a rush to spend at the end of the fiscal year. Others maintain spending and will find supplementals totally inadequate. These agencies will be forced to employ a reduction-in-force (RIF) of personnel. Since civil service regulations protect senior employees by allowing them to "bump" those with less tenure (who, in turn, receive severance pay if they are separated) and retain their pay rate, the result is highly paid, demoralized people doing much less skilled work. A new wrinkle on quick economizing on payroll was undertaken in FY 1982: the furlough. Under this arrangement employees are, in effect, forced to take a number of days' leave without pay in each pay period.[2]

None of this is to say that force reductions or temporary conversions of some jobs to part-time status are always un-

Table 3

Supplemental Appropriations for Federal Pay Raises
Fiscal Years 1970–1980
(budget authority in millions of dollars)

Fiscal year	Fully increased costs*	Absorption required by the president (through OMB)	Absorption required by Congress	Enacted supplemental
1970	5,600	1,200	400	4,000
1971	5,000	600	300	4,100
1972	2,900	300	300	2,300
1973	1,400	400	100	900
1974	4,100	500	300	3,300
1975	2,400	400	200	1,800
1976	3,300	1,200	200	1,900
1977	2,800	600	100	2,100
1978	3,800	500	100	3,200
1979	3,700	1,200	100	2,400
1980	4,200	200	300	3,700

Source: Congressional Budget Office 1981, p. 13.

*CBO estimates.

warranted. As part of a substantial reordering of priorities, they may in fact be necessary. But when these personnel changes are driven by belated budget action that forces haste—well, it makes waste.

Comparability

The largest short-term budget saver is a cutback in the annual pay raise. Two percentage points is over $1 billion earned in the budgeteer's savings account (more if absorption is forced). In recent years every budget proposal by the president and every final budget outcome has featured such salary reductions as a major form of budget saving.

"Reductions" in salary means pay raises less than the standard in federal law, which specifies that the level of pay in each work grade be set equal to pay in comparable jobs in the private sector. (Obviously it would be desirable to get comparable output from the public work force, but government output is not valued in an ordinary marketplace, so productivity measures are necessarily partial.) The law also allows the president to promulgate a pay raise different from the salary comparability standard; since 1977 every pay raise has been below comparability.

In 1978 and 1979 President Carter discovered inflation and promulgated a voluntary wage restraint program for everyone; as a token of the government's serious purpose, he proposed to hold down the federal pay increases for those years. By the summer of 1979 the Carter administration knew that its voluntary program was dead, but the need to restrain federal pay—largely for budgetary reasons—would persist. Conveniently, in June 1979 the Carter administration proposed a pay reform bill that would establish a new federal pay standard—total compensation comparability (TCC). The TCC standard would adjust federal *salaries* so as to equate *total compensation* in the federal and nonfederal sector. By proposing this bill, the administration had a new excuse to hold down the pay increase. Since everyone knew that federal retirement was more costly than private pensions and social security combined, pay would have to be restrained to achieve TCC. (To be fair, the Carter proposals had many other quite legitimate objectives.) Thus in the January 1980 budget Carter was able to point to his pay reform proposal as the source of nearly $3 billion in savings.

Then a funny thing happened. First, in September 1980 Candidate Carter flinched and raised the pay increase due in October to 9 percent rather than the 6 percent in his January budget. Second, the Office of Personnel Management (OPM) finally was able to get some data on private sector fringe benefits, and when it computed (in early 1981) the pay raise required for TCC in 1980, the computer spit out 8.8 percent. President Carter had hit it almost on the head— total compensation comparability (on the average) had been attained.[3]

Enter Ronald Reagan. If President Reagan had endorsed 100 percent TCC, he would have had to propose about an 8.5 percent pay hike for 1981. This was obviously not simpatico with the severe budget restraints being proposed. Thus the Reagan administration invented yet another standard. In 1981 it proposed a pay reform law that would set the standard for federal employees' compensation at 94 percent of total compensation in the nonfederal sector, presumably to reflect the greater security of federal jobs. (Reread the last section and see how secure you'd feel about your pay!) This standard justified holding pay raises to under 5 percent in 1981 and to about 7 percent in the next two years.

By the time of the budget unveiling in early 1982, even 7 percent pay raises were too rich in light of the massive federal deficits being proposed by the Reagan administration. Apparently it was deemed inadvisable to invent a new, lower standard for federal compensation (84 percent of private compensation?) by pointing to the greater security of RIFs and furloughs, so the administration simply arbitrarily projected 5 percent annual increases in pay, withdrew its comparability legislation, and promised a comprehensive reform proposal by early 1983. At this writing, Congress appears unwilling to accept the extreme domestic program cuts that Reagan proposed, with one exception: federal pay retrenchment.

This minihistory of federal pay has two important points. First, proposed legislation—even though it is not enacted or even taken very seriously—has been used in the area of federal employee compensation to justify what are at bottom arbitrary restraints on employees' salaries largely to meet short-term budget targets. Second, the repeated departures from existing law have created a mess: federal pay rates have fallen progressively behind salaries in the private sector.

The requested hold-downs in federal pay and the practice of giving all employees the same percentage pay raise have created enormous distortions. In the upper part of the General Schedule (GS)[4] range—say, people making over $30,000, mostly male professionals and managers—salaries were on the order of 14 to 23 percent below those of the private sector in March 1981, according to the government's comparability survey. In the lower and middle grades, pay in the aggregate is less out of line. But since everyone at a given grade (and step) is paid the same rate regardless of occupation, many clerical workers in these lower grades are—by the government's own numbers—somewhat overpaid compared to the private sector. Professional workers (mostly entry level) in these grades, by the same token, are underpaid. These distortions give rise to more distortions. To hire a really well-qualified professional at an uncompetitive wage, federal bureaus promise (and produce) rapid promotions. And this adds to grade creep and a loss of integrity in the civil service system.

Why don't the "underpaid" professionals in the upper grades quit? Answer: retirement benefits. High-earning career workers in the federal civil service have an enormous advantage over their private counterparts. They participate in a retirement program that (unlike social security) contains no tilt in favor of low earners. As a result, the GS 14 is sitting on a future pot of gold. If he or she quits before retirement eligibility age, all that is available is a deferred annuity based on final salary while employed—in short, the deferred annuity is worth zilch in an inflationary era. So they stay. (Until eligible for retirement—then they leave immediately.)

Lower-wage federal employees meanwhile are badly served by their retirement program compared to what would be obtainable under social security. So they take their inflated salaries and quit later—just in time to qualify for social security anyway, and to double dip their way through the Golden Years.

Executive pay ceiling

The ordinary federal worker has been better treated in salary decisions than his boss. At the top of the federal pyramid are federal judges, members of Congress, cabinet and subcabinet officials, and heads of major independent agencies and commissions. Pay rates for these officials are set annually upon recommendation of the president, who is supposed to recommend the same pay hikes for them as those proposed for the General Schedule. Although this payroll is not a legitimate budget issue (their pay being .02 percent of federal spending), in recent years these pay raises have been caught up anyway in the budget crunch. The crux of the problem has been that members of Congress have been unwilling to vote themselves significant annual raises and they have refused to let the officials of the other two branches move ahead. The result is that between 1977 and early 1982 there was only one pay raise of 5.5 percent for executive branch officials at the same time that other federal workers received five raises totaling 38 percent.[5] The significant problem created by this "pay cap" is that the rates of pay for top officials are also, by statute, the ceiling on basic pay for Senior Executive Service members (the 7,000 mainly career officials who are just above the General Schedule and are regarded as the mainstays of the government) and on pay for the top grades of the General Schedule. In 1981 virtually everyone in the Senior Executive Service and as many as 43,000 others were all earning the same rate of pay (about $50,000).

This log jam was broken in the middle of the budget mania late in 1981 when Congress finally allowed the ceiling for executive branch employees to be raised to $58,000 without raising their own salary. However, to demonstrate their recollection of the true meaning of total compensation, the congressmen did vote themselves a huge tax deduction for the costs of dual residences and they also liberalized rules governing limitations on receipt of speaking fees and the like. The very nature of the quid pro quo here makes it evident that the adjustment is very much like putting a dormer in the roof: it's very hard to do twice. So the problem of many employees with pay compressed at the ceiling is likely to recur.

Compression of pay at the top of the federal service not only creates obvious problems of morale[6] and of supplying incentives for promotions (why take a promotion if the pay is the same?), but it has had a devastating impact on retention of experienced officials. Retirement rates for workers at the pay ceiling rose to 75 percent of those eligible in the age class 55–59 years in 1980, largely because retirement benefits were indexed automatically while pay rates—used to determine the initial retirement benefit—were frozen.

RETIREMENT BENEFITS AND THE BUDGET

Most federal white-collar employees participate in the Civil Service Retirement System (CSRS).[7] They are exempt from social security.[8] The CSRS provides a full annuity at 55 years of age with thirty years of service, at age 60 with twenty years of service, or at age 62 with five years of service. The retirement benefit is fully indexed, being adjusted for inflation once a year (twice a year until 1982), and is taxable after the employee recovers his contribution. Most employees currently contribute 7 percent of salary to the CSRS.

The pension is based on a formula that combines years of service and salary. The salary component is based on the highest average pay of any three consecutive years of employment (High-3). A worker retiring after thirty years of service would get about 56 percent of High-3; after thirty-five years, about 66 percent; and after forty-two years, 80 percent, the statutory maximum. Before, during, or after federal service a worker may qualify for social security and/or a private pension by working in a covered job. The CSRS pension is not reduced when other benefits are received, nor is it reduced if the employee works while in retirement status.

Civil service retirement is financed through a trust fund in the federal budget, a fund with four major sources of income: employee contributions, matching contributions from the employing agency, appropriations, and interest earned on the trust fund surplus that is invested in U.S. Treasury bonds. By conventional standards, the CSRS trust fund is in good shape. At the end of fiscal year 1981 the trust fund surplus was over $80 billion and growing, since the income of $28 billion from the four sources above significantly exceeded annual benefits now running at nearly $18 billion.

The apparently healthy status of the CSRS trust fund for the most part obscures what is a sizable and growing burden on taxpayers. Most of the CSRS trust fund "income" is simply a bookkeeping, intragovernmental transaction. When the CSRS trust fund receives interest ($6 billion in 1981), for example, the U.S. Treasury Department is simultaneously debited for that payment. The only true *income* (that is, received from *out*side the government) is the 7 percent of payroll charged to employees.[9] In 1981 these receipts amounted to $3.8 billion, compared with the $17.7 billion in benefits paid. Thus the CSRS fund is already running at a deficit, and that deficit will grow sharply in future years.[10]

Even piercing the veil of intragovernmental payments does not do justice to the net liabilities taxpayers are incurring under the CSRS, because we are comparing today's benefit payments made to *former* workers with contributions from *current* employees. The annual liabilities of the CSRS are best appreciated by calculating the projected value of *future* benefits and contributions of the *current* cohort of employees. When this concept of cost was most recently estimated by the Board of Actuaries of the CSRS, the benefits promised amounted to about 36 percent of payroll.[11] After the employee cost of 7 percent of payroll is subtracted, the net employer cost is about 29 percent, or over $14 billion as the net annual liability to the taxpayer. This liability can be reduced only by changing the benefit rules of the CSRS or by raising the charge on the employee.

Unfortunately, the imperative of annual budgeting has not focused attention on the fundamental features of the CSRS that give rise to the large taxpayer liability. In recent years only relatively minor changes have been made. One change, in the mid-1970s, eliminated a "kicker" in the indexing formula that boosted retirement benefits by an extra 1 percent (the kicker) whenever an inflation adjustment was made. More recently, beginning in 1982, the inflation adjustment for the CSRS was put on an annual rather than semiannual basis. These changes essentially put federal retirees on the same footing as social security recipients with regard to indexing. Finally, also in 1982, new beneficiaries under the social security minimum benefit were eliminated. This minimum benefit provided a particularly handsome return on contributions to workers with a low average career wage, including those whose career wages were low because of only a few years of coverage. Former civil servants were a major target of this reform.

In its fiscal year 1983 budget, the Reagan administration proposed yet another set of restraints on federal retirees. It proposed to change the indexing rule for CSRS beneficiaries (and military retirees) so that the annual increase would be the lesser of the rise in consumer prices or the average rise in General Schedule pay. In addition, any retiree whose CSRS annuity exceeded by 20 percent or more the annuity to be earned by a new retiree entering the rolls from the same grade and length of service would get no inflation adjustment at all. (Existing annuitants receiving up to 20 percent more than newly retired counterparts would get three-quarters of the inflation adjustment otherwise due them.) OMB estimates these changes would reduce CSRS benefits by $1 billion in 1984, rising to $2 billion in 1987.

These proposals highlight the quick-buck approach to retirement reform. The only sense to be made of linking a retiree's annuity to the pay rate of his job is that it discourages people from retiring prematurely. It is true that the present CSRS encourages such premature retirement by providing (a) a relatively young eligibility age, (b) no reduction in CSRS benefits for earnings or other annuities after retirement, (c) double dipping if the employee can qualify for social security after retirement, and (d) larger cost-of-living adjustments than wage raises in recent years. The first three listed factors are crucial structural flaws of the current compensation system that can be alleviated only by fundamental reform of the system. In particular, coverage of federal employees under social security and a deliberalization of retirement age would be two elements of such a reform.[12] As we have all learned from President Reagan's ill-fated social security proposals, such fundamental reforms must be phased in slowly, and that means budgetary savings do not materialize for some time.[13]

The Reagan administration's proposal to reduce the

deleterious effect on retirement decisions of divergent movements of pensions and pay has only one virtue—quick-
budget effect. A fair assessment of the problem would note
that a major reason federal pay has risen less than pensions
is that salaries have been held down because it was argued
that retirement benefits are too generous. It is a cruel hoax
to first lean on salaries because retirement payments are too
high, and then turn around and say we have to reduce retirement benefits because their growth relative to salaries has
caused problems. Moreover, it is bizarre to penalize the most
aged retirees (those most likely to be receiving 20 percent
above their new retiree counterparts) in order to correct current employees' retirement incentives. A long-run structural
view would surely have produced a different reform package
that would have been fairer and more effective.[14]

TOWARD FUNDAMENTAL REFORM

Fundamental restructuring of federal personnel compensation practices would involve major innovations for both pay
and retirement components. The personnel ceilings coupled
with loose budget control for salaries should be replaced, as
advocated by the GAO, by a strict budget limit on payroll.
Salary schedules for clerical workers should be separated
from salaries for professional and managerial occupations
(with the legitimate concerns about sex discrimination addressed directly). Closing underpayment gaps should be the
occasion for much tighter controls over job classification and
for introduction of some geographic pay differentials. On the
retirement front, coverage of federal workers under social
security with deliberalization of retirement age is long over-
due. An adequate supplementary retirement program
modeled after existing individual retirement accounts
(IRAs) could be offered with some employer subsidies at

much lower cost, in combination with social security, than the current CSRS.

But all these reforms take time. Because they do not (or should not) affect current retirees, they cannot lower retirement benefit outlays in the short run. And because the long-term salary reform probably involves some short-term budget costs, the net result is that fundamental reform does not help short-run budget deficit control.

CONCLUSION

Federal personnel policies are in a crisis stage. Key employees are underpaid, demoralized, and jumping ship as soon as possible. Others are overpaid, promoted too rapidly, and underqualified for highly responsible jobs. The retirement system is costly, is not well integrated with social insurance, and produces counterproductive immobility for those employees waiting for retirement eligibility and equally counterproductive incentives to quit immediately when eligibility is attained. These problems need to be addressed through a fundamental overhaul of the system, the major consequence of which would probably be short-term budget increases as inadequate salaries are raised but long-term budget savings from scaling back the Civil Service Retirement System. The current domination of federal policy by short-run budget considerations exacerbates existing problems and distorts rational public policy choices.

13

HERSCHEL KANTER

The Defense Budget
Process

**McNamara, Laird, Brown, and defense programs. The
military services and the Reagan administration. The
programming system and national security. Budget
reviews. The acquisition process. Weapons development and service flexibility. Reform problems.**

For the last decade an intense debate has centered on the
defense budget. The debate has included issues of foreign
policy, fiscal policy, budgetary reform, and distribution of
federal government largess, as well as the more direct
issues—what the assigned tasks of the military establishment should be and whether that establishment can carry
out those tasks.

It is difficult enough to come to grips with the larger questions of whether the defense budget is serving appropriate national purposes and whether the taxpayers' dollars are being spent efficiently. But those issues are often obscured in the public debate by the symbolic importance attached to a single annual defense budget. This was underscored when the Reagan administration presented its defense budget as a sign of its shift in national priorities and as a pillar of its new foreign policy, though the changes—which emphasized investment in weapons to be delivered in two, five, or ten years—would have no major, direct, and immediate impacts.

Despite substantial increases in the defense budget, there are problems in the budget process that are likely to prevent the United States from spending those increases so as to achieve a consistent set of foreign policy goals. It is therefore useful to review the history of the budget process, to examine the process itself, and then to see how the military services— the army, navy, air force, and marines—operate within that system. Because the difficulties of such a system are inherent in the management of a large budget with such a diffuse task, we end with only modest suggestions on how the process might be improved.

THE PAST IS PROLOGUE

Since World War II various attempts have been made to bring coherence to strategy and to make strategy and budget consistent. Some of these attempts were based on formal studies; others were based on the views of the president, secretary of state, or secretary of defense. Some were comprehensive while others were piecemeal, examining one mission at a time or one major weapon at a time. The defense budget was not derived as part of a coherent strategy within realistic fiscal limitations. Rather, it was a series of ad hoc adjustments to strategic and fiscal realities.

In the 1950s there was no formal method of examining the defense program over a number of years to see the implications of current decisions. Fiscal constraints were introduced only on an annual basis as the budget was reviewed each year. When Robert McNamara became secretary of defense, he introduced the planning, programming, and budgeting (PPB) system, which gave him a tool with which to view the whole program within the context of a five-year plan. But the planning system did not include a formal budget constraint for the five-year period, or even for one year, so it lacked an element vital to the functioning of a reasonable process. Indeed, Secretary McNamara took the public position that no such constraint existed and that he was buying everything that was needed without regard to cost. Such constraints did, in fact, exist, and were applied in an informal way in the annual budget review rather than as a formal part of the five-year PPB system.

Melvin Laird, who became secretary of defense in 1969, began by framing the defense debate within the terms of National Security Study Memorandum 3 (NSSM 3), a study—directed from the White House—that included both strategic and budgetary considerations. Although the study failed to bring the policy coherence that one might have hoped for, it served to underscore that defense policy must involve the simultaneous determination of weapons, strategy, and budgets. Following that initial effort, Secretary Laird instituted a resource planning system that defined "strategy guidance," and then gave the services explicit budget constraints or "fiscal guidance" for planning their five-year time horizon. Within the confines of that fiscal guidance they were to offer a five-year projection in the form of a "Program Objectives Memorandum" (POM). However, the services were unable to offer a POM that was within the requirements of fiscal guidance and at the same time consistent with strategy guidance. Still, the exercise was valuable because the services were forced, for the first time, to lay out a fiscally constrained program that could be examined for its consistency with both a broad national security strategy and a financial plan.

Setting fiscal guidance to cover a five-year period has focused the Department of Defense (DOD) on its long-run fiscal problem but has not solved it. Three difficulties that have always existed have become more obvious: first, the five-year POMs have continued to be too ambitious, forcing major changes in the program each year as it is translated into an annual budget; second, in looking ahead five years, costs of purchasing and operating future programs have consistently been underestimated by the armed services; and third, five years has proved to be an insufficient period for full implications of the current program to become manifest—there has been no long-term coherent strategy that encompassed resource limitations, technology, and threat.

The first problem—changes during the annual cycle—has come about because the secretary of defense has approved more programs than could be bought, given what the president was likely to spend. Secretary McNamara's programs were approved without a formal budget constraint, so the discrepancy was not obvious until the budget review each October. Once formal fiscal guidance was introduced into the system, the secretary of defense set such guidance, not according to his estimate of how much the DOD was *likely* to get from the president in the following years, but rather on the basis of what he *hoped* to get. This problem has continued through to the Reagan administration and has become even more severe this past year, requiring an amendment six months after the new administration submitted its 1982 budget. In past administrations, such changes have been generally aimed at the next budget to be submitted to Congress rather than at the one before Congress at that time. These many quick fixes will continue as long as fiscal guidance continues to be set at levels the secretary of defense hopes to get (or feels compelled to establish for bargaining purposes) and not at levels the president is willing to spend over the long term. When this unrealistic guidance is combined with an attempt to fine-tune the economy by means of the defense budget, the problem is made worse because it emphasizes outlays, the economic measure of defense impact, rather than total obligational authority, the normal tool for controlling defense spending.

The second problem is that even when the POMs are within the parameters of fiscal guidance, they consistently underestimate the costs of what they include. Moreover, the services are able to exclude support programs that must eventually be bought. The costs of individual programs — such as the F−18 fighter plane or the M−1 tank — are underestimated from the inception of the program through all its stages. Beyond that, the services neglect the manpower, spare parts, and other operating costs that support these complex weapons systems. Thus each year, as the services produce new five-year programs, they find that they either need more money or must cut back or postpone purchases.

The third problem is that five years is not a sufficient period for a planned force structure when it takes ten to fifteen years to develop a weapon system and another five to ten years to introduce it in large numbers. In the mid-1970s another planning tool — the extended planning annex (EPA) — was introduced to extrapolate the force and financial figures in the POMs for an additional ten years. However, the implications of the EPA calculations — that the DOD will not be able to sustain its force levels with the weapons it is planning to buy — have not been heeded.

Thus we see that within a year, from one year to the next, and over a longer period, there are built-in pressures for the military services — and indeed, for the secretary of defense — to plan for too much. More research, development, and acquisition programs are set in motion than can be afforded within the levels of funding that the president and Congress will accept. In fact, Secretary of Defense Harold Brown made a virtue of this overcommitment. In forwarding some figures from his five-year defense program to Congress, he pointed out that:

The [five-year defense program] detail upon which we depend for [the enclosed] displays is significantly different from the [overall budget] projections contained in President Carter's FY 1979 budget; the differences will be resolved each year during the programming and budget processes as the various programs compete for funds. The uncertainty about how we will make future choices among competing claims . . . requires us to plan each of such programs at a level whose sum exceeds what we plan as the total defense program.

Although there might be nothing wrong in principle with a system in which "programs compete," the method described by Secretary Brown contains major drawbacks. Such an approach as he describes will not judge program competition on the long-term criteria of cost and capability. Programs will be selected, instead, on narrow financial criteria that are necessary to make the long-range plan fit into this year's budget limitation. Indeed, the zero-based budgeting system was a formalization of this very technique of program ranking based almost entirely on cost impact in the coming budget and neglecting even the budget implications of the next few years.

THE REAGAN ADMINISTRATION

The Reagan administration came in with two major defense thrusts: first, to increase the budget, and second, to decentralize the PPB system—giving more discretion to the military services. The Reagan budget increases of March 1981 allowed the services to buy in significant numbers most of the weapons they had developed in the 1970s and to buy the ordnance and spare parts to support them. However, it did not allow for the expansion of the strategic forces that had been promised in the 1980 campaign, nor did it allow for added U.S. Army divisions and U.S. Air Force wings that seemed to be implied by the policy statements of the new administration.

Following these increases, the secretary of defense instituted two major reviews: one of the planning, programming, and budgeting system and the other of the acquisition system (the latter being the management system for developing and procuring weapons). As a result of these reviews, memoranda were issued emphasizing "decentralization and accountability" through a "system of centralized control of executive policy direction and more decentralization of policy execution." This was commonly understood to mean that the services had been given considerably more power and discretion to choose programs within a centrally determined budget constraint. The meaning of the "centralized . . . policy direction," and particularly the extent to which this policy direction will constrain the services, is still to be determined.

It was only the army and navy that received their promised freedom to exercise their judgment on what to buy within the higher budget levels. The decisions to build a variant of the B–1 strategic bomber and to cancel the multiple protective shelter basing mode for the MX missile were of such political importance that the air force was not allowed to exercise its preferences. By the fall of 1981 the combination of these decisions on strategic programs and difficulties with the economy—particularly the prospective deficit—led to cutbacks in some programs that had been funded earlier in the year at close to levels deemed adequate by the services. The process of disrupting long-range plans continues, but with an added wrinkle: a new emphasis on outlays.

Outlays—checks drawn on the Treasury—are the figures used to compare the defense budget to the total budget, the deficit, or the gross national product (GNP). The more

meaningful figure, however, for measuring the U.S. commitment to defense programs is total obligational authority
(TOA), the legal limit on obligations to buy and operate the
defense program as finally approved by Congress. The TOA
figure is used by the Department of Defense, the president
and his advisers, and the armed services and appropriations
committees of Congress to review the details of the defense
budget and to set its level. Outlays lag the TOA, particularly
for procurement programs. For example, $1 billion of ship-
building results in $30 million of outlays in the first year and
$130 million in the second, etc. (table 1). Thus, outlays for
procurement in a particular budget year are substantially
determined by past defense policy decisions rather than current ones. Nevertheless, outlays, revenues, and deficits are
the stuff of economic policy and the budget resolution in Congress; they cannot be ignored.

The Reagan administration, in its October 1981 budget
revisions of the 1982–1984 budgets and its subsequent fall
review of the 1983–1987 program, used outlays as major
decision criteria for the defense budget. This added to the
already confused state that existed from formulating the
1982 budget for the third time (January, March, and October). Programs were not competing on long-term cost and
capability, not even on short-term cost based on TOA, but on
1982 and 1983 outlays.

Thus despite the reforms of Secretaries McNamara and
Laird (which helped to bring policy and budget in line with
each other), problems remain that have plagued the DOD
and kept it from attaining this ideal. We now examine in
more detail the formal resource planning system to see how
it might be modified to provide a more satisfactory outcome.

Table 1

**Outlays per Dollar of TOA for
Selected Budget Categories**

Category	Year				
	1	2	3	4	> 4
Shipbuilding	.03	.13	.14	.14	.55
Aircraft	.10	.40	.30	.10	.10
Missiles	.30	.55	.14	.01	–
Research and development	.59	.34	.05	.01	.01
Military personnel	.98	.02	–	–	–
Other operating costs	.83	.14	.03	–	–

Source: OSD comptroller.

THE RESOURCE PLANNING PROCESS

The only externally fixed item in the DOD annual calendar is the delivery date of the federal budget to Congress, usually around 20 January but postponed in 1982 because Congress convened two weeks late. However, the process that produces the budget begins years earlier. Once submitted, the budget must run a gauntlet involving three budget resolutions, several authorization bills, and several appropriations bills. Once approved, the funds must be obligated (contracted for) over a period that, for some budget appropriation categories, covers up to five years. Final payment of the bills may take as long as ten years after the funds are first approved by Congress.

A *single* defense budget within a wide range will not have a major influence on the U.S. military posture. Weapons that take five to ten years to develop are bought for another five or ten years and operated for twenty. Thus it is the decisions of the programming system and the acquisition process that, because of their influence over a number of years, significantly change the U.S. military posture. A series of annual budgets does influence the military posture by undermining—or at least modifying—decisions that result from the programming and acquisition systems. After all is said and done, it is the annual budget review that results in the "real" proposal to Congress.

The programming system should be the bridge between long-term national security goals and the annual budget. Operating on an annual cycle, the DOD programming process generates a five-year resource program and eight years of forces, well short of the time it takes to fully develop and buy a weapon system. The process begins in January when the secretary of defense sends his policy guidance to the services. This document includes budget constraints or fiscal guidance for five years—measured in terms of TOA—as well as guidance on selected specific weapons, support programs, and missions, and the more general policy guidance on anticipated scenarios or situations.

The services (and defense agencies) then respond with their POMs, which form the basis of the new budget. For example, the first year of the 1983–1987 POM was supposed to be, with some additional elaboration, the basis of the 1983 budget proposal to be submitted to Congress in January of 1982. The POM may contain more or less detail, depending on how much is demanded from year to year in guidance from the secretary of defense and how well the services respond to that guidance.

Even if the guidance is minimal, the secretary of defense will still want to have his staff review the POMs to ensure that cost estimates are realistic and that no missions are neglected, particularly those supporting other services. For example, both airlift in the air force and sealift in the navy must support army deployments. He will wish to oversee coordination of common acquisition programs—navy and air force missile programs, or army and marine corps helicopter programs. Finally, there are highly visible and sensitive programs on which he may want to oversee service decisions or even make such decisions himself; the MX missile basing program, the B–1 bomber, the F–18 fighter aircraft, and the M–1 tank are well-known examples of this type.

Decisions are normally issued by the secretary of defense in program decision memoranda (PDMs) that cover a five-year period, as do the POMs, but with considerably less detail. If the PDM budget levels are reduced below the level in the original fiscal guidance, then the services must juggle the many interacting programs in their POMs to accommodate the reductions. This past year (1981) the revised economic package, issued at the end of the summer, included reductions in the 1982, 1983, and 1984 defense budgets below the levels previously proposed by the president. The services had to change many programs in their POMs and even in the 1982 budget, which was already before Congress. Moreover, the decisions on strategic nuclear programs—a major part of the air force budget—were made by the secretary of defense and the president in early October, requiring a complete restructuring of the air force budget and five-year program as contained in its POM submitted in the late spring.

The PDM becomes part of the guidance for submission of the services' new budget to the Office of the Secretary of Defense (OSD). The budget is reviewed by OSD and the Office of Management and Budget together. The president and the secretary of defense can then once more change their minds about budget levels and about detailed programs. Normally, they take advantage of that opportunity to make changes during the budget review. Finally, because the previous budget (1982 in this case) passes Congress so late, the services are not able to consider the impact of congressional decisions until the end of the budget review.

In any case, the budget is delivered to Congress each January along with elements of a five-year program that ordinarily has not been reviewed in a comprehensive fashion by the secretary of defense because of time constraints. It is this budget that is reviewed in considerable detail by four congressional committees—the two armed services committees and the two appropriations committees. These committees produce six bills: authorization bills and appropriation bills for military construction, for the rest of the defense budget, and for supplemental spending to cover at least the annual pay increases. These bills must then be approved by both houses of Congress. The committees are themselves constrained by the budget resolutions that are approved by the budget committees of the House and Senate and then by the two houses.

Parallel with all this programming and budgeting activity is the acquisition process that governs the development and procurement of new weapons. The acquisition process begins with the earliest conceptual phases of looking at new weapon system requirements, and continues through development to the acquisition of major weapons. Every weapon that will cost over $100 million in research and development or over $500 million in procurement (both expressed in fiscal year [FY] 1980 dollars) is given special treatment that includes both a standard set of program review papers and meetings of most of the senior DOD officials in a body called the Defense System Acquisition Review Council (DSARC). These meetings are for the purpose of approving higher and higher levels of commitment, ending with consideration of whether a weapon should go into production.

This process involves project managers, the service materiel commands, the service staffs, and the service secretaries, as well as the secretary of defense and his staff operating through the DSARC. It is this review process that governs the program manager and the contractors in developing weapons, including the characteristics, cost, and schedule. The review takes place one weapon system at a time, with weapons examined at major milestones. Since these reviews are part of a separate system outside the program and budget, the POM and budget reviews provide one more opportunity for disruption.

The secretary of defense approves the annual budget, the five-year program through the mechanism of the PDM, and the DSARC acquisition decisions. Despite his centralized responsibility, the three systems—budget, program, and acquisition—operate under the guidance and control of separate bureaucracies. Past secretaries of defense treated decisions generated in each of these processes as separate decisions, setting policy with little regard for long- and short-term fiscal realities, setting five-year fiscal guidance with little regard for policy choices or short-term budget realities, and making individual acquisition decisions with little regard for other choices. Since the decisions are sequential, a secretary of defense is free to do this, relying at each stage on the staff responsible for that stage.

In addition, the president feels free to change his mind several times per year, as is his prerogative, and Congress feels free, as is its constitutional right, to change the defense budget in detail. Thus the problem is made considerably worse than if the organizational problems were confined to the Department of Defense itself.

THE SERVICE ROLES IN RESOURCE PLANNING

The purpose of the budget and resource planning process is to provide funds for the four armed services that do the work of the DOD. It is the services that develop and buy the weapons, train the people, operate and support the weapons, and (when necessary) use them.

The services have objectives that involve, on the one hand, the execution of military missions and the readiness to perform those missions and, on the other, the responsibility to develop, design, acquire, and support the weapons to carry out those missions. These two objectives, while they result in many complementary contributions to national security, also compete.

Indeed, this dichotomy between military and technical skills causes a major difficulty in weapons development. Rather than being guided by military missions, the technologist may determine the nature of weapons based on his technological goals. On the other hand, the military officer may follow prevailing military doctrine, neglecting the effects of new technology.

Further, the services have major missions upon whose success the future of careers and of the services themselves are dependent. This may lead to the neglect of some missions and to overemphasis on others. Within the services, particular sections will support the weapons associated with their sections.

The services compete for funds and, to some extent, for missions. Their major missions, weapons, or skills become ends in themselves: strategic bombing (a mission), aircraft carriers (a weapon), or flying (a skill) become important for their own sake. On the other hand, less important missions, weapons, or skills that are secondary to the services are neglected. Examples include those missions that are primarily supportive of another service, such as the air force's airlift and close air support missions, or those missions that do not require what are thought to be the most demanding or traditional skills—e.g., flying from land bases rather than aircraft carriers (in the navy) or operating a missile installation rather than flying an aircraft (in the air force).

The secretary of defense promised in the spring of 1981 that he would give the services greater flexibility in choosing their programs within the new higher fiscal ceilings that were announced last March by the Reagan administration. The services responded with enthusiasm to this offer. However, they failed to note the fact that if they were given more authority, they would be responsible for more consistent planning, tighter control over their programs, and better coordination with their counterparts in other services.

The changing of budget levels by the president and secretary of defense during 1981, the reserving of some major decisions to the secretary of defense with little service advice, and the continued congressional micromanagement of details have tended to negate these increased freedoms. Still, the services have had a great deal more freedom to choose their programs than in the past. It will be interesting to see whether they can manage any better under this new system of partial decentralization.

PROSPECTS FOR REFORM

Over the last thirty years, many reforms have been undertaken to improve the operation of the Defense Department.

The reasons for the reforms are the continual frustration with stop-and-go planning and budgeting, the concern about duplicate development programs and cost overruns, the frustration of the service chiefs of staff at their inability to affect civilian priorities, and the lack of coherence of the whole system.

The problems come about for several reasons. The political system in which the DOD operates is one in which the president and Congress make detailed decisions that often are inconsistent both internally and between the two institutions. The DOD's job and its environment are so complex that the organization finds itself unable to make the smooth transitions from long-range resource programs to annual budgets, or from long-range resource programs to individual acquisition programs. The services, which have their own goals appropriate to their assigned tasks, find themselves in conflict with each other and with the overall goals of the DOD. Even within the services there are major bureaucratic conflicts among military branches and between the doctrinal and technical establishments.

In making changes, it is typical that new problems are created to replace the old. If this were not so, then the last thirty years of reforms might have been more successful than, in fact, they have been. Some changes that might improve the situation include the following:

- Set fiscal guidance at levels that will be acceptable to the president rather than selecting levels that are too high and then lowering them for reasons that have little to do with national security.

- Resolve the conflict between the programming, budgeting, and acquisition systems by placing them under the responsibility of a single under secretary for resources rather than the deputy secretary who now has that and many other responsibilities.

- For those missions that cut across the services—e.g.,

airlift and sealift—assign budgetary and program responsibility for provision of resources to cross-service operational commands rather than to the services.

The first proposal is one that would provide a more stable environment in which the DOD could operate, but would work only if the president and his immediate staff were willing to cooperate. The second might make it clearer that the three systems are not as independent as secretaries of defense have treated them. And the third proposal would introduce more competitors into the allocation process, downgrading the services relative to the military commands that cut across them by giving those components more responsibility for resource management.

Even if the internal Department of Defense processes were more efficient, no changes or reforms would relieve the DOD of the outside constraints that face it. Nevertheless, making the environment more stable—particularly with respect to funding levels and to interference with individual acquisition programs—and making more positive use of bureaucratic competition should lead to a more effective use of funds.

IV

Structural Reforms

14

MELVYN B. KRAUSS

Financing "Forced" Increases in Government Spending

Government growth and external influences. Growth of the economy. Financing public debt—three views. Inflation and the money supply. War taxes, good taxes, and tax reform. Government purchases. A consumption tax.

Judging from the 1980 election results, an apparent consensus exists in this country for reducing the growth of government spending. The Reagan administration's approach is an attempt to implement this consensus. Indeed, in its first year in office the rate of growth of nondefense government spending has been significantly reduced by comparison with what former President Jimmy Carter proposed.

Notwithstanding the administration's commitment to limit the growth of government, unforeseen changes in the external environment could force a dramatic and rapid budget expansion during President Reagan's term in office. Increased uncertainty about the continuity of oil imports could necessitate an accelerated buildup of this country's strategic petroleum reserve (SPR), for example. Or an unexpected deterioration in world geopolitics might make rapid U.S. military expansion irresistible. In any case, this chapter is concerned with the problem of financing public expenditures that could not be avoided because of changes in the external environment—that is, "forced" (and temporary) increases in public expenditure.

To give an idea of the order of magnitude involved in a forced temporary increase in spending, consider that Congress has authorized an SPR of 750 million barrels by 1989. The present reserve is approximately 100 million barrels. To implement the 750-million-barrel target in one year instead of eight because of a national emergency would entail an expenditure of about $26 billion, assuming today's per barrel price of oil at $35 with storage costs at $5 (Adelman 1981).

A QUESTION OF RESOURCES

The first question concerns the *source of resources* to support forced increases in public expenditure. Economic growth and resource transfer are two alternatives. The former does not seem feasible for at least two reasons. First, increasing the growth rate takes time, and if the forced expenditure increase must be rapid, time will be lacking. Second, an analysis that assumes a fixed—and optimal—growth rate makes more sense intuitively; otherwise, it would have to be explained why the economy had a suboptimal growth rate prior to the change in external circumstances. Increases in public expenditure forced by external changes therefore will imply resource transfer from other sectors of the economy to the expanding sector.

Where can these resources be obtained? The answer is elsewhere in the public budget, in the private community, or abroad. This chapter will analyze various issues raised by these alternatives.

The first point to be made is that a forced increase in public expenditure need not imply an increase in the overall budget if there is the congressional will to adjust other budget items downward. Without Congress, however, it is doubtful that the president could impound sufficient funds from other programs to prevent the overall budget from increasing *pari passu* with the forced increase in expenditure. In times of national emergency, history has shown that Congress does support the president. Some part of the resources to finance the forced increase in public spending can therefore be expected to come out of nonvital parts of the budget.

Though it might seem that a national crisis induced by external events would provide the perfect excuse for cutting normally sacrosanct domestic programs, it must be remembered that a national sense of fair treatment looms larger in times of national emergency. This factor, plus the fact that poor people constitute a most important part of the armed forces, could provide a protective shield about federal programs directly bearing on the poor. The distributional consequences of reallocating resources within the public budget, therefore, are likely to be of even more concern in time of emergency than normally.

TO TAX OR TO BORROW: THREE VIEWS

If the forced increase in government expense cannot be fully or partially financed elsewhere in the public budget, economic policymakers face two alternatives: to tax or to borrow. This choice really comes down to taxes today or taxes tomorrow, since government will have to increase taxes in the future to pay for current borrowing. An important question of economic debate has concerned the differences between these two alternatives.

To analyze this question, let us assume a given level of government expenditure and a shift from tax to debt finance. There are at least three different views as to the economic effects of such a shift—the Ricardian, the classical, and the Keynesian. The Ricardian view has been clearly stated by Robert Barro (1978, p. 2):

In a Ricardian setting where future taxes implicit in the public debt are fully capitalized by current generations, the shift from tax to debt finance would have no initial expansionary effect on aggregate demand. It is then immediate that the rise in the government deficit would have no effect on the price level, rate of return, level of output, or the capital/labor ratio. Any shift from current to future taxation implied by debt issue does not involve a burden on later generations because of the implicit connection—via operative private intergenerational transfers—between the old and the young. Hence, there would be no burden of the public debt in a Ricardian setting.

In this view there is thus no economic difference between financing a given level of government expenditure by taxes or by debt.

The classical view of the public debt differs. It argues that a shift from tax to debt finance, for a given level of current spending, would lead to an increase in perceived private sector wealth and hence to an increase in aggregate demand. With the supply of commodities fixed in the classical setting at full employment, the restoration of market clearing requires a decrease in aggregate demand via increases in the price level and/or the rate of return. The reduction in capital accumulation implied by a higher rate of return in turn implies lower future values of the capital/labor ratio—one definition of the true burden of the public debt. Even without this capital stock reduction, moreover, the shift from current to future taxation would imply a shift in the tax burden to later generations, as manifested for currently living generations in a transfer of lifetime disposable income from currently young to currently old individuals.

The classical analysis of the public debt assumes a "closed economy"—an economy cut off from world capital markets. Accordingly, one factor this analysis does not include is that the shift from tax to debt finance can attract foreign savings. The above-described increase in capital's rate of return thus can attract private foreign savings to domestic shores, which over subsequent years yields income to foreign capitalists in the form of dividends and/or interest. Allowing for the world capital market dramatically alters the conclusions of this analysis. Once the mobilization of foreign savings for domestic purposes is considered, the classical view no longer implies a burden either in terms of a reduced future capital stock or in terms of shifting taxes from present to future generations. The liabilities incurred from importing foreign capital are private—so they impose no future tax liabilities—and future values of the economy's capital/labor ratio need not fall.

According to Barro (1978), the difference between the traditional classical and Keynesian views is much less than that between either one of those two and the Ricardian view. The difference between the classical and Keynesian views simply is that, in the Keynesian setting, the initial expansion in aggregate demand induced by the switch from tax to debt finance leads to increases in output rather than to increases in the price level and/or the rate of return. Given the initial assumed "underemployment equilibrium" in a Keynesian setting, the rise in output and employment means that current and future generations will be better off because of the debt expansion. This contrasts sharply with both the Ricardian view, where there is no effect from the switch, and the classical view, where the effect is negative.

While the difference between the classical and Keynesian views of the public debt problem turns on which theory of macroeconomic output one supports, the difference between both these views on the one hand and the Ricardian on the other rests on different assumptions as to the rationality of individual economic agents in the respective models. According to the classical position, for example, private individuals suffer from an asymmetrical view toward taxes; current taxes are seen as burdens while future taxes are not. This type of "selective" rationality is not convincing.

In contrast to the classical position, private individuals, in the Ricardian view, are characterized by "universal" rationality. Private citizens understand that the switch from tax to debt finance does not give them a "free lunch." Liabilities to the government in the form of taxes simply are shifted from the present to the future. Moreover, this shift is not conceived to transfer a burden onto future generations.

Because of the possibility of private intergenerational transfers, any shift of taxes between generations can—indeed, must—be offset in a model where the preferences of present wealth holders for the disposal of their wealth after their demise (i.e., their bequest motives) are assumed not to change. In other words, why would a current, rational wealth holder who has made no new decision to shortchange his heirs do so anyway by shifting present taxes onto them? If the wealth holder's preferences are fixed, any increased burden on future generations caused by shifting from tax to debt finance simply will be offset through an increase in private bequests.

While the Ricardian view of the public debt benefits from its assumption of rational private citizens, the analysis based on this model has not been complete. Its particular message is that the shift from tax to debt finance will be neutral with respect to present wealth holders and thus the several economic variables discussed above. But consistent with its assumption of rationality and wealth neutrality is an intertemporal substitution effect influencing the distribution of economic activity over the life cycle, though not necessarily its total.

For example, switching taxes from the present to the future makes work today more attractive than work tomorrow. One would therefore expect worker-consumers to work more today and less tomorrow than otherwise would be the case. Present output of goods and services would increase as a result, just as in the Keynesian case. The substantial difference between the two, of course, is that in the Keynesian view the increased output today is assumed to make present and future generations better off, while in the Ricardian it simply represents borrowing output from the future.

There is a special case, however, where the intertemporal substitution effect assimilates the Ricardian and Keynesian models. This is when—*a la* Arthur Laffer—the increase in work effort in the present period due to the switch-over is so great that tax revenues derived therefrom make future tax increases unnecessary. Taxes will be less in the future than people expect, and work effort greater than anticipated. Switching from taxes to debt finance in this case can increase the amount of work effort over the entire life cycle rather than merely effectuating an intertemporal redistribution of effort. Similar to the standard Laffer analysis, for the increase in work effort to occur in the Ricardian model, the elasticity of work effort with respect to tax must be greater than one.

FORCED GOVERNMENT EXPENDITURE
AND MONEY CREATION

Based on extensive empirical research, Barro (1978, p. 10) argues that "the principal link from the federal budget to money creation in recent U.S. experience involves the departures of federal spending from normal—especially the positive response to wartime spending—rather than the surplus position (of the budget) or the level of federal spending *per se*." This statement strongly implies that money creation has been the favored means in the United States for financing forced increases in government spending, especially those related to the military.

The result of an unanticipated increase of the money supply to finance a forced increase in government spending is inflation. This means that the source of resources absorbed in the military buildup, for example, will be holders of money cash balances denominated in the inflated currency. Thus, if the United States is the inflating country, holders of U.S. dollar cash balances pay for the increase in government spending. No future tax liabilities are created—nor is recourse to explicit "defense taxes" required. The mechanism of resource transfer is inflation, which taxes the cash balances of private wealth holders.

There can be no doubt that President Johnson chose the "inflation tax" to finance the Vietnam War because he apparently felt an explicit tax increase would make an already unpopular war even more so. An unintended—and favorable—by-product of this policy, however, was to "export" some of the burden of financing the war to our trading partners abroad. This could occur during Vietnam because of the fixed exchange rate policy existing under the Bretton Woods international monetary system. As long as foreigners were willing to accept inflated U.S. dollars at a fixed rate of exchange for their own currency, we could extract real resources from abroad through running deficits in our international balance of payments. Ironically, many unsophisticated political economists argued at the time that our balance of payments deficit was a "problem" (for us, not for the Europeans) that constituted yet another cost of the war. Rather than a cost, however, our foreign deficit was one way the United States passed the war's true costs on to others.

If our partners in the Organization for Economic Cooperation and Development (OECD) were as clever as they thought they were, they never would have clung to fixed exchange rates as long as they did. To protect their resources from U.S. "expropriation," they should have let their currencies float as soon as we flooded the world with Vietnam dollars.

The United States is not likely to get a chance like that again, if only for the fact that the Western world has gone off fixed exchange rates (the creation of the European Monetary System can be interpreted as an indication that the Europeans are determined not to repeat their mistake). Thus, the only argument in favor of financing forced increases in government spending by money creation—that foreigners will pay for it—no longer is applicable. The remaining arguments are all negative.

Inflation taxes savers. As economists have consistently pointed out, to tax something is to reduce its supply. Using the inflation tax to finance forced increases in government spending therefore can be expected to reduce the savings ratio in a country that already has an anemic savings ratio relative to the tasks it faces. This is an important argument against recourse to the inflation tax.

Another is that inflation increases the size of government relative to the overall economy. Progressive income taxes mean that inflation increases tax revenues faster than it inflates incomes. The proportion of personal income accruing to government increases as a result. In addition, government gains from inflation because claims on government—pensions and salaries—tend to be fixed in monetary terms.

Inflation whittles down the real value of these claims, which often are owned by the poor and elderly. On the other hand, the biggest gainers from the post-Vietnam inflation have been U.S. citizens lucky—and rich—enough to have owned their own houses. The redistribution effects of inflation do not conform to accepted standards of national equity.

ECONOMISTS AND POLITICIANS

Economists have one view of the world, politicians another. In his budget message to the English Parliament over whether the Crimean War should be financed by taxes or debt, Gladstone made the following statement (Hirst 1931, p. 160):

The expenses of the war are the moral check which it has pleased the Almighty to impose upon the ambition and lust of conquest that are inherent in so many nations. There is pomp and circumstance, there is glory and excitement about war, which, notwithstanding the miseries it entails, invests it with charms in the eyes of the community, and tends to blind men to those evils to a fearful and dangerous degree. The necessity of meeting from year to year the expenditure which it entails is a sanitary and wholesome check, making them feel what they are about, and making them measure the cost of the benefit upon which they may calculate. It is by these means that they may be led and brought to address themselves to a war policy as rational and intelligent beings, and may be induced to keep their eyes well fixed both upon the necessity of the war into which they are about to enter, and their determination of availing themselves of the first and earliest prospects of concluding an honourable peace.

Gladstone clearly was no Ricardian. To meet the war finance, he continued the income tax (which had been introduced by Pitt as a war tax) at the doubled rate of one shilling, two pence, on the pound.

The British experience with the income tax in the nineteenth century is very instructive. New taxes introduced for purposes of national emergency—such as a "war tax"—tend to become permanent features of the fiscal landscape. In the United States there have been calls in recent years for a "defense tax" to finance military buildup for a "peace through strength" policy. During the Carter years, I argued for a federal tax on consumption—a U.S. sales tax, for example—to finance such a buildup (Krauss 1980). Recent newspaper reports indicated congressional interest in a "defense tax"—no doubt due to the perceived need to increase defense expenditures without further increasing federal deficits (apparently there are as few Ricardians in the U.S. Congress today as there were in the English Parliament one hundred and thirty years ago).

If a defense tax takes the form of a federal tax on consumption, perhaps the strongest argument that can be made in its favor is precisely that the tax would become a permanent feature of the U.S. fiscal landscape. Gimmicks like defense taxes may be the only way "good taxes" like the consumption tax can be wedged into our federal fiscal structure, since "tax reform" understandably no longer carries a decent name and supply-siders argue that increasing the tax raises budget deficits rather than reducing them. The point is that once a defense tax were in place alongside the federal income tax, an increasing share of the federal fiscal burden could be shifted over time from income to sales taxation (which would be beneficial for the anemic U.S. savings ratio and provide "automatic" indexation of federal taxes to boot). Admittedly, this has little to do with our national defense or, for that matter, with financing forced increases in public expenditure. But that type of tax reform would be good for our economy.

TEMPORARY VERSUS PERMANENT CHANGES IN GOVERNMENT PURCHASES

This chapter so far has concerned itself with issues of the

economic differences of financing a given increase in government expenditure by taxation, borrowing, or money creation.
Attention next focuses on the related—though theoretically
separate—issue of the economic effect of an increase in
government purchases regardless of how that increase is financed. The essential question here is whether government
purchases do play an important role in influencing aggregate
demand and thus output and employment, or whether, as
Martin Baily (1971) argues, the expansionary effect of
government spending is offset by simultaneous decreases in
private consumption expenditures.

In analyzing the macroeconomic output and employment
effects of government purchases, the critical factor, according
to Barro (1981) and Robert Hall (1980), is whether the increase in purchases is temporary or permanent. Hall argues
that temporary changes in government purchases—the concern of this chapter—can have an important stimulative
effect, because they induce intertemporal substitution of work
and production. These effects are most important in the case
of transitory expenditures that are not close substitutes for
private spending (the basis for Baily's argument), such as
those in wartime, but would not apply to long-run changes in
government spending. Barro also argues that the response of
output is likely to be larger when the change in government
purchases is temporary rather than permanent.

Barro estimates the division of defense purchases into permanent and temporary components by considering the effect
of war and of war expenditures. Defense spending associated
with wars is considered largely transitory, while other
changes in defense spending are viewed as permanent.
Shifts in nondefense federal, state, and local purchases are
also mostly permanent.

Analysis in Barro's paper of real gross national product
(GNP) reveals a significant expansionary effect of temporary defense purchases. There is evidence that temporary
movements in defense expenditures produce roughly double

the response in output of equal-sized but permanent shifts in defense purchases. Barro stresses intertemporal substitution variables as the channel for the strong positive output effect of temporary shifts in government purchases. Temporary shifts, he argues, increase the real rate of interest, motivating the postponement of consumption and leisure from the present to the future. The reduction of present leisure means a greater work effort and an increased supply of goods and services. A permanent rise in government expenditure, on the other hand, leaves the real rate of interest unaffected— thus the absence of an intertemporal substitution effect. England during World War II would appear to be a case where there was a substantial redistribution of work effort over the life cycle: the English worked extra hard during the war and have taken leisure ever since.

SUMMARY AND CONCLUSIONS

A forced increase in government expenditure is defined as contingent public expenditure made unavoidable by reversible changes in external circumstances. Thus forced government spending is conceived to be temporary.

The evidence is that such temporary expenditure increases, particularly those related to defense, have been financed by increases in the money supply—that is, inflation. There is also evidence that temporary increases in defense expenditure increase the output of goods and services through an intertemporal substitution effect. This should be understood not as an increase in the rate of economic growth, but as a reallocation of work effort over the life cycle. During the Vietnam War, expropriation of foreign resources also was possible due to the fixed exchange rate international monetary system.

It is doubtful that expropriating foreign resources to finance future forced increases in government spending will be possible. Nor is the evidence that temporary spending needs can be met by increases in the current supply of goods and services as convincing as one would like. If these two sources of resources are not available to finance temporary government purchase increases, the private community must bear the brunt of the resource transfer through taxation of some form or other.

Inflation—the favored tax so far—is a bad tax. Regardless of whether the choice is made to tax today or tax tomorrow, there should be a shift from money creation to explicit taxation. The introduction of a U.S. consumption tax into the federal tax structure as a "defense tax" during a geopolitical crisis could be very opportune.

15

ARNOLD J. MELTSNER

Budget Control through Political Action

A consensus on budget control? The deficit as political
liability. The aggregate and its components. A reform
amendment. Tinkering with the system. Outside
strategies. Public participation in budgetary control.

After President Reagan's tax-cut and budget-cut victories in
the summer of 1981, an examination of political options
available to control the federal budget would seem to be unnecessary. From now on, all a president has to do is assemble
a majority in Congress to execute his will; treat the budget as

an aggregate, obscuring the merits or demerits of individual programs and offering political rewards for cutting; and call the process reconciliation, thereby making the cuts appear to be part of routine congressional budgetary procedures. All this, and a president is well on his way to fiscal happiness — or is he?

Without taking away from President Reagan's excellent exercise of leadership skills, the pulling together of a majority, a coalition, to pass legislation is the way we usually conduct the public's business. The present problem for the president, however, is whether or not he is going to be able to get that coalition or some other one to continue the cutting. He has not much choice but to try, with the short-term prospects of a diminished revenue due to tax cuts and later provisions for indexing. Yet the conditions for holding together a coalition bent on cutting are not promising.

First, the pain from the initial set of cuts is just being felt and expressed in constituent pressures, making it more difficult to get additional cuts from the same budget targets. Second, the advantages of the president's economic recovery program will take some time to be felt. The costs of the program will be intensely felt by some, while the benefits are likely to be diffuse and spread among the many. Third, there is going to be severe disagreement over which additional programs to cut and how to cut them. Big programs—those making up the safety net—with big constituencies, such as social security and Medicare, will have to be tackled. Nor is it a secret that increased defense spending is in conflict with domestic program cuts.

Gypsy Moths and Boll Weevils feed on different vegetation, and the president is going to find it difficult to keep everyone's eye on the aggregate instead of on the program components where the heat and politics are. It is ironic, but if the economy improves and inflation recedes, the appetite for further belt tightening will diminish. It will appear less necessary to take draconian measures and there will be a tendency to return to past spending habits.

Ultimately, the president's ability to control the budget depends on public support, and President Reagan has been quick to solicit that support. But is there a consensus in this country for controlling the budget? If the election of the president represents the emergence of a consensus on budgetary control, then a selection of the means of control becomes a secondary matter. Most options will work because the political support exists to make them work. But suppose the election marks an ephemeral consensus in which the special interests and legislative incentives that have acted to create uncontrollable budgets are still with us; then what? It is one thing to support a president when he first comes into office; it is quite another to continue doing so when constituents are not pleased with the president's actions. One suspects that the consensus, if there is one, is not extensive, deeply held, nor likely to last. Moreover, in the past it has not been unusual for citizens to want both reduced taxes and increased spending. We will not get a better fix on this question until the results of the 1982 congressional elections are in. In the meantime, those who are interested in controlling the federal budget would be foolish to rely solely on a president to form one-time legislative majorities.

DEFICITS ARE BAD

Any political analysis of limiting budgets must consider the deficit. A few years ago the deficit was something that a few conservatives and budget-balancers could rant about, but today the deficit is a driving force behind political behavior. Some primitive cultures, after counting from, say, one to four, use the concept "many" for the rest of the numbers. So, too, is the present deficit thought of as "many." It really is beside the point whether the Congressional Budget Office estimates a fiscal year's deficit at $60 or $120 billion; the

numbers are sufficiently large to be beyond one's com-
prehension. They appear simply too large. Nor does com-
prehension increase when efforts are made to put the deficit
in perspective by pointing out that it is only a few percentage
points of the gross national product. No amount of trying to
put the deficit on an understandable scale will reduce its
political liability.

Obviously, adverse economic and financial consequences
of deficits contribute to the embarrassment that political
leaders experience when they adopt unbalanced budgets. But
the problems of financing the deficit or its possible relation
to high interest rates, inflation, and our other economic mal-
adies are not at issue. Indeed, economists are not likely to
agree on whether the deficit *is* an economic problem. We can
all agree, however, that deficits are a political problem.

To be sure, a number of years ago the same numerical deficit would not have caused a ripple in the political decision-
making stream, but now the likelihood of a deficit is a sign of
fiscal irresponsibility, both current and future. Political rhetoric, such as it is, equates deficits with a lack of stewardship
and a violation of the fiduciary relationship that citizens expect of their leaders.

When the Reagan administration went back to the well for
an additional $16 billion in cuts and revenue, its objectives
were to reduce the deficit and to keep it declining until the
budget is balanced. It was a politically risky move to suggest
more holes in the safety net before the previous cuts were
felt, but also politically risky not to do so. Politicians, irre-
spective of party and spending desires, cannot appear to be
contributing to the deficit. Planning to be so much in the red
for fiscal year 1983 and beyond is a certain route to being politically dead.

Besides acting as a partial brake on spending, the deficit
will motivate budgetary reform. Political actors will feel the
pressure to do something, as they have in the past. In 1909,
for example, President Taft had a deficit of $89 million from

a budget of $694 million. He subsequently got some money from Congress and appointed the Commission on Economy and Efficiency. The work of that commission became a significant milestone in the history of budgetary reform and led to the Budget and Accounting Act of 1921. If President Reagan is unable to bring his budget into balance as planned, his failure will probably provide the conditions for structural reform of federal budgeting. Of course, we should recognize that despite President Taft's efforts and the subsequent reforms, the long-run trend for government was to spend more.

AN AMENDMENT TO THE CONSTITUTION

Before President Reagan's election, there was considerable interest in amending the Constitution to control the budget. For a short time, this interest in mechanical rules for balancing the budget or linking spending to economic growth subsided as people waited for the president to develop and push his economic programs. However, this patience did not last long, and by July 1981 the Senate Judiciary Committee had issued a report on Senate Joint Resolution 58, which linked the various approaches together by amending the Constitution to require a balanced federal budget and to tie taxation to economic growth.

Amending the Constitution, at least on the surface, seems an attractive political option. It provides a rule that will constrain public spending and provide an excuse for those elected officials who need it. The official can say to a disgruntled constituent, "I wanted to get money for your program but I couldn't; the amendment made us balance the budget." Supposedly, the mechanical rule will take the heat and at the same time build character and provide some backbone to officials who have caved in to citizen demands in the past.

Of course, it is not easy to amend our federal Constitution. Unlike the situation with some state constitutions, we have infrequently amended the federal—witness the recent problems that have confronted the passage of the Equal Rights Amendment. One wonders whether controlling the budget has the same appeal as temperance once did.

Most of us worry generally about pieces of the budget and not about the aggregate. Thus a small, organized group of intense proponents of the amendment would probably confront a large, initially unorganized, and diffuse set of opponents. Those who believe in the importance of maintaining discretion and flexibility for official action would join other opponents who might see a programmatic threat in the amendment. The battle would likely be fought by experts, and it would probably not be a situation where large numbers of citizens would be banging on the door for this reform.

With the prevailing fear about deficits, the amendment might get the necessary two-thirds vote in Congress and be proposed to the states. Yet why should state legislatures go along? On the one hand, most states have a constitutional or statutory provision to avoid deficits, and in the aftermath of California's Proposition 13 many of them adopted some form of limitation upon state expenditures and revenues. Polls have shown that citizens do react favorably toward the notion of balanced budgets, and in recent years thirty-one states have applied for a convention to consider a balanced budget amendment—and several more may soon join them. On the other hand, note that many of the states are already increasing their sales and gasoline taxes just to make ends meet. Indeed, the Tax Foundation reports that thirty states increased their taxes by a net of $2.5 billion in 1981. If state legislators perceive that they will get less federal financial help once the amendment passes, they may be reluctant to ratify it. They certainly will not do so if they see the amendment as a way of dumping problems, without money, on them.

Suppose the amendment still passed; then what? Would the public's desire for spending be brought to heel? In the short term, the amendment would work as intended. But as time eroded political support for control and the escape features became less flexible than they were thought to be, people would start thinking about ways of repealing the amendment. Not finding that route so easy, they could subvert and undermine it. All an official would have to do is change a few definitions, or alter a few estimates, or shift recording expenditures to a more promising fiscal year, and the budget would appear to be in balance. If you doubt that willful political officials would do so, just look at the antecedents of New York City's fiscal crisis of 1975. The city had plenty of rules and laws to encourage fiscal conservatism, but officials manipulated these rules until the crisis became visible to the nation. Public attention and state and federal oversight, not rules alone, made it more difficult to engage in creative accounting.

In 1973 then-Governor Ronald Reagan proposed a Tax and Expenditure Limitations Constitutional Amendment (Proposition 1) to the voters of California. At that time I opposed this tampering with the state's constitution because I wanted to create a favorable climate of trust and flexibility so that the legislators could do the job they were elected to do. The voters defeated the proposed amendment, but it was only five years after the governor's proposal that the voters passed the financially capricious and draconian Proposition 13. In retrospect, the proposed amendment was a more thoughtful response to the problem of controlling governmental expenditures than Proposition 13, whose full consequences have yet to be experienced or understood. Today it may make more sense to pursue amending the federal Constitution, whether by tax limitation or some combination, than to wait for some more spasmodic and ill-conceived response.

The success of an amendment strategy, however, will depend on developing and maintaining political support for

budgetary control, support that must continue if it is to be
effective; otherwise, officials will have sufficient incentives
to undermine and circumvent its intentions. The proponents
of the amendment strategy believe that an amendment, once
passed, would alter expectations about governmental spending and thereby create the conditions for maintaining and
expanding political support. They hope that with appropriate
public vigilance, the symbolic and practical effects of an
amendment would change the character and behavior of
public officials. Nobody really knows if they are right—
whether their proposed reform will follow the path of the income tax (the 16th Amendment), which today is an accepted
feature of the nation's life, or the path of the prohibition of li-
quor (the 18th Amendment), which is not.

TINKERING

If we are seriously going to consider changing the Constitution, we should also consider other ways of tinkering with our
system of politics and budgets. From the standpoint of political feasibility, the ideal change would help control the
budget without shifting political power—which may be a
contradiction in terms. In the past, as we changed from a legislative to an executive budget, we did shift political resources to the executive branch by encouraging the president to set the legislative agenda and frame the important
budgetary issues. Today, proposals to give the president an
item veto or the authority to impound funds would certainly
increase his political resources. While members of Congress
would like the president to take the heat for unpopular cuts,
they do not want to make him more powerful, particularly at
their expense.

   One notion—an almost politically neutral move that
would dampen budgetary aspirations—is to lengthen the

period covered by the budget. Some state governments operate on a two-year budget, and the federal government could
do the same. As presently practiced, budgeting eats up
tremendous amounts of everybody's time. It is a wonder that
public servants have any time left to do anything else. From
an efficiency perspective, therefore, a two-year budget
makes sense, though several problems would be hard to
avoid. Budgeting over a two-year period would not be as flexible as our one-year budget; but we already have supplemental appropriations to deal with the unexpected. It is also true
that old programs would have an edge over new ones because
it would take the newcomer more time to get into the cycle.
Generally, old programs have developed constituencies, and
a two-year budget—or, for that matter, a balanced budget
amendment—would give them appropriate respect and thus
an advantage.

The potential for tinkering is endless when ingenious
people set their minds to it. For example, use a less expensive
cost-of-living index; reduce the frequency of adjusting for inflation; get the millions of dollars that are off budget back on
budget (so everyone can see who the spenders are); shift
open-ended entitlements to fixed allocations; cut by object
class (e.g., travel, personnel, maintenance) so program
effects are obscured; get rid of self-inflicted costs of previous
internal management control schemes, and so on.

The trouble with tinkering is that it is nothing more than
tinkering: it changes procedures, rules of the game, and
rhetoric. No slight accomplishment, but still it does not get at
basic attitudes. It does not develop a basic constituency and
political support for budgetary control. There will still be
those who honestly believe that their program is different.
There will still be elected and civil service officials who will
align their policy objectives with programs that have political support. Trees will be preserved in the name of national defense.

USE OF THE BUREAUCRACY

As time goes on, a more surgical approach to budget cutting is necessary. Rather than being able to lop off billions, budget cutters start looking for millions, the rounding-off errors of the process. At that point, it is no longer possible to operate solely outside an agency. Newcomers to the Office of Management and Budget simply will not know enough. They will not know which reports, activities, and programs can be dispensed with. They will suspect that the fat is there, but they will not know where it is.

A typical response to such a situation is to levy a percentage cut on the agency—say, 5 percent. Operating on a fair-share norm, every agency is expected to cut its budget by 5 percent. The trouble with this response is that the outsiders do not know whether the chosen number is appropriate. For some agencies, it may be terribly low; for others, the cut cannot realistically be made. Nor can the administration know the difference between real and fake complainers. It will need informants.

Most bureaucrats are loyal to their agency. Rarely will they go outside or make an end run, and when they do it is usually to defend a program from cutting, not to suggest a candidate for elimination. That is why the agency itself has to be in charge of its own cutting and that is why its members have to be enlisted to help. It is one thing to make the bureaucracy the enemy when running for office; it is another to continue to do so when governing. Of course, each agency contains bureaucrats who will push for expanding programs when they can; but each agency also contains people who want to run things efficiently and, as part of their professional ethos, want to give the taxpayer his or her money's worth. Lumping these people together and treating the agency as a monolithic spending machine is a serious mistake, as it deprives the agency head of valuable sources of expertise and information. The agency head should be given the leeway to enlist internal help from his or her agency. It is the people on the inside who know where to make the surgical cuts. As long as the main mission is left intact or appears to be so, bureaucrats can be used to hold the line or cut the budget. Most of them would rather cut their budgets in what they view as a sensible way than to live with the uncertain consequences of meat-ax cuts.

SHIFTING THE FOCUS: OUTSIDE STRATEGIES

To control spending in the long run, we have to shift the focus of our efforts. We need to get outside of Washington and pay attention to the citizens and to their expectations and aspirations about government. We need to disaggregate the budget and examine its components. Right now we have been concentrating on the aggregate budget because many of its components seem meritorious—at least, to somebody— while the total is seen as out of control.

The use of the reconciliation procedure as an aggregate approach was quite appropriate to the politics of the moment. There was a new president in office whose election seemed to indicate substantial support for checking the growth of the federal budget. The president was willing and able to take the heat for budget cutting. Using the reconciliation procedure, programs were lumped together and then subjected to fair-share notions of cutting, while interest groups and their legislative supporters were unable to make the case for the special circumstances of their programs. Reconciliation, as in many other aggregate approaches using revenue constraints or expenditure limits, puts the emphasis on cutting and not on what is cut (or on the likely effects of the cuts). In the rush to meet the president's agenda, there is little time to do otherwise than to find sufficient cuts to meet the desired amount.

This use of the reconciliation procedure will not work so easily in the future. For the 1983 budget cycle and beyond, the president will not be as popular as when he first came into office. The interest groups will be mobilized to assert their case. Congress will not continue to allow one of its procedures to be subverted to increase presidential power at its own expense, particularly when constituents see few benefits from the president's economic policies and can see benefits from increased spending. Nor can we expect that the reconciliation procedure will bind behavior by itself in the short run. At any point in time, legislators can use the appropriations process to undermine previous agreements to a point at which the president will be in the trenches fighting on the ground of a particular program to keep the integrity of his aggregate budget.

It should be recognized that not much has been done to change the underlying political forces and beliefs that make for uncontrolled spending in the first place. *A widely shared public philosophy on the appropriate scope of governmental activity and its associated expenditure level does not exist.* Many of us would prefer, at least some of the time, a balanced budget, but few of us would agree about the level at which the budget should be balanced. We can see the desirability of controlling spending, but a consensus on the means to do so has not yet emerged. Nor do we have in office a cohort of public officials who are prepared to sacrifice their pet programs to reduce the rate at which spending is increasing. We are in a period of transition when the signals are mixed and political support is uncertain. To be sure, the administration has to act as if the support is there, and as if it is simply implementing a popular mandate. Short-term outcomes then depend on the skill of our leaders and the transparency of their actions. Long-term outcomes, however, will depend on the emergence of a public consensus about the limits of governmental action.

Most of the current options for controlling the budget focus on changing the rules by which Congress and the bureaucracy operate. We focus on what goes on *inside* these institutions—and rightly so, because that is where the problem of public spending is visible and the levers of control seem close and convenient. Solutions are usually found close to the problems. To augment these inside options, however, it is essential that we turn our attention to the *outside*. We cannot rely solely on expecting behavior to change because we have changed the rules. The desired behavioral change—a belief in the necessity to limit governmental activity and to control federal spending—must also be reinforced from the outside.

Consider the several national tax organizations that have tried to raise our tax consciousness. As citizens, we are told that we have to work so much of the year just to pay our taxes. From such efforts we are likely to wish that our taxes be reduced, but not all of us will convert that wish to a reduced appetite for public services. Of course, cutting taxes does act as a constraint on spending, and this has been part of the logic of the Proposition 13 movement as well as of the president's program. Yet efforts on the tax side tend to divide the nation into taxpayers and spending beneficiaries, with the possibility of increased social conflict. Such efforts also encourage a further separation of taxes from spending, as if it makes sense to decide on one without considering the other.

Besides emphasizing tax burdens, national and particularly state interest groups should try to link taxes with spending, and where this fails, then emphasize the disadvantages of spending for its own sake. Making the connections between taxes and spending is no easy task; it probably involves adopting a user-charge mentality, even where the imposition of such a charge seems politically impossible. Citizens must understand that they are paying for public services. If citizens become cost-conscious, their appetite for governmental services might be reduced.

Now cost consciousness need not be raised to the point that one group is at the throat of another. We have enough trouble avoiding constituent backlash and infighting every time a new sewerage system or child care program or library or public education program is proposed for funding. The point of cost consciousness is to realize that public services are not free; they cost all of us something. Because they do cost, we as citizens have to make a choice between potential programs. If we insist on selecting and approving programs sequentially, independent of each other and one at a time, we are bound not to like the aggregate result. We are like kids in a candy store eating one candy bar after another, without much thought as to the capacity of our stomachs, until we get sick. Public budgeting operates much the same way; each program has some merit as we put it into the budget—until we add up the total. If citizens would be more careful about their initial demands for governmental services, then the effects of the aggregate budget would be tolerable and we could avoid a stomach ache.

The way things are now, citizens reward legislators for bringing spending projects to their districts. Few scream about the profligacy of such actions; certainly no one gets punished for bringing the proverbial pork back home. It seems as if we have accepted this distributional ethic of national politics forever. But why should we continue to do so when we believe that the effects of the total barrel are bad for us? If interest groups would forget about liberal/conservative distinctions—which are often misleading because they do not help to identify the spenders— some legislators might not get reelected and the message would get around. The unsung hero in this context would be the one who fights *not* to bring the water project to his or her state or the unnecessary freeway to the city just to have federal money. The battle is not fought over a mysterious aggregate budget total but over a specific program or project, and the political conflict is at the appropriate level where it can be felt and understood.

In the long run, a more certain way of balancing the budget is to elect and appoint men and women to office who deeply believe in the value of doing so. They must *want* to control the budget, and not be forced to. For these people to come forth and do the job, citizens have to be convinced that it is in their own self-interest to constrain the scope of government.

CONCLUSION: A PUBLIC CONSENSUS

It is no easy matter, however, to convince citizens of what is in their long-run interest. After all, many citizens do benefit from the programs that we would encourage them to live without. It seems somewhat abstract to point out to them how some programs might dampen individual initiative or constrain the range of choice. Moreover, there are no simple answers to how much we should spend on defense or on health. Even the adverse economic effects of ever-expanding federal budgets and their deficits will not convince citizens of the necessity of budgetary restraint unless leaders and officials can convert these effects to persuasive political language and symbols.

There are those who believe that appealing to the self-interest of citizens to control the budget is impractical and even silly. They see the individual citizen as caught between a conflict of two interests: an intense preference for a specific benefit from government and a less intense, general taxpayer interest in reduced taxes and a healthy economy. The way this conflictual situation is analyzed, specific interests are likely to win over general ones, but this analysis, while perhaps accurate, is not helpful. It tells us little about how to appeal to citizens—only that our appeals will be frustrated.

There must be some way to appeal to citizens so that the conflict, at least sometime, is at the same level of specificity and intensity. Is it that difficult to convince a retired person that inflation is eroding his or her savings? Cannot the argument be made in such a way that the benefits of reducing inflation are as specific and compelling as the benefits of Medicare? One wonders how many people would be willing to give up their mortgage interest deduction on their income tax or their social security and veterans' death benefits in exchange for increased economic stability.

In order to develop a consensus on public spending, discussion has to proceed at multiple levels of argumentation. First, the aggregative negative and positive effects of budgetary totals should be explained. Second, these aggregative effects must be translated to specific consequences for specific groups in our population. At the same time, discussion should proceed on the major programmatic choices that we must make to meet domestic and international needs.

The problem of developing a consensus on public spending is so difficult—some would say, impossible—that reformers would just as soon sidestep it. That is why there is so much interest in tax limitation amendments and the like. I support these attempts, but I also believe we would all be better off if we could encourage the use of available democratic processes. To do so, as I have urged in this last section, is not to engage in wishful thinking or utopian prescriptions, as some might conclude. My objective is much more modest: to shift attention to outside public strategies that complement the inside budgetary control efforts of officials and experts.

It is essential that, in and out of elections, we discuss the appropriateness of public spending totals and programs, the suitability of the federal, state, or local level of government to deliver a specific service, and the relative efficiency of using the various sectors of our complex economy and society. While there are important economic issues to be discussed, fundamental questions about individual freedom and the role of the state must also be raised.

We cannot blithely continue to assume that all the activities of government have merit and that only the deficit or aggregate spending is bad. Ultimately, the question of controlling the budget is the question of the appropriate role and scope of government. Ultimately, our ability to control the budget rests on the public's understanding and support for doing so.

16

ALVIN RABUSHKA

Fiscal Responsibility: Will Anything Less Than a Constitutional Amendment Do?

The national tax bill. Voter rebellion. The federal budget, receipts, and expenditures. The triple spending bias. Reforms—institutional and constitutional. Three proposed amendments. Senate Joint Resolution 58.

Reforming the federal budget process is a much pursued but elusive goal for politicians, Washington-watchers, congressional and public finance scholars and, last but not least, tax-payers. Several conferences a year address the question of whether the growth of federal taxes, expenditures, and deficits can be brought under control. A burgeoning literature offers a variety of institutional, statutory, and constitutional reforms to stem and reverse the upward spiral.

In 1929 federal spending of $3 billion consumed 3.1 percent of the gross national product (GNP). In successive decades it grew to 10.0, 15.6, 18.5, 20.3, and 23.1 percent by 1980.[1] In money terms, it was as recent as fiscal year 1962 that federal spending passed the $100 billion mark. A $200 billion budget was reached only nine years later. In rapid-fire succession came $300 billion (1975), $400 billion (1977), $500 billion (1980), $600 billion (1981), with estimates of $1 trillion by 1985.

To pay this massive bill, taxes increased sharply. Taxpayers contribute 22 percent of GNP to the federal government in taxes, compared with 15 percent in 1949. Taxpayers also face much higher marginal rates on income. Households in the 70th percentile of taxpayers have seen their average top marginal rate rise from 20 percent in 1966 to 28 percent by 1981; for those in the 95th percentile, from 25 to 46 percent.

Deficits have been even more dramatic. The government has run a budget deficit in nineteen of the past twenty years. Eight deficits in the 1970s exceeded $40 billion. The total national debt of the United States has grown from $383 billion, following the 1970 fiscal year, to surpass $1 trillion on 21 October 1981. Nor does the figure include the growing unfunded liability of social insurance programs and the implicit obligations of loan guarantees.

Nearly invisible in 1929, the federal government has now become the dominant economic institution in the United States. Along with rising federal deficits, taxation, and spending have come inflation, stagnation, and low levels of savings and capital formation. These have bred unemployment, reduced profits, and lowered real household disposable incomes (after adjusting for inflation and taxes).

THE REACTION

On 6 June 1978 voters in California said "enough."[2] Landslide passage of Proposition 13 highlighted public concern over rising taxes and runaway government spending. Proposition 13 was contagious. In November 1978 voters in 20 states confronted a tax or spending limit measure on their ballots. One year later another rash was proposed and adopted. By the end of 1980, 8 states had adopted a constitutional limitation and 10 states had imposed a statutory restraint on permissible levels of taxing or spending.

State legislators heard the message, too. During the 1978 and 1979 sessions, 37 states reduced property taxes, 28 states cut income taxes, 13 states restricted sales tax collections, and 12 states cut or repealed other taxes. Six states adopted some form of income tax indexing. State and local taxes as a share of personal income fell from 12.1 percent in 1977 to 10.9 percent in 1979.

A counterpart trend aimed at the federal government got under way in 1975. Led by the National Taxpayers Union, state legislatures passed resolutions calling for a constitutional convention to write a balanced budget amendment. By January 1982, 31 states had so resolved. Under Article V of the Constitution, Congress is "obliged" to call a convention upon the applications of 34 of the present 50 states.

A companion effort to limit permissible levels of federal spending was pushed by the National Tax Limitation Committee—including such distinguished economists as Milton Friedman—which sought to extend successful states' amendments to the federal Constitution. These campaigns prompted the Senate Judiciary Subcommittee on the Constitution early in 1979 to develop its own constitutional proposal, trying to reconcile a broad range of proposals requiring balanced budgets or spending and taxing limits. Its "consensus" measure is a combination balanced budget/tax limitation measure (discussed below) that was reported to the full Senate on 19 May 1981. This marks the first time in the postdepression era that either chamber of Congress will have had an opportunity to debate a constitutional amendment to impose fiscal restraint.

The most recent push to bring the budget under control is President Reagan's attempt to cut both spending, some $40 billion from nondefense programs in fiscal 1982, and taxes, a major reduction in individual rates followed by indexing of the tax brackets to inflation beginning in 1985. The spending cuts were achieved by aggregating cuts through the little-used reconciliation provision in the 1974 Budget and Impoundment Control Act, whereby passage of a House or Senate budget resolution issues instructions to committees for specific reduction levels. This, however, is a bruising process (see Panetta 1982).

Despite approved spending cuts for fiscal 1982, several estimates of the budget deficit exceed $100 billion with promises of bigger deficits to come in subsequent years. There is, of course, good reason for these deficits: recession, tax cuts, and increased defense spending. But there have always been good reasons for the deficits in nineteen of the last twenty years.

BIAS IN THE BUDGET PROCESS

Throughout most of our history, revenue estimates were typically dealt with before expenditure estimates. It was generally believed that public expenditure should be fit to available public revenues, set at a low level, and that revenues should not be extended to fit expenditure. Public officials supported new spending only when they were prepared to reduce other spending programs or raise new revenues.

Spending decisions in the twentieth century have become increasingly divorced from constraints of revenue. With practically unlimited access to deficit spending, members of Congress have responded to the demands of spending interests. The federal budget process has become a regime of permanent and continuing deficits, having yielded steadily higher levels of public spending. Even annual deficits projected at $100 billion or more for several years to come no longer seem to force Congress to enact modest, much less draconian, spending cuts. In addition to nearly unlimited access to deficit spending, the Treasury has collected automatic annual increases in tax receipts. Our progressive tax code works to transfer more and more of our personal income to the government, because as individual income increases, people are taxed at progressively steeper rates. This rising share of national income paid in taxes is due to real increases in income or to inflation. Such a tax system allows Congress to raise taxes without ever having to vote an explicit increase. Indeed, the progressive tax system has permitted Congress to enact eight postwar tax cuts and still collect an increasing share of income in tax receipts. The process should end in 1985 when full indexing of the tax brackets takes effect.

The spending bias can be explained in several ways. The first concerns the relationships between concentrated benefits and dispersed costs. The benefits of any given spending program are concentrated within a relatively small class of beneficiaries, while the costs of such a program are dispersed through a large class of taxpayers. Those who benefit from a particular spending measure stand to do so greatly, while those who bear the costs are affected insignificantly. It is not as worthwhile for an individual taxpayer to spend much time and effort to save a few dollars in taxes as it is for the spending interests to secure millions or billions of dollars for themselves. Thus as programs are considered one by one, there is a bias toward growth in the size of government spending.

A second bias is the clash between short-run benefits and long-run costs. Sitting congressmen can enjoy the immediate political benefits of spending programs, abetted by deficit spending, while the costs—in the form of potentially higher future taxes, higher future inflation, or higher future interest rates—will be evident only at some distant time, to be borne by a future Congress.

A third bias appears in the structure of Congress itself (Shepsle 1981). The committee system, whatever its original intentions, finds members of Congress gravitating to those specific committees that allow them to serve their geographic constituencies by bringing home their "fair share." Farm state members serve on the agriculture committee, and so forth. Each congressman is rewarded with reelection if he successfully serves his constituency, even if the collective actions of Congress yield overall harmful financial and economic results. Congress may not be doing a responsible job even as each congressman is separately applauded. There is, in short, a mismatch between budget objectives and the budget process. Despite the 1974 Budget Act, the broad objectives of budget making clash with the incentives congressmen face as individuals. The collective need to curtail spending gives way to each individual's need to increase it.

INSTITUTIONAL REFORM

Changes in the operating structure of Congress are one technique to restrain its propensity to spend or practice deficit financing. One such reform has been suggested by Allen Schick (1982), longtime congressional budget expert. Schick suggests modification of the 1974 Budget Act into a two-step process. First, Congress would consider the budget totals in light of the condition of the economy and overall needs of the government. Total outlays would be fixed at the start of the process by supermajority vote. Second, the functional allocations allotted within the total would then be binding upon the

entire Congress and the separate committees. Each committee would determine how the moneys are apportioned within
its functional categories. This would create a strong incentive to bring so-called "uncontrollables" under control, since
these items would compete directly with discretionary programs. Uncontrollables are those categories of expenditure
that rise automatically with changes in inflation and eligibility, requiring no changes in the law to fund these higher outlays. Social security, food stamps, and unemployment benefits exemplify these entitlement programs. To enforce this
two-step process, Schick recommends that the president
have authority to withhold funds when the budget's overall
objectives are threatened, but without undoing program
priorities set by Congress. Of course, for Schick's reform to
work, Congress must not set annual outlays at ever-higher
levels. Nothing in his two-step modification alters the incentives to spend that each member faces.

Kenneth Shepsle offers another type of reform in four sets
of recommendations that could strengthen the executive, the
House Appropriations Committee, the House Budget Committee, and party leaders. He recommends granting the
president a variant of the item veto. Instead of allowing an
executive to blue-pencil any given item in any appropriation
bill, as in the item veto, the president could propose an omnibus reconciliation measure—an omnibus of item vetos—
that he would return to the legislature for up or down approval on the whole package. An omnibus veto, subject to
congressional approval, would allow the president to coordinate fiscal policy across committee jurisdiction, and thus
take budget aggregates into account.

Other reforms would grant to the full committee chairman
and ranking minority member of the Appropriations Committee absolute power over subcommittee assignments,
which might prevent subcommittees from domination by
those with purely provincial concerns. (This measure would
undo recent reforms that are popular with most members of

Congress, and is thus an unlikely suggestion.) All thirteen money bills in Shepsle's recommendations should be disposed of in the House at the same time, rather than receiving drawn-out, independent consideration. This would provide the opportunity for total comparison of costs and benefits.

Finally, Shepsle would upgrade the House Budget Committee to a full-ranked standing committee and give party leaders power over assignments to it. A strengthened Budget Committee might play a more constraining role on actual outlay decisions during the First and Second Budget Resolutions.

Critics of statutory law changes or internal institutional reforms note the failure of the 1974 act, under which record deficits have accumulated. They claim that no Congress can bind a succeeding Congress by simple statute, and that statutes do not possess the imperatives of constitutional limitation. None of these proposed changes imposes effective constraints on deficits or on the ability to levy new taxes to increase spending. Growing concern that Congress cannot and will not become a responsible budgetary agency has prompted the current movement to impose a constitutional constraint.

CONSTITUTIONAL REFORM

Constitutional restraints assume three forms: the balanced budget amendment, a tax or spending limitation, or a combination of the two.

The balanced budget amendment: pros and cons

A balanced budget amendment would solidify the link between spending and revenue.[3] It would compel public officials, first, to determine what resources are available to government and, against that constraint, to choose among the many competing claims on public spending.

Under the amendment, if politicians voted new spending programs, they would have to eliminate old programs or raise additional taxes. Resistance to the elimination of existing programs or to tax increases would discourage many new spending proposals and eliminate the current bias toward overspending. It would end future deficits and reduce the inflationary effect of creating new money, which has in past years financed a portion of these deficits. In turn, reduced inflation would moderate the tax increases caused by bracket creep.

Although some regard any tax increase as inherently undesirable, a balanced budget amendment would still permit an increase in public spending if there were an overriding democratic consensus. In practical terms, few politicians would want to campaign on a platform of higher taxes to finance more spending. The balanced budget would require that tax increases be explicitly voted, rather than implicitly imposed by deficit spending and its stimulus to inflation.

Political values and perceptions are important determinants of government action. For this reason, a balanced budget amendment is especially attractive. It is easy to understand—every housewife understands the need for living within her means. It is also widely supported. Polls show overwhelming support for a balanced budget, often by margins of 6 to 1.

Most supporters of a balanced budget amendment are keenly aware of practical difficulties in its implementation. Every proposed amendment contains an escape hatch clause, based on some declaration of emergency and a two-thirds or greater vote by Congress, to suspend the requirement in the event of war or serious economic downturn. Some proposed amendments suggest the creation of a "rainy day" reserve fund from budgetary surpluses for periods of temporary deficit.

Although practical difficulties are acknowledged, most proponents regard continuation of present fiscal policy—

deficits and concomitant inflationary pressure—to be far more dangerous than grappling with the implementation of a balanced budget constraint.

Opponents of a balanced budget amendment include those who oppose a constitutional restraint on fiscal flexibility. Paul Samuelson[4] argues that economics is an inexact science and that it would be unwise to freeze policy rules for the indefinite future and thereby limit the flexibility required to deal with future problems. In his view, moreover, the present system of American democracy can cope with any national trend toward unreasonably large government. And if the escape clause is too lenient, the amendment would become merely a pious resolution cluttering the Constitution.

Other criticisms of a balanced budget highlight its conceptual difficulties. What does "outlays" mean? How does one prevent the emergence of "off-budget" spending or the separation of current and capital expenditures now found in several state budgets? How does Congress cope with the general unreliability of economic forecasts? What are the appropriate enforcement provisions if a projected balanced budget becomes unbalanced in the course of the fiscal year? How and by whom will the budget subsequently be made to conform to the constitutional prohibition?

Nor does the experience of the fifty states suggest that a constitutional prohibition on deficits prevents rapid growth in public spending. By late 1980, thirty-nine state constitutions forbade deficits. Despite ostensible success—the states rarely sustain prolonged deficits—budget balance typically comes with higher, not lower, levels of spending and taxes. The reason is that most states reap rising revenues from progressive state income taxes and inflation-fueled property taxes, and many have enacted tax rate increases. The result is that state and local tax revenue as a share of personal income almost doubled since 1952 from 8.4 percent to 15.1 percent of GNP in 1978. In the absence of some revenue limit, a balanced budget amendment may eliminate federal deficits, but it will not necessarily arrest government growth. Progressive income taxes hold for the federal government until indexing takes effect in 1985, which largely eliminates the automatic "kicker" in revenues. If indexing is repealed, a purely balanced budget amendment at the federal level might duplicate the experiences of the states, resulting in higher levels of taxing and spending. Ending deficits does not prevent more spending.

Spending limitation amendment: pros and cons

Proponents of a spending limitation often advance the same arguments as those who advocate a balanced budget. The fundamental defect in present budgetary procedure is that Congress considers spending programs on a piecemeal basis and the public cannot express its views as to the size of the budget.

The major objective of a spending limitation amendment is to link the growth of government to growth in the private economy, either in terms of GNP, personal income, or changes in the consumer price index (CPI). Specific clauses could allow for upward or downward adjustments in the level of government spending to cope with emergencies.

Advocates of a spending limit amendment emphasize its feasibility.[5] The amendment would adeptly avoid a pitfall of the balanced budget. Since outlays would be based on the calendar year preceding the current fiscal year, spending growth would be based on actual data and not on economic forecasts, which are notoriously unreliable. The twenty-one-month difference between the fiscal year and the calendar year on which it is based would incorporate, in the view of its advocates, an automatic countercyclical element in federal spending. Slow economic growth would slow federal spending twenty-one months later when the economy might be booming. Conversely, rapid economic growth would increase government spending twenty-one months later when the economy would most likely be slowing down.

Critics of a spending limitation are of two minds. One group opposes any constitutional limitation on federal fiscal policy or flexibility. The second claims that a balanced budget amendment is superior to a spending limitation.

There is nothing inherent in a spending limit that would prevent future deficits. Projections showing that inflation or economic growth would produce a balanced budget under a spending limitation (because under our progressive tax structure, tax revenues increase faster than GNP) would prove false if Congress voted tax reductions. Thus the pressure on monetary inflation from deficits would not be eliminated.

Another defect in many of the proposed spending limitation measures is their complexity. The Heinz-Stone Spending Limitation Amendment, originally drafted and supported by the National Tax Limitation Committee, contained a very complicated inflation penalty clause and was inordinately long. Typically, complex proposals lose support as ratification nears. Moreover, some critics object to the inflexibility of these measures, which would prevent desirable increases in expenditures unless a state of emergency were declared.

The experience of state constitutional tax and expenditure limits (TELs) is extremely limited. The first of these measures was adopted in Tennessee in March 1978. By the end of 1980, eight states had imposed some form of limit, but most are too recent to judge their effects. Preliminary evidence in California reveals a variety of maneuvers by local governments and the state legislature to evade a constitutional limit on spending adopted in November 1979, thus rendering it ineffective (see Rabushka and Ryan 1982, chapters 7 and 10).

Balanced budget/tax limitation amendment

Since 1979 members of the Senate Judiciary Subcommittee

on the Constitution have sought to develop a consensus measure that would attract the support of as many proponents of a constitutional initiative as possible. Senate Joint Resolution 58 (S.J.Res. 58 [see appendix A]), a combined balanced budget and tax limitation amendment, was voted out of the subcommittee by a 4–0 vote on 6 May 1981, and reported out of the full Senate Committee on the Judiciary by an 11–5 vote on 19 May 1981. The measure enjoys the support of both the National Taxpayers Union, progenitor of the balanced budget constitutional convention movement, and the National Tax Limitation Committee, formerly sponsor of the Heinz-Stone Spending Limitation Amendment.

S.J.Res. 58 has several key provisions.[6] Section 1 establishes the norm of a balanced federal budget. It requires that Congress adopt a "statement" or budget of planned receipts and outlays, in which planned outlays do not exceed planned receipts, prior to each fiscal year. A planned deficit can be adopted only by a three-fifths vote of the "whole number" of each house of Congress—that is, a constitutional three-fifths. In contrast, a simple majority may plan a surplus. Section 1 also mandates that actual outlays do not exceed the outlays set forth in the statement.

It bears restating that the amendment establishes a *planned* balanced budget as the fiscal norm. It does not seek to establish an *actual* balanced budget as a fiscal norm. Actual outlays may exceed actual receipts. For example, a recession may reduce actual receipts below statement receipts, which is permissible under the amendment. Deficits caused by increased spending, however, will not be permitted, since actual outlays cannot exceed statement outlays. Although statement outlays may not exceed statement receipts, a surplus may be adopted to permit redemption of public debt.

If circumstances warrant, Congress may adopt an amended statement of receipts and outlays for the fiscal year (provided that outlays do not exceed receipts) at any time during that fiscal year. An amended statement containing a deficit will require a three-fifths vote only if such deficit is greater than the deficit in the previous statement.

Section 1 imposes upon Congress and the president a mandate to prevent total actual outlays from exceeding statement outlays. For example, should the economy perform below expectations—leading to increased spending on "entitlements" or debt service due to higher interest rates— Congress will be called upon *either* to increase statement outlays and approve a deficit, or to postpone spending programs and/or reduce eligibility for "entitlements." If, when the final accounting for a fiscal year is completed, actual outlays exceed statement outlays through unintentional and presumably modest error, an obvious remedy will be a planned surplus of equivalent size during the subsequent fiscal year. The amendment also restrains spending "off budget" because the term "outlay" makes no distinction between on- and off-budget expenditures.

Congress is expected to adopt the most accurate estimates of receipts and outlays that it can, but in all cases a congressional majority will be the final arbiter among the choices of estimates. As the fiscal year unfolds, actual receipts may or may not meet expectations. An unexpectedly more robust economy may yield actual receipts above statement receipts; an unexpectedly weaker economy may yield actual receipts below statement receipts. Either result is permissible. The amendment imposes no obligation upon Congress to react to the flow of actual receipts during the fiscal year—only to the flow of actual outlays.

Recent years have witnessed congressional failure to adopt a budget by the 1 October date on which a new fiscal year begins. Congress has funded government operations in such instances by adopting continuing resolutions. Under the amendment, this practice will be banned. Failure to adopt a statement of receipts and outlays by the 1 October deadline will be construed as an implied adoption of a statement in which both receipts and outlays are zero. In that event, Congress and the president will be mandated constitutionally to ensure that fiscal year outlays also will be zero.

Loans for which the federal government guarantees repayment of principal and/or interest, in whole or in part, impose no funding obligation on the Treasury unless and until such loans come into default and the Treasury must discharge the guarantee obligation. Such a discharge is intended to be construed as an outlay in the fiscal year of discharge.

Section 2 establishes the norm that tax receipts should not grow more rapidly than the general economy. This puts an effective halt to higher taxes arising from bracket creep and other sources, unless a "whole" majority of the membership of both houses votes to permit receipts to outpace general economic growth—that is, enacts a bill expanding a specified tax base and/or increasing specified tax rates.

Put another way, section 2 states that the balanced budget in section 1 should not be balanced at levels of receipts and outlays that consume an increasing proportion of the national economy. It attempts to achieve this by requiring that receipts reasonably expected to be received by the government not increase by a percentage greater than the percentage increase in the national income during the calendar year just prior to the beginning of the fiscal year. If reasonably expected receipts in any fiscal year are greater than allowable statement receipts, Congress must modify the revenue laws to reduce anticipated receipts. If circumstances warrant, Congress may permit a more rapid growth in receipts, but only upon a recorded vote of a majority of the membership of both houses.

Under current revenue laws, stabilizing the share of national income available to the federal government requires that Congress enact annual tax cuts until 1985 when indexing becomes effective, unless it is prepared to vote annually for tax increases that would increase the federal government's share of the economy.

The relationship between the growth of national income during the prior calendar year and the growth of receipts during the following fiscal year provides Congress with reasonably precise guideposts in its budgeting process. Quite accurate estimates of the growth in national income are available by mid-July prior to the beginning of the fiscal year.

Take fiscal year 1982, for example, which began 1 October 1981. The rate of increase in statement receipts for fiscal year 1982 is limited to the rate of increase of national income for calendar year 1980. If, say, national income rose 10 percent in 1980, statement receipts for fiscal 1982 could exceed fiscal 1981 statement receipts by only 10 percent. Any higher estimate would force a tax cut.

Statement receipts may also rise by less than the proportionate increase in national income. Coupled with the balanced budget mandate in section 1, this decision will force lower outlays than otherwise permitted. The smaller than proportionate increase in statement receipts will then become the base for statement receipts in subsequent fiscal years, until Congress votes a rise in allowable receipts.

The relationship between the growth of income during the prior calendar year and the growth of receipts also establishes the federal budgetary process as a mildly countercyclical instrument of fiscal policy. The twenty-one-month lag between the midpoint of the prior calendar year and the midpoint of the fiscal year leads to receipts' being able to grow more rapidly than the fiscal year national income during periods of recession, thus moderating downturns in the economy, and more slowly than the fiscal year national income during periods of expansion, thus moderating the economy.

While there are no sanctions contained expressly within S.J.Res. 58 for the violation of any particular provision, it must be recognized that Congress and the president are expected to act in accordance with the Constitution. The amendment is designed to promote its own enforcement through the political process. By shifting the focus from hundreds of individual spending measures to two or three critical votes each year relating to aggregate levels of taxation and deficits, the amendment is designed to enable the electorate to better identify those members of Congress most responsible for higher levels of spending, taxing, and deficits.

Sections 1 and 2 are jointly linked to the growth of federal outlays. Since taxes cannot grow faster than the economy and since outlays cannot exceed receipts, the proposed amendment will also establish the fiscal norm that federal outlays cannot grow faster than the economy—a *de facto* spending limit that includes both on-budget and off-budget expenditures.

S.J.Res. 58 overcomes the spending bias in present arrangements by restoring the link between federal spending and taxing decisions. It does not stipulate any specific level of spending or taxing. Rather it eliminates both planned deficits and nonvoted tax increases. The measure contains a wartime emergency waiver, and requires that Congress provide compensation equal to the additional costs of any activities it mandates on the states.

FUTURE PROSPECTS

In past statements, President Ronald Reagan has supported the amendment approach to constraining government spending. "Excessive Federal spending and deficits have become so engrained in government today that a constitutional amendment is necessary to limit this spending. I shall continue to emphasize the need for such an amendment" (Senate Judiciary Committee 1981, p. 4).

In 1981 the Reagan administration took no stand on S.J.Res. 58 or any such amendment. Budget Director David Stockman argued that the president's tax and spending reduction proposals took precedence over an amendment (despite Congressman Stockman's prior endorsement of an amendment).

Critics of S.J.Res. 58 number many in the ranks of leading supply-side tax cutters, with their emphasis on tax rate reductions to restore incentives to work, save, and invest. Since any revenue feedback effects from tax rate reductions take time, Congress would have to vote a planned deficit under S.J.Res. 58 to enact major tax rate cuts. An amendment thus might preclude passage of needed tax rate cuts and further damage the economy.

But it should be just as difficult or easy to vote a planned deficit for more spending. The price of supply-side tax cuts today could by 1985 turn out in practice to be new spending and bigger government. At least the amendment would tend to freeze what have been long-run trends toward higher government spending.

One might argue that supply-siders suffer short-term myopia. To oppose this consensus amendment now, on the ground that it frustrates major tax cuts, will risk accepting a renewed string of deficits in search of renewed social spending should political fortunes change. Once the idea that deficits don't matter becomes engrained as a fiscal norm, the distinction between "good" deficits arising from tax cuts and "bad" deficits arising from more social spending will doubtless become reversed or irrelevant.

The likely $100 billion deficits for both fiscal years 1982 and 1983 make the political climate for Senate approval of S.J.Res. 58 especially propitious. It is less likely that a Democrat-controlled House of Representatives would go along with the Senate. But should both houses of Congress approve the amendment, I would expect ratification by the states in quick succession. Much depends, of course, on the administration's support for or opposition to the measure.

APPENDIX A

SENATE JOINT RESOLUTION 58

Report No. 97-151

97th Congress, 1st Session

JOINT RESOLUTION

Joint resolution proposing an amendment to the
Constitution altering federal budget procedures

Resolved by the Senate and House of Representatives of
the United States of America in Congress assembled (two-
thirds of each House concurring therein),

That the following article is proposed as an amendment to
the Constitution of the United States, which shall be valid to
all intents and purposes as part of the Constitution if ratified
by the legislatures of three-fourths of the several States
within seven years after its submission to the States for
ratification:

ARTICLE —

Section 1. Prior to each fiscal year, the Congress shall adopt a statement of receipts and outlays for that year in which total outlays are no greater than total receipts. The Congress may amend such statement provided revised outlays are no greater than revised receipts. Whenever three-fifths of the whole number of both Houses shall deem it necessary, Congress in such statement may provide for a specific excess of outlays over receipts by a vote directed solely to that subject. The Congress and the President shall ensure that actual outlays do not exceed the outlays set forth in such statement.

Section 2. Total receipts for any fiscal year set forth in the statement adopted pursuant to this article shall not increase by a rate greater than the rate of increase in national income in the last calendar year ending before such fiscal year, unless a majority of the whole number of both Houses of Congress shall have passed a bill directed solely to approving specific additional receipts and such bill has become law.

Section 3. The Congress may waive the provisions of this article for any fiscal year in which a declaration of war is in effect.

Section 4. The Congress may not require that the States engage in additional activities without compensation equal to the additional costs.

Section 5. Total receipts shall include all receipts of the United States except those derived from borrowing and total outlays shall include all outlays of the United States except those for repayment of debt principal.

Section 6. This article shall take effect for the second fiscal year beginning after its ratification.

V

Conclusion and Summary

17

MICHAEL J. BOSKIN

AARON WILDAVSKY

The Worst of Times/ The Best of Times in Budgeting

Budgeting confusion and promise. Tax preferences. Consumption taxes. Defense budgeting and domestic spending. Social security. Indexing. Congress and the Budget Reform Act of 1974. Compromise, not surrender.

Our amusement at the discovery of deficits by Democrats and the Republican retreat from balanced budgets is tempered by the realization that both sides have good reasons for their about-face. For the Reagan administration, deficits are not desirable, merely less pernicious than other alternatives. Reflation by hugely expanding the money supply would take the country back to "stagflation." Doing away with the proposed three-year across-the-board tax cuts would result in actually increasing taxes (social security increases, "windfall" excise taxes on oil, bracket creep) during a deep recession. It would also deprive the administration of its main claim to have done something different. Aside from holding the Republican party responsible for the recession, the Democratic party has to be concerned about inheriting such huge deficits that, when in control of Congress or occupying the presidency, it has to spend all its time (and political capital) in raising taxes and reducing spending growth.

There is no agreement among economists on exactly how harmful deficits are or how large they have to be to become a major threat. Suffice it to say that few economists, politicians, or citizens are sanguine about the prospect of continuous deficits of between $100 and $250 billion, averaging about 5 percent of gross national product (GNP). Compared to private saving of only $300 to $400 billion, deficits may dwarf potential investment. If we recall that budget balance stands in many minds as a sign of social balance as well, huge deficits are near-universally considered bad omens. Hence there is widespread agreement on the desirability of reducing them—though the closer one gets to specifics, the less agreement there is. For us, the problem is one of figuring out how to use whatever agreement there *is* to move public policy on taxing and spending, the basic decisions that determine the deficit, in more desirable directions.

DISARRAY

No book can catch up with current events, and we shall not try. As we write, the third budget resolution for last year (actual 1981, fiscal 1982) has not yet been passed and the first resolution for this year (actual 1982, fiscal 1983) has not yet been formulated. Congress and the president have been unable to agree on a program of tax additions and spending cuts to reduce a deficit of some $180 billion. Soon, we suspect, Congress will show that its members cannot agree. What then?

We can recall no time since the Great Depression when there has been less consensus on what to do about our economic difficulties. Past patterns offer little guidance, since the spread between the price level and the premium demanded for loans has widened far beyond experience or expectation. Last year's budget is still to be passed in full; continuing resolutions, which are a sign of dissension, bid fair to become a way of life. Accusations fill the air about who is to blame, as do dire predictions of disaster if this or that nostrum — budget balance, a gold standard of some sort, constitutional spending limits, an end to expenditure indexing, and more — is not adopted.

But there is also promise. For if everyone is worried and opinion is unsettled, there is also a rare opportunity to make changes with a large, lasting, and (hopefully) desirable impact. In the midst of all this flux, therefore, it is of the utmost importance that short-run expedients not overwhelm longer-run considerations in establishing a sounder footing for future budgeting. The creative task is to make short-term necessities speak to longer-term desirabilities. Before specifying what we think should be done now, therefore, we wish to set out criteria for substantive and structural change in budgeting.

CUT TAXES AND TAX
PREFERENCES, TOGETHER

First, a word about taxation, a subject missing from this book because spending is itself a large enough topic. Both those who emphasize more progressive taxation to achieve equality and those who stress incentives to encourage economic growth believe that the system of taxation is inimical to their desires. The high rates generated by progressivity have led to a proliferation of tax preferences, commonly called loopholes, and the effort to stimulate investments has spawned innumerable special provisions whose effects are only dimly understood. It dawns on people that they should invest to make money, not to generate tax losses. The public is bombarded by advice to make use of tax shelters like Individual Retirement Accounts, rather than give over their income to Uncle Sam. It is all legal and respectable. Yet taxes used to be called the "price" of civilization, not the defect (at least, not in America) of legal tax avoidance. Many people believe other people are getting out of paying their fair share. Perceived fairness and public legitimacy, the hallmarks of a good tax system (in addition, of course, to yield), are manifestly missing. Why has there been no reform?

High progressive rates powerfully induce affected interests to find ways of retaining their income. A structure of interests is built up (viz., insulators and the energy industry, minority restaurant help and the business lunch) that is difficult to tear down. And we barely mention the industry that has grown up around reducing taxes.

What should be done? Within an overall context of progressive taxation, tax rates should be lowered so that over a period of years they decline to a range of something like 10 to 30 percent. Most tax dodges would disappear without anyone's lifting a finger against them because they would no longer be worth the effort. As tax rates are reduced across the board, tax preferences should decline along with them. Vexatious problems can be mitigated merely by lowering rates. To be more precise, once we have a relatively comprehensive personal consumption tax, rate cuts should in general be across the board for corporations and for real people; they should not usually be designed to "fine-tune" investment in one sector or another of the economy. For one thing, "fine-tuning" merely generates new tax preferences. For another, knowledge of consequences for different people and industries, variously situated, is poor; first- and second-order effects — on which their rationale depends — are missed, let alone the seventh and eighth orders. Instead of arguing about which method of depreciation is least distorting, we favor integrating corporate and personal taxes by taxing the recipients of corporate income at the personal level.

Why do we think there is a chance to combine across-the-board cuts with reduction in tax preferences? Because the current chaos occurs in a context in which not all desires can be satisfied; certain compromises will have to be made. The Reagan administration (and likely, future ones) knows it has to contribute to reducing the deficit. Rather than give up the income tax cut at the heart of his program of limited government, the president will be disposed to find the funds elsewhere, especially as he wishes to hold down cuts in defense. His choices vary between new charges (see the section on energy) or reduction of old preferences. The Democratic party opposition, anxious not to be against tax cuts and desiring as well to hold down further declines in domestic spending, must also agree either on new revenues or on diminution of old preferences. The difficulty will be in agreeing on exactly whose tax preferences are to decline. This is the best opportunity in decades to mobilize necessity — i.e., choice among disagreeable options — in support of lower tax rates and lesser tax preferences.

This reduction in rates and preferences should be done in the context of a gradual move to a comprehensive consumption tax. A personal consumption tax could be implemented with a "qualified account," whereby taxpayers would be allowed to deduct from (a more comprehensive measure of) income all of their saving (details are discussed by Break 1978). This would leave a tax base of income minus saving, i.e., consumption. The advantages of such a tax system for both equity and efficiency (particularly regarding neutrality in the consumption/saving choice) are now well documented (see Mieszkowski 1978). The tax would also be much less costly to administer, in terms both of the government and of private resources, than the current income tax. However, the transition to such a tax must be done carefully and gradually to avoid capricious windfall gains and losses.[1] Further attempts to include various preferences must be resisted. The lower the tax rates and tax preferences (the one cannot be had without the other) while maintaining revenue, we would add, the better the tax system.

It is increasingly self-evident that the complex structure of rates and preferences in the tax code is causing substantial resource inefficiency in the name of a redistribution of tax burden that is more myth than reality. The bulk of federal spending is now on transfer payments; the redistribution of income to those temporarily or permanently distressed through spending *swamps* the modest redistribution that occurs through the tax system. A simpler, more efficient tax would almost certainly accomplish at least as much redistribution to the poor, without the enormous unnecessary costs the current tax system imposes in the name of minor shifts in the tax burden among different nonpoor income classes. We thus strongly favor serious consideration of a comprehensive *flat rate* personal consumption tax. If a single rate is impossible to implement politically, perhaps two or three rate classes could be established (hopefully, only on an interim basis).

LONG-TERM CONSENSUS ON LONG LEAD-TIMES ESSENTIAL IN DEFENSE

The "secret" of defense budgeting is long lead-times. Unsustained effort is less than useless. Better to spend somewhat less and sustain that spending than to play a losing "stop/go" game. Long lead-times, it should be obvious, require a lasting consensus as to the level of defense spending. Aside from the truism (which, nevertheless, bears repeating) that defense policy depends on domestic support, failure to achieve a bipartisan consensus results in the extreme budgetary uncertainty that stultifies defense planning. The essential political task is to agree, not only on this year's, but on this decade's level of support so that a change of party does not automatically mean a drastic change in defense spending.

Yet it must be said that the current administration has not been persuasive on defense, not only with Democrats but also with Republicans. Citizens, as well as specialists, fail to see a coherent connection between articulated strategy and spending consequences. The short-run pressure to reduce the projected growth in defensive outlays—so Democrats will agree to domestic cuts and investors will see progress in reducing deficits—has the potential, we believe, of compelling a reconsideration of priorities, which would make the administration more persuasive to its critics and, equally or more importantly, to itself.

We do not presume to specify the size of the cut, but rather speak to the process by which it is made and to its content. Top officials in the Department of Defense plead that if cuts are to be made, they be allowed to say where. Their rationale is that they not be left with the same size of military establishment yet with a smaller budget. After all, their strategic task is to meld force structure with available resources. We agree, especially as this will encourage establishment of priorities. Here the simplest action Congress could take—a lump-sum rather than an across-the-board cut—would be most helpful.

Alternatively, if there is agreement in Congress on substance, it could mandate a reduction in forces. Our prime candidate would be a reduction in troop levels with officers bearing half the necessary cuts. This reduction in force (say, 50,000 in number) would at once compel consideration of American commitments abroad and of the composition of its fighting forces at home—altogether a salutary experience. There is no magic number of troops for the United States to maintain in Europe, for example, to deter attack. The number there was not so much chosen as observed after the fact as a number we once had that was henceforth to be treated as an index of our resolve. Perhaps modest reductions in Europe and Asia would do more to persuade allies to become more interested in their own defense than the endless, fruitless, and unseemly expostulation that now surrounds this subject. Such an approach would also aid in improving the caliber of fighting forces while winnowing out overstaffed officers and underqualified enlisted men.

DOMESTIC REDUCTIONS CAN ALSO BE MADE

Let us suppose that around $50 billion of deficit-reducing revenues and defense cuts are (both now and for the foreseeable future) achieved in the manner we have just discussed. How can equivalent reductions come out of domestic spending? Taking defense, debt interest, and large entitlement programs out of consideration leaves only about a quarter of the total. This remainder, largely composed of general governmental expense, has already been hard hit. This is the current dilemma of domestic spending. Once we decompose it into various elements, however, the opportunities as well as the obstacles will become more apparent.

The place to begin is with programs that aid people of above-average income. "Socialism for the rich," whether it be loan guarantees or purchase guarantees or trade policies, is an obvious target. Robert Reischauer's article (chapter 11) provides a good list with which to begin. Of course, these benefits are wound up with others for lower-income people. Since the spending growth—and hence deficit reduction—must come from somewhere, as everyone says, starting at the top is more politically palatable than the reverse.

The same principle applies to subsidized medical care. While inflation in general is running at about 7 percent, it is more than double that in medicine. The reason is that public and private money is being pumped into medical care faster than the factors of production. Hardly anyone (see the articles by Enthoven and Seidman, chapters 7 and 8) pays directly for the services received; hence, no one has sufficient incentive to seek cost-effective care. A first step the federal government might take is to restructure the tax preferences for medical care, most of which go to people with higher incomes. This would also increase the fairness of placing spending caps on Medicare and Medicaid. Should Medicaid be federalized as part of the president's new federalism program, the stream of spending could gradually be cut down from this central source.

Obviously, domestic spending cannot contribute substantially to reducing the deficit without the "big ticket" items— the entitlement programs, especially social security. In the last decade the real income of social security recipients increased by about half, while the average for working people was only a few percent. If one asks whether this increased amount is sufficient to live on, the answer is "not really." But if one asks about the relationship between the retired and the employed, clearly the retired are doing a lot better than they once did.

In response to these situations, there is a rash of proposals for reducing the real increase in social security so as to improve the financial security of its trust fund and to help lower the general deficit. Rather than fund social security from general revenues, which would keep income taxes permanently high and risk a tax revolt along the lines that occurred in Denmark when a similar action was undertaken, we would encourage a return to the original notion of social security as the bottom tier of a multitiered retirement income system. It would provide the bulk of income for low-income retirees, but be supplemented by private saving (including pensions) for the nonpoor. A two-tier system proposed by one of the authors (Boskin 1977a) would do much, when combined with gradual changes in the age structure of benefits and our consumption tax proposal, to strengthen the ties between benefits and taxes, draw transfers out into the open where they can be more easily evaluated, and increase our private saving rate.

ALTERING INDEXING

Policy merges imperceptibly into process. Altering indexing is one of the basic ways to alter budgetary outcomes in an inflationary environment. It would hardly be an exaggeration to say that the budgetary process since the late 1960s has been driven by the presence of indexed spending on social welfare (against price rises) and the absence of indexed tax brackets. The lack of tax bracket indexing, within a progressive income tax structure, meant that governmental revenue rose around 1.6 times the increase in the price level. The higher the inflation, the higher the tax revenue. The presence of indexing has meant that welfare programs have expanded more rapidly than those subject to yearly scrutiny through the appropriations process. No doubt it was a sense of national priorities that defense should remain in a steady state and welfare should grow from 1955 to 1979, but it was also a fact that defense was not indexed and welfare was.

The simplest approach to budget balance, and by far the most conservative in terms of requiring the least disruption in existing institutions, would be to restore the old status quo: no indexing of either spending or taxing. Congress would be free (as free as it ever could be) to reprogram taxes and spending year by year or even more frequently. Alternatively, tax indexing (now scheduled for 1985) could be combined with indexing of spending. The result would be large deficits as revenue grew only slightly faster than spending due to real growth. Diminishing expenditure indexing, while establishing tax indexing, would gradually drive spending growth down, thus eventually producing spending levels consistent with tax revenues raised.

CAN CONGRESS CONTROL ITSELF?

What are the chances, we might ask, without indexing or any other automatic pilot to steer the budgetary process, of Congress's keeping control? Will it be able to arrive at totals and priorities so that members and constituents will feel well served? Before asking about the budget, one must ask whether Congress can control itself, with or without presidential action.

The basic rule has been budgeting by addition, not by subtraction. Budgeting item by item, program by program, without a cost constraint, has led to logrolling on a massive scale. Why should program advocates act as if more for one means less for another when they can add their requests together, thereby passing these on to taxpayers (or to higher interest costs and hence future taxpayers)? Why should any

agency or its clientele heed the call of a purported public interest in expenditure growth reduction when no one else has
to do the same and when, without all those others, the total
cuts do not add up to enough to make a difference? And why
should they worry about taxpayers when the cost of their
programs is so small, when prorated among millions of citizens, that no one has a sufficient stake to protest?

This argument—that there is an inherent pro-spending
bias in budgeting—is made by the proponents of constitutional spending limits. They argue that, left to its own
devices, Congress cannot impose limits on spending. It has,
they say, neither centralized leadership able to impose limits
nor the incentive to abide by them. Thus Congress in its
parts can will individual items of spending, but as a whole it
cannot control total spending. Hence, one spending rule currently favored by many (e.g., Senate Joint Resolution 58)
would limit federal spending to the prior year's level times
the percentage increase (or decrease) in gross national product. With this rule in play—that is, with a standing constitutional rule imposing a spending limit—they expect Congress
to be able to determine priorities in the knowledge that big
increases in some places must be accompanied by equivalent
cuts elsewhere.

If those who believe that Congress cannot discipline itself
in the absence of a constitutional spending rule are correct,
then doing away with indexing altogether will not lead to
long-run budget balance.[2] Spending will continue to rise relative to national product and will rise faster than revenue.
How will we know whether Congress has the required
desire and capability to control its budget?

Leaving aside for the moment the question of the appropriate level of federal spending, Congress can be seen to be in
control when it sets a spending ceiling within which it lives
and toward which, with whatever surplus or deficit it deems
desirable, taxation is turned. Under the Budget Reform Act
of 1974, Congress passes a first budget resolution that sets a

target and then a second budget resolution to accommodate what has actually been done. (When this no longer fits, a third resolution may be proposed to provide a total justifying the sum of its parts.) The Budget Reform Act has its successes: by providing another source of expertise on numbers through the Congressional Budget Office, competition has, on average, created greater accuracy; by requiring resolutions, a few more congressmen have become concerned with the relationship between expenditure, revenue, and the economy; and by considering the kinds of calculations that can be done by a large and heterogeneous body of legislators, the Budget Reform Act has made decision making feasible. But by all accounts, it has neither effectively controlled spending growth nor cut down on end runs around the Treasury (since 1974, guaranteed credit and entitlements have burgeoned); nor, so far as may be ascertained, has it had much influence on total spending at all (see Fisher 1982).

The crux of the matter is that, in order not to be defeated, the House and Senate budget committees made the first resolution ample enough to accommodate almost all demands and, where that proved insufficient, ratified the overshoot in their second resolution. In short, the Budget Reform Act did not disenthrone budgeting by addition. That can be done only by establishing effective ceilings below the level of demand so that the doctrine of opportunity cost—a thing is worth what one has to give up for it—actually applies, and resource addition gives way to resource allocation.

Conceptual changes, such as capital accounting, inflation adjustments for both assets and liabilities, and biennial budgets, would enable Congress to better control budgets if (and it is a big "if") it had the incentive to do so. We do not recommend a separate capital budget, for that would create an additional pocket of spending and an agency interested in its expansion. It is important, however, in conceiving of budget balance, to do separate calculations for capital assets. Adjusting for inflation on both the asset and the liability side should add to available information. And a biennial budget, while it would not change much directly, would give the participants time to think. Time is a commodity increasingly in scarce supply as budgets are reconfigured and deadlines missed.

What is the probability that Congress will collectively decide upon—and enforce on itself—a ceiling that bites? The answer is: not very high. After all, a committee of leaders that sets and enforces policy is called a cabinet in a parliamentary form of government. There is no need to tell a sophisticated audience that the federal system—the separation of powers, the fact that congressmen do not owe their elections to one another or to the president, that they do not stand or fall together (hence the weakness or absence of party discipline)—mitigates against collective rule. Yet there are circumstances that alter cases, and the present mega–Battle of the Budget may be one of them.

RECONCILIATION WILL
RESURRECT ITSELF

President Reagan achieved his extraordinary success in cutting some $30 billion from the fiscal year 1982 budget by aggregating all the cuts and convincing Congress to consider them together. Instead of finding themselves in the shopworn situation in which the incentive to accept cuts dissipates because relevant others do not have to do it, spending advocates this time were disadvantaged because their measly programs—amounting to only a few billions of dollars—got lost in the overall totals. How were interest groups to determine friend from foe when votes were not taken on a program-by-program basis?

The hurried nature of this reconciliation process (reconciling items of expenditure to a preconceived total or target), and the radical change in habits of thought and action it represented, led observers to predict it would not soon be used again. We think otherwise. How, for instance, would whatever agreement might be reached between the Reagan administration and its budget critics be enforced if it were not proposed and acted upon in Congress as an indivisible package? Should such an agreement be unreachable or should it fall apart, the congressional opposition—to consider a contrary rationale—might well find reconciliation useful in pinning the president between his desires to reduce domestic spending and their desire to cut defense spending by putting the two together in a package. Even if a declining economy puts the current administration on the run, resulting in its loss of Congress and the presidency, Democrats will still have to preside over a decline in the size of the deficit. They, too, may then find the interstices a useful place to hide from retribution or, putting the point positively, to place the general over more partial and particular interests. Democratic party reluctance to give up freewheeling spending might be tempered by the approach of constitutional spending limits. Rather than allow states to hold a constitutional convention, Democrats may prefer to spend less so as to retain discretion in the future. Our point is that if ever Congress is going to take collective action, now is the time.

IF CONGRESS CANNOT CONTROL SPENDING, CONSTITUTIONAL LIMITS ARE DESIRABLE

Should Congress show that it cannot cope with spending and taxing other than by making them larger, we would then support Senate Joint Resolution 58 (see Wildavsky 1982), giving spending limits a constitutional mandate. Those who are aware of the tenor of our past work (Wildavsky 1980) or who have read this far can hardly be surprised to hear that we are in favor of limited government; we would prefer government not to increase in size relative to the private sector. Those who agree with this position need not go further: if Congress cannot act reasonably without a spending limit, then either it must impose one on itself or the people— through the amending process—must do so for it. For those who disagree, however, we have one more word: unless there is no limit to the level of spending (and hence, taxing) they would prefer, they must also face these issues. After total spending at all levels of government rises from the current 34 percent of GNP to 44 or 64 percent, they will also have to figure out how to impose limits at a time when the forces benefiting from spending will have grown much larger than they are today. Better, our advice is to start now.

COMPROMISE, YES; PREEMPTIVE SURRENDER, NO

Talk of compromise fills the air. Allowing the expenditure budget to go unpassed, kept going only by continuing resolutions, and allowing the deficit to go unreduced except as economic conditions might improve, appears irresponsible. Agreement along the lines we have discussed is no doubt preferable to drift. But we do doubt that any agreement at all—agreement for its own sake—is preferable to the status quo. Reflation and increases in income taxes (rescinding scheduled tax cuts would mean actual increases) are worse than the status quo. The stage will be set for another round of inflation and unemployment. Investors, who are concerned about deficits, will be even more concerned about declining sales. Unions will seek wage hikes to keep pace with inflation. Continuing resolutions, by contrast, will keep domestic spending down and the decline in inflation will lessen the effects of indexing on entitlements. Defense will not be able to go up as much as planned, but there is some doubt whether all the available funds can be spent, and it may be worth taking time to work out a longer-range consensus for the future.

No one can say when, if ever, there will be as good an opportunity to restructure budgetary relationships. For out of the ashes of burned budgetary hopes there may yet arise the Phoenix of opportunity. What other time has opened up the prospect of reducing tax preferences, lowering tax rates, altering the rules for indexing (or abolishing them altogether), enhancing congressional control of its own budget, or adjusting to constitutionally mandated ceilings? For those who favor budget opportunities, this is the best of times.

VI

Notes,
References,
About the Authors,
Index

NOTES

1. Aaron Wildavsky: "Introduction: Toward a New Budgetary Order"

1. See the author's chapter entitled "Budgets as Compromises among Social Orders."

2. For Felix Frankfurter's efforts in this direction, see Hirsch 1981, p. 113.

3. See Wildavsky 1981a, pp. 329–50. A shorter version can be found in idem 1981b, pp. 47–57.

4. Wildavsky 1973a. A revised version is in idem 1973b, pp. 84–108.

4. Michael J. Boskin: "Assessing the Appropriate Role of Government in the Economy"

1. An expanded definition of government outlays amounts to over 40 percent of gross national product in the United States. See Boskin 1980b.

2. Essentially, the size of the project should be enlarged to the point where its marginal benefits equal its marginal or incremental costs; a project should be built or undertaken in a period in which the discounted present value of benefits minus costs is maximized; the project should be undertaken if, and only if, the present value of benefits exceeds the present value of costs, each discounted appropriately to the present.

3. It is important to point out that decisions similar to these are made all the time in the private sector, and that the private sector decision-makers face a somewhat different type of discipline—namely, that of profit and loss and potentially being driven out of business—than does the government. Those at Ford Motor Company who were projecting the demand for Edsels several decades ago were no more accurate than those who projected oil price increases for purposes of estimating the revenue from the "windfall profits tax."

4. For example, the bottom quintile of the distribution of total compensation in 1979 received only 2.2 percent, whereas the top quintile received 48 percent. However, the total income, including cash and in-kind transfers, of the lowest quintile was 6.4 percent of the total. Further, in 1980, 6 percent of persons lived below the poverty line, once in-kind transfers were included. Excluding all transfers would increase this estimate to about 20 percent (ignoring feedback effects on labor force participation, etc.). See Danziger 1981.

5. See Eisner and Pieper 1982 for a discussion of government net capital formation in the United States.

6. The classic reference on these adverse incentives is Feldstein 1975.

7. Preliminary estimates for fiscal year 1983 for all of social security amount to $170 billion.

8. See Boskin and Robinson 1980 for a discussion of this debate.

9. I have elsewhere discussed my views concerning social security reform—see, e.g., Boskin 1977*a*. Suffice it to say that I strongly favor separating the welfare and annuity aspects of the system, using the latter to provide an identical and reasonable real return on total lifetime contributions for all persons, and calling for strong income-testing of the former (welfare). Gradually phasing in, after a grace period, higher eligibility ages (while maintaining a strong disability program at younger ages) is also highly desirable. These two reforms would do much to alleviate the immense long-term financial problems of social security (see chapter 9 by Avrin) and to target funds for their appropriate purposes. The current and prospective continued enormous haphazard income redistribution occurring through social security in a veiled and ill-understood manner is simply indefensible.

10. Indeed, Hansen (1969) estimates that discretionary fiscal policy has often worsened the business cycle in many countries.

6. Michael J. Boskin: "Macroeconomic versus Microeconomic Issues in the Federal Budget"

1. See Congressional Budget Office 1981*b*, which estimates revenue losses of $228 billion in 1981, projected to increase to $403 billion by 1984.

2. See Stiglitz and Boskin 1977 for a discussion of conceptual problems with tax expenditures.

3. The CBO (1982*b*) analyzes credit activity as listed in the official budget.

4. See Boskin 1980*b* for further discussion.

5. See Boskin, Avrin, and Cone 1982. The 1982 *Economic Report of the President* unfortunately used a closed group estimate of $6 trillion for social insurance debt, thereby assuming that all of the shortfall would be assumed to be paid by future generations of workers.

6. CBO estimates that a percentage point of increase in real growth increases revenues and decreases outlays by over $30 billion a year after two years; corresponding figures for a percentage point higher inflation, unemployment, and interest rate are $20 billion, $30 billion, and $5 billion.

7. Indeed Hansen (1969) estimates that discretionary fiscal policy has often worsened the business cycle in many countries.

8. See, for example, Barro 1968, Kochin 1974, Lucas 1976, Lucas and Sargent 1979, and Sargent and Wallace 1975.

9. Such a curve relates the inflation rate and unemployment rate, which at one time was presumed to be a stable relationship indicating that lower employment implied higher inflation.

10. I have elsewhere (Boskin 1978, idem 1980*b*) discussed some pros and cons of balanced budget and spending limit proposals.

7. Alain C. Enthoven: "Federal Health Care Spending and Subsidies"

1. The estimate has been updated for the effect of the Economic Recovery Tax Act by personal communication with Dr. Ginsburg. This estimate includes a $16.5 billion income tax revenue loss and a $6.5 billion payroll tax loss. See also U.S. Treasury Department 1982. The Treasury does not include payroll tax losses in its so-called "Tax Expenditures."

2. Health Incentives Reform Act of 1979. S. 1485, 96th Congress, 1st session, 12 July 1979. See also S. 433, 97th Congress, 1st session, 5 February 1981.

3. Comprehensive Health Care Reform Act. S. 1590, 96th Congress, 1st session, 26 July 1979. Also S. 139, 97th Congress, 1st session, 15 January 1981.

4. Health Maintenance Organizations Medicare Reimbursement Amendments of 1979. H.R. 4444, 96th Congress, 1st session, 13 July 1979.

5. Voluntary Medicare Option Act. H.R. 4666, 97th Congress, 1st session, 2 October 1981.

6. In the Federal Employees Health Benefits Program (FEHBP), Blue Cross/Blue Shield (BCBS) recently claimed that they were suffering from adverse risk selection and threatened to withdraw from the program. The design of the FEHBP does have correctible defects that contribute to adverse risk selection, including the side-by-side offering of high-option and low-option plans and requirements that some participating health plans offer more comprehensive benefits than others. BCBS claims that they attract a disproportionate share of retirees whose costs are higher. The Public Employees Retirement System has used a "supplemental annuitant premium" mechanism to compensate the health plans that attract a disproportionate share of retirees.

7. National Health Care Reform Act of 1980. H.R. 7527, 96th Congress, 2d session, 9 June 1980. See also H.R. 850, 97th Congress, 1st session, 16 January 1981.

9.   Marcy E. Avrin: "Financing Retirement Income"

1. It should be noted that early retirement benefits are not included in these figures, since they are paid to individuals under age 65.

2. The Census Bureau in these projections assumes a birthrate of 2.1 children per woman, a constant 400,000-person rate of net immigration each year, and a life expectancy increase of 2.7 years for males and 4 years for females by the year 2050.

Some argue that the problem of aged dependency is somewhat alleviated by the fact that total dependency—population 65 years and over and 0–17 as a percent of population aged 18–64—actually decreases for a number of years and only increases slightly about the year 2030. See Torrey 1981*a* for a discussion of this issue.

3. Future birthrates will largely determine the size of the labor force in the 21st century. Considerable controversy exists as to birthrate predictions. The predictions have far-reaching implications because the resulting age distributions under the various assumptions are significantly different. A comparison of the Census Bureau's high- and low-fertility assumptions shows that under the low-fertility assumption the baby boom generation is still a significant age "lump" in the year 2000, but under the high-birth assumption the baby boom is dwarfed by the number of its own children.

4. In order to understand this intergenerational transfer component, it is useful to examine the most extreme case: the first cohort of retirees under the system. Consider an individual who was age 62 in 1937 and retired in 1940 at age 65.

For a worker making average earnings and investing the sum of employer and employee contributions at interest rates then prevailing, the accumulated retirement principal in 1940 would have been only $68.36, yielding an annuity of $6.59 per year. Clearly, benefits far in excess of contributions would be required if any substantial benefits were to be paid. The actual average annual benefit paid in 1940 to a male aged 65 years was $270.60. Since an annuity would have yielded only $6.59, $264.01 of the benefits was a pure transfer, or welfare payment (see Parsons and Munro 1977).

Since the benefits may—and, in fact, did—change over the retirement period, it is more convenient to compare capitalized savings and benefits over the expected time span than to compare annuity payments and annual benefits. For the individual in question, the present value of lifetime benefits was $2,962.09, of which $2,893.73 was a transfer. Thus this individual paid for only 2.3 percent of the benefits received. This percentage has been increasing for individuals over time. Those retiring at age 65 in 1970 paid for approximately 32 percent of the benefits received (see Boskin et al. 1980, 1981, for estimates of these transfers).

5. Indexing benefits to the CPI is intended to alleviate any inflation-caused decrease in the real purchasing power of benefits. Using the CPI, however, probably over-indexes benefits because the purchases of the retired are impacted less by inflation than those of the general population on which the CPI is based.

6. The fund ratios, or the amount in the funds expressed as a percentage of a year's expenditures, were at the beginning of 1981 only 18, 20, and 46 percent for OASI, DI, and HI, respectively (Social Security Administration 1981a, p. 67; idem 1981b, p. 27).

7. This estimate is based on the 1980 intermediate assumptions of the trustees of the social security trust funds (see Boskin et al. 1981).

8. Each year the trustees of the OASDI and HI trust funds make short-term and long-term financial projections for the funds. They base these projections on four combinations of economic and demographic assumptions ranging from optimistic to pessimistic. The assumptions include real gross national product, wages in covered employment, Consumer Price Index, hospital costs, annual unemployment rate, and total fertility rate. See Social Security Administration and Health Care Finance Administration 1981 for a summary of the projections.

9. Barbara Torrey, a fiscal economist at OMB, estimates that 58 percent of the projected growth in the share of the federal budget devoted to the elderly between 1980 and 1986 is due to Medicare alone (Torrey 1981b, p. 2).

10. Projections for the HI trust fund do not go beyond twenty-five years because of the high degree of uncertainty about the trend of future hospital costs relative to the rest of the economy.

11. Besides these direct expenditures, social security also involves a tax expenditure by the federal government because of the forgone revenue from the nontaxation of benefits. The Treasury estimates that tax expenditures will amount to $9.19 billion in fiscal 1981. This estimate is extremely sensitive to several highly debatable assumptions. For an explanation of the calculation of this estimate, see Munnell 1982, ch. 3, p. 20.

12. These figures do not necessarily imply that the retired population has become better off relative to workers over the years. Such a comparison cannot be made without including other factors such as income from investments.

13. For example, working wives with low covered earnings pay social security taxes but collect spouses' benefits based on their husbands' earnings. They receive nothing in return for their own tax payments.

14. There is considerable debate as to the existence and extent of these adverse incentives. See President's Commission on Pension Policy 1981 for a discussion of them.

15. Considerable debate exists as to the future growth of coverage. The President's Commission on Pension Policy projected little future growth. This projection is challenged by work performed at the Employee Benefit Research Institute.

16. Debate exists as to whether pension plan contributions are, in fact, a substitute for wages as this calculation assumes. Also, the calculation has been criticized for failing to capture the essential nature of the tax concession where tax payments are deferred. See Munnell 1982, ch. 3, p. 17, for a discussion of this point.

17. Deferral is equivalent to an interest-free loan from the Treasury to the employee—the higher the tax bracket, the greater the loan. For example, if an employee is in the 25 percent bracket, the annual interest-free loan from the Treasury amounts to 25 cents for each dollar of employer contributions, while for an employee in the 50 percent bracket, the loan is 50 cents per dollar of contribution. Not only is the Treasury loan per dollar of contribution greater for high-wage workers, but because larger pension contributions are made on behalf of high-income workers, the absolute amount of their dollar loan is much greater.

18. With this structure, the average age of nondisability retirement was 42 in 1978 (President's Commission on Pension Policy 1981, p. 18).

19. The mean benefit for those who are married and age 65 or over was $9,393 for military retirement compared with $3,689 for private plans in 1978. For comparison, the average social security retirement benefit was $2,196 (President's Commission on Pension Policy 1981, p. 16).

20. The system allows normal unreduced retirement benefits at age 55 with thirty years of service and a full cost-of-living adjustment to benefits that averaged $8,951 for a married couple in 1978 or double that of the benefit in the average private employee plan. The average retirement age was 61 in 1978. The federal plan differs from most private plans in that employees make a tax-deductible contribution of 7 percent of salary to the plan (President's Commission on Pension Policy 1981, p. 17).

21. The average benefit to married participants in state and local plans was $4,957 in 1978 or more than 25 percent higher than that of private plans. Many state and local plans, however, require employee contributions.

22. Although 70 percent of state and local workers are covered by social security, few of the plans are integrated. The extent to which private employee plans are integrated is not known conclusively. A 1978 study conducted for the Treasury found that two-thirds of all defined benefit plans were integrated. A 1980 survey of large plans by Bankers Trust found that 89 percent of plans with benefits based on final pay and 70 percent of those with benefits based on career-average pay were integrated (Bankers Trust 1980).

23. Under current integration rules, a private pension plan is considered nondiscriminatory if the ratio of combined private pension and social security benefits to earnings is no higher for employees whose wages exceed the taxable social security wage base than for those whose wages are fully covered.

24. See President's Commission on Pension Policy 1981 for surveys of the literature regarding these issues.

25. See Boskin et al. 1981 for calculations of the return on contributions that various groups of individuals can expect to receive from social security.

26. For the other recommendations of the commission, see President's Commission on Pension Policy 1981.

27. See Avrin and Woodruff 1981 and ICF 1981 for discussions of the MUPS.

28. See Boskin 1978*b* for a discussion of the correlation between the rate of taxation of interest and the rate of saving.

29. See Boskin and Shoven 1980 for a proposed simple method of implementing a consumption tax.

30. See Kurz and Avrin 1979 for further discussion of a hypothetical system such as this.

31. The system, despite its ad hoc nature, has helped to decrease the percentage of over-65 individuals below the poverty line from 35 percent to 15 percent since 1960.

10.   James W. Abellera and Roger P. Labrie: "Budgeting for Defense: The Original Reagan Five-Year Spending Program"

1. Alternative views of the impact on the economy of the increased spending levels in the Reagan FY 1982–1986 program (especially in the area of procurement) can be found in Capra 1981, pp. 27–30.

2. See Office of the Assistant Secretary of Defense (Comptroller) 1981 a; idem 1981 b. Weapons systems included in the Reagan increases are those for which quarterly selected acquisition reports (SARs) are required by Congress (weapons systems whose estimated total program cost exceeds $300 million), and other major procurement programs.

3. The remainder, $6.7 billion of $70.9 billion in total FY 1980 personnel costs, included expenditures for family housing, medical support, overseas dependent education, individual training, recruiting and examining, half of base operating support, and a miscellaneous category. See Brown 1981, p. 269.

11.   Robert D. Reischauer: "The Federal Budget: Subsidies for the Rich"

1. Congressional Budget Office (1982c) estimates the federal subsidy to freight transportation modes as a percent of total cost as follows: pipeline 0%, truck 1%, railroad 6.2%, inland waterway 29.5%.

2. The allocation factor is the estimated number of acres needed to meet the nation's domestic and international requirements for the commodity divided by the total number of acres actually planted. The secretary of agriculture sets the allocation factor.

3. All of the estimates in this section are taken from Lin, Johnson, and Calvin 1981.

4. The Omnibus Reconciliation Act of 1981 increased from 7 to 9 percent the interest rate charged on loans once the borrower has left school, instituted a 5 percent origination fee, and instituted a "needs analysis" for borrowers from families with incomes over $30,000.

12.   Robert W. Hartman: "Federal Employee Compensation and the Budget"

1. This chapter deals exclusively with federal civilian white-collar employees. Military and blue-collar workers (mainly employed in the Department of Defense) and postal workers present different problems beyond our scope.

2. In the case of some agencies—the Office of Personnel Management (OPM), for example—only employees whose pay derives from the salaries and expenses appropriation are forced on furlough. Those whose salaries derive from a revolving or trust fund such as, for example, the Civil Service Retirement Fund are untouched because the 1982 budget cuts did not (in general) affect such funds.

3. The government's definition of comparability includes a one-year lag in federal salaries. Thus when comparability was "attained" in October 1980, it meant that federal compensation at that time was equal to private sector compensation as of March 1980. The federal compensation was thus six months behind. By the following September, federal pay would be eighteen months behind the private sector. Thus the average lag is one year.

4. The General Schedule (GS) is the largest civilian pay system in the federal government. About 1.5 million employees hold jobs classified from GS-1, paying in 1981 $8,342, to GS-15, paying the top rate of $50,000.

5. Judges have done better as a result of a technicality.

6. In the Senior Executive Service (SES) and for managers in the upper GS grades, bonuses and merit pay in excess of basic pay could serve as a morale enhancer. For the GS, however, merit pay has not been implemented, while the SES bonuses given since 1980 have created such resentment among nonrecipients that it is problematic whether such payments can really replace basic salary increases.

7. Postal workers, even though they work for an off-budget agency, also are in the CSRS. There are many smaller retirement funds for special groups of federal employees, such as the Foreign Service.

8. The military forces have their own retirement plan and participate in social security as well.

9. In addition, it may make sense to count as true income the contribution made by the U.S. Postal Service, as employer, because that service is now off budget. This amounts to another $1.5 billion in 1981.

10. The CSRS trust fund is often compared to the social security trust funds (OASDI). Both are pay-as-you-go systems, but the crucial difference is that OASDI income really is made up of receipts from nongovernmental entities (the Federal Insurance Contributions [FICA] tax), not from internal transactions. OASDI is in bad shape—but at least its shape is clear from the accounting.

11. These estimates are based on an assumed inflation rate of 6 percent, a nominal interest rate of 7 percent, and wage increases of 8.8 percent.

12. For discussion of civil service retirement reforms, see Congressional Research Service 1982, Hartman 1980, and House Committee on Post Office and Civil Service 1980.

13. Many people favor universal coverage under social security for federal workers precisely for its short-term remedial effect on the social security trust funds. They forget the short-term negative effect on the CSRS trust fund.

14. The administration's proposals should not be confused with efforts to change indexation so as to reflect the growth of prices or wages, whichever rise least. This proposal stems from the general proposition that the real income of the retired population should not be guaranteed when the working population is suffering real wage declines. Such a proposition would be implemented by applying the alternative indexing to all retirees—social security recipients as well as civil servants—and the relevant wage index would be economywide, not just restricted to federal pay rates. The Reagan administration did not endorse this proposal in its budget program.

16. Alvin Rabushka: "Fiscal Responsibility: Will Anything Less Than a Constitutional Amendment Do?"

1. *Economic Report of the President,* 1981, computed from table B-17, p. 252, and table B-73, p. 318. When the numbers are adjusted for inflation, the dollar totals are not quite so staggering. It might also be noted that the spending totals exclude off-budget outlays, which have grown 50 percent faster than on-budget outlays since 1974, thereby understating the total current dollar amount of recent government spending.

2. For a detailed examination of the causes and consequences of California's Proposition 13, see Rabushka and Ryan 1982.

3. Balanced budgets and spending limits are discussed further in Rabushka 1980, pp. 98–102.

4. *AEI Economist,* April 1979, pp. 4–6. For a thorough critique of both federal spending and balanced budget amendments, see Shrum 1982.

5. The best-known example of a federal spending limit amendment was Senate Joint Resolution 56, drafted and sponsored by the National Tax Limitation Committee, including Milton Friedman. It was introduced in the 96th Congress, 1st Session, by Senators Heinz and Stone.

6. For a thorough analysis of this proposed amendment, see Stubblebine 1982; also see Senate Judiciary Committee 1981.

17. Michael J. Boskin and Aaron Wildavsky: "The Worst of Times/The Best of Times in Budgeting"

1. The U.S. Treasury has carefully detailed the potential mechanics of such a transition. See Department of the Treasury 1977.

2. Appropriately defined with a separate capital account and adjusted for inflation.

REFERENCES

Aaron, H., and Boskin, Michael J., eds. 1980. *Economics of Taxation.* New York: The Brookings Institution.

Abellera, James W., and Labrie, Roger P. 1981. "The FY 1982–1986 Defense Program: Issues and Trends." *AEI Foreign Policy and Defense Review* 3, 4/5.

Adams, Henry Carter. 1899. *The Science of Finance: An Investigation of Public Expenditures and Public Revenues.* New York: Henry Holt & Company.

Adelman, M. A. 1981. "Coping with Supply Insecurity." Address to third annual meeting of International Association of Energy Economists, 12–13 November, Houston, Texas.

Alexander, Arthur; Becker, Abraham S.; and Hoehn, William H., Jr. 1979. "The Significance of Divergent U.S.–U.S.S.R. Military Expenditures." *Rand Note N–1000–AE,* February.

Astin, Alexander W.; King, Mayo R.; and Richardson, Gerald T. 1981. "The American Freshman: National Norms for Fall 1980." Research paper. Los Angeles, CA: Laboratory for Research in Higher Education, University of California at Los Angeles.

Avrin, Marcy E., and Woodruff, Thomas. 1981. "Retirement Policy in an Income Distribution Framework." In *Coming of Age: Toward a National Retirement Income Policy,* Appendix, ed. President's Commission on Pension Policy. June. Washington, DC: Government Printing Office.

Baily, Martin J. 1971. *National Income and the Price Level: A Study in Macroeconomic Theory.* 2d ed. New York: McGraw-Hill.

Bankers Trust Company. 1980. *Corporate Pension Plan Study: A Guide for the 1980's.* New York: Bankers Trust.

Barro, Robert J. 1974. "Are Government Bonds Net Wealth?" *Journal of Political Economy* 82, November/December.

———. 1978. "Comments from an Unreconstructed Ricardian." *Journal of Monetary Economics,* August.

———. 1981. "Output Effects of Government Purchases." *Journal of Political Economy* 89, December.

Barth, James R.; Cordes, Joseph J.; and Watson, Harry. 1981. "The Economic Determinates and Implications of the Size and Allocation of Pension Fund Capital." In *Coming of Age: Toward a National Retirement Income Policy,* Appendix, ed. President's Commission on Pension Policy. June. Washington, DC: Government Printing Office.

383

Bassett, Preston C. 1981*a*. "Federal Pension Programs." In *Coming of Age: Toward a National Retirement Income Policy,* Appendix, ed. President's Commission on Pension Policy. June. Washington, DC: Government Printing Office.

———. 1981*b*. "State and Local Pension Plans." In *Coming of Age: Toward a National Retirement Income Policy,* Appendix, ed. President's Commission on Pension Policy. June. Washington, DC: Government Printing Office.

Baumol, William J., and Bowen, William G. 1966*a*. "The Audience." In *Performing Arts—The Economic Dilemma,* by William J. Baumol and William G. Bowen. Cambridge, MA: MIT Press.

———. 1966*b*. *Performing Arts—The Economic Dilemma.* Cambridge, MA: MIT Press.

Beck, Morris. 1981. *Government Spending: Trends and Issues.* New York: Praeger.

Biles, Brian; Schramm, Carl J.; and Atkinson, J. Graham. 1980. "Hospital Cost Inflation under State Rate-Setting Programs." *New England Journal of Medicine* 303, 18 September.

Blau, Joseph L., ed. 1954. *Social Theories of Jacksonian Democracy.* New York: Bobbs-Merrill.

Blue Cross/Blue Shield Associations. 1981. "A Third Party Payer's Perspective—Medicare Vouchers." 28 September. Washington, DC: Blue Cross/Blue Shield Assns.

Borcherding, Thomas, ed. 1977*a*. *Budgets and Bureaucrats: The Sources of Government Growth.* Durham, NC: Duke University Press.

———. 1977*b*. "A Hundred Years of Public Spending, 1870–1970." In *Budgets and Bureaucrats: The Sources of Government Growth,* ed. Thomas Borcherding. Durham, NC: Duke University Press.

Boskin, Michael J. 1977*a*. "The Alternatives before Us." In *The Crisis in Social Security,* ed. Michael J. Boskin. San Francisco, CA: Institute for Contemporary Studies.

———, ed. 1977*b*. *The Crisis in Social Security.* San Francisco, CA: Institute for Contemporary Studies.

———. 1978*a*. "The Economics of the Tax Revolt." *National Tax Journal.*

———, ed. 1980*a*. *The Economy in the 1980s.* San Francisco, CA: Institute for Contemporary Studies.

———. 1982. "Federal Government Deficits: Myths and Realities." *American Economic Review,* May.

———. 1980*b*. "Federal Government Spending and Budget Policy." In *The Economy in the 1980s,* ed. Michael J. Boskin. San Francisco, CA: Institute for Contemporary Studies.

———, ed. 1978*b*. *Federal Tax Reform: Myths and Realities.* San Francisco, CA: Institute for Contemporary Studies.

———. 1980*c*. "Interrelationships among the Choice of Tax Rates, Tax Base and the Unit of Account in the Design of an Optimal Tax System." In *Economics of Taxation,* ed. H. Aaron and Michael J. Boskin, New York: The Brookings Institution.

————. 1978*c*. "Taxation, Saving and the Rate of Interest." *Journal of Political Economy* 86, April.

————; Avrin, Marcy E.; and Cone, Kenneth. 1982. "Modelling Alternative Solutions to the Long-Run Social Security Financing Problem." In *Behavioral Simulations of Tax Policy,* ed. Martin Feldstein. Chicago, IL: University of Chicago Press.

————; Avrin, Marcy E.; and Cone, Kenneth. 1980. "Modelling Alternative Solutions to the Long-Run Social Security Funding Crisis." NBER Working Paper No. 583. November. Cambridge, MA: National Bureau of Economic Research.

————; Avrin, Marcy E.; and Cone, Kenneth. 1981. "Social Security Simulations Using the Assumptions of the Trustees of the OASDI Trust Funds." Mimeo, February, available through the authors.

————, and Hurd, M. 1982. "Are Inflation Rates Different for the Elderly?" NBER Working Paper, Stanford, CA.

————, and Robinson, M. 1980. "Social Security and Private Saving: Analytical Issues, Empirical Evidence, and Policy Implications." U.S. Congress, Joint Economic Committee, Washington, DC: Government Printing Office.

————, and Shoven, John B. 1980. "Issues in the Taxation of Capital Income in the United States." *Proceedings of the American Economic Association* 70, 2 (May).

Break, George F. 1978. "Corporate Tax Integration: Radical Revisionism or Common Sense?" In *Federal Tax Reform,* ed. Michael J. Boskin. San Francisco, CA: Institute for Contemporary Studies.

Breit, William. 1978. "Starving the Leviathan: Balanced Budget Prescriptions before Keynes." In *Fiscal Responsibility in Constitutional Democracy,* ed. James M. Buchanan and Richard E. Wagner. Leiden/Boston: Martinus Nijhoff Social Sciences Division.

Brown, Harold. 1981. *Department of Defense Annual Report, FY 1982.* Washington, DC: Department of Defense.

Brunner, K., and Meltsner, Arnold J. 1976. *The Phillips Curve and Labor Markets.* Carnegie-Rochester Conference Series on Public Policy. New York: North Holland Publishing Company.

Buchanan, James M., and Wagner, Richard E. 1978. *Fiscal Responsibility in Constitutional Democracy.* Leiden/Boston: Martinus Nijhoff Social Sciences Division.

Capra, James R. 1981. "The National Defense Budget and Its Economic Effects." *Federal Reserve Bank of New York Quarterly Review* 6, 2 (Summer).

Carlson, Keith M. 1981. "Trends in Federal Revenues: 1955–86." *Review* (Federal Reserve Bank of St. Louis), May.

Collins, John M. 1980. *U.S.–Soviet Military Balance.* New York: McGraw-Hill.

Committee on the Budget (U.S. Senate). 1982. *Tax Expenditures: Relationships to Spending Programs and Background Materials.* 17 March. Washington, DC: Government Printing Office.

Congressional Budget Office. 1982*a. Baseline Budget Projections for Fiscal Years 1983–1987* (February). Washington, DC: Government Printing Office.

————. 1982*b. Federal Credit Activities.* Washington, DC: Government Printing Office.

————. 1980*a. Five-Year Budget Projections: Fiscal Years 1981–1985.* February. Washington, DC: Government Printing Office.

————. 1979. *Profile of Health Care Coverage: The Haves and Have-Nots.* March. Washington, DC: Government Printing Office.

————. 1981*a. Reducing the Federal Budget: Strategies and Examples, Fiscal Years 1982–1986.* Washington, DC: Government Printing Office.

————. 1982*c. Reducing the Federal Deficit: Strategies and Options* (February). Washington, DC: Government Printing Office.

————. 1982. *Restructuring the Civil Service Retirement System: Analysis of Options to Control Costs and Maintain Retirement Income Security.* Washington, DC: Government Printing Office.

————. 1982*d.* "Statement of Alice M. Rivlin before the Committee on the Budget, U.S. Senate, 10 March." Washington, DC: Congressional Budget Office.

————. 1981*b. Tax Expenditures.* Washington, DC: Government Printing Office.

————. 1980*b. Tax Subsidies for Medical Care: Current Policies and Possible Alternatives.* Washington, DC: Government Printing Office.

Crecine, Patrick. 1961. "Defense Budgeting: Constraints and Organizational Adaptation." Discussion Paper No. 6. Ann Arbor, MI: University of Michigan Press.

Danziger, Sheldon. 1981. "The Distribution of Income: An Account of Past Trends and a Projection of the Impacts of the Reagan Economic Program." U.S. Congress, Joint Economic Committee. Washington, DC: Government Printing Office.

————; Haveman, Robert; and Plotnick, Robert. 1981. "How Income Transfers Affect Work, Savings and the Income Distribution." *Journal of Economic Literature* 19, 3 (September).

Davis, Jerry S. 1981. "The Impact of Guaranteed Student Loans on Student Financing of Educational Costs at Pennsylvania Post-Secondary Institutions, 1977–78 and 1980–81." Research paper. Harrisburg, PA: Pennsylvania Higher Education Assistance Agency.

Department of Defense. 1977*a*–1981*a. Department of Defense Annual Report, FY 1978, 1979, 1980, 1981, 1982.* Washington, DC: Department of Defense.

————. 1981*b. Soviet Military Power.* Washington, DC: Department of Defense.

Department of the Treasury. 1977. *Blueprints for Basic Tax Reform.* January. Washington, DC: U.S. Treasury.

————. 1981. *Statistics of Income Bulletin* 1, 1.

Dorfman, Joseph. 1959. *The Economic Mind in American Civilization, 1918–1933.* New York: Viking Press.

Duignan, Peter, and Rabushka, Alvin, eds. 1980. *The United States in the 1980s*. Stanford, CA: Hoover Institution Press.

Economic Report of the President. 1981. Washington, DC: Government Printing Office.

Eisner, R., and Pieper, P. 1982. "Government Net Worth: Assets, Liabilities and Revaluations." Mimeo. Evanston, IL: Northwestern University.

Enthoven, Alain C. 1981. "Design for Comprehensive Reform of Medicare." Memorandum for Assistant Secretary Robert Rubin, Department of Health and Human Services, 1 July.

———. 1980. *Health Plan: The Only Practical Solution to the Soaring Cost of Medical Care*. Reading, MA: Addison Wesley.

———. 1978. "Shattuck Lecture—Cutting Cost without Cutting the Quality of Care." *New England Journal of Medicine* 298, 1 June.

Federal Aviation Administration. N.d. "Selected Statistics for General Aviation for 1978." Unpublished. Washington, DC: Federal Aviation Administration.

Feldstein, Martin, ed. 1982. *Behavioral Simulations of Tax Policy*. Chicago, IL: University of Chicago Press.

———. 1981. *Hospital Costs and Health Insurance*. Cambridge, MA: Harvard University Press.

———. 1974. "Unemployment Compensation: Adverse Incentives and Distributional Anomalies." *National Tax Journal* 27, 2 (June).

Ferry, Thomas P.; Gornick, Marian; Newton, Marilyn; and Hackerman, Carl. 1980. "Physicians' Charges under Medicare: Assignment Rates and Beneficiary Liability." *Health Care Financing Review*, Winter.

Fisher, Louis. 1982. "The Congressional Budget Act: Does It Have a Spending Bias?" Paper prepared for the Carl Albert Congressional Research and Studies Center Conference on the Congressional Budget Process, University of Oklahoma, February.

———. 1981. "In Dubious Battle? Congress and the Budget." *The Brookings Bulletin* 17, 4 (Spring).

Fitzpatrick, Edward A. 1918. *Budget Making in a Democracy: A New View of the Budget*. New York: Macmillan Company.

Forsythe, Dall W. 1977. *Taxation and Political Change in the Young Nation, 1781 and 1833*. New York: Columbia University Press.

Friedman, Milton, and Schwartz, Anna Jacobson. 1963. *A Monetary History of the United States, 1867–1960*. Princeton, NJ: Princeton University Press.

Fuchs, Victor R., and Kramer, Marcia T. 1972. *Determinants of Expenditures for Physicians' Services in the United States, 1948–68*. DHEW publication (HSM) 73–3013. December. Washington, DC: Department of Health, Education, and Welfare.

Gibson, Robert M., and Waldo, Daniel R. 1981. "National Health Expenditures, 1980." *Health Care Financing Review*, September.

Ginsburg, Paul B. 1976. "Inflation and the Economic Stabilization Program." In *Health: A Victim or Cause of Inflation?* ed. Michael Zubkoff. New York: Prodist Publishing.

Gordon, Michael R. 1981. "Rubles for Defense—Are the Soviets Really Outspending the Pentagon?" *National Journal*, 11 April.

Hall, Robert E. 1980. "Labor Supply and Aggregate Fluctuations." Carnegie-Rochester Conference Series on Public Policy. New York: North Holland Publishing Company.

Halloran, Richard. 1981. "New Cuts to Claim Missiles, Warships, and Army Divisions." *New York Times*, 24 September.

Hamburger, M., and Zwick, B. 1981. "Deficits, Money and Inflation." *Journal of Monetary Economics* 7.

Hansen, B. 1969. *Fiscal Policy in Seven Countries.* Paris: Organization for Economic Cooperation and Development.

Harberger, A. 1971. "Three Basic Postulates for Applied Welfare Economics." *Journal of Economic Literature* 1x, September.

Hartman, Robert W. 1980. "Retirement for Federal Civil Servants: Down from the Incomparable." In *Industrial Relations Research Association, 33rd Annual Proceedings.* Madison, WI: IRRA.

Hirsch, H. N. 1981. *The Enigma of Felix Frankfurter.* New York: Basic Books.

Hirst, Francis W. 1931. *Gladstone as Financier and Economist.* London: Ernest Benn, Ltd.

House Committee on Post Office and Civil Service. 1980. *Report of the Universal Social Security Coverage Study Group.* WMCP: 96–54. Washington, DC: Government Printing Office.

Huntington, Samuel P. 1961. *Common Defense: Strategic Programs in National Politics.* New York: Columbia University Press.

Hurd, M., and Boskin, Michael J. 1982. "The Effect of Social Security on Retirement in the Early 1970s." NBER Working Paper 659, rev. Stanford, CA.

ICF. 1981. "Analysis of the Potential Effects of a Minimum Universal Pension System." In *Coming of Age: Toward a National Retirement Income Policy,* Appendix, ed. President's Commission on Pension Policy. June. Washington, DC: Government Printing Office.

Internal Revenue Service. 1981–1982. *Statistics of Income* 1, 3. Winter. Washington, DC: Department of the Treasury.

Ippolito, Dennis S. 1981. *Congressional Spending: A Twentieth Century Fund Report.* Ithaca, NY, and London: Cornell University Press.

Joint Committee on Taxation. 1982. *Estimates of Federal Tax Expenditures for Fiscal Years 1982–1987.* 8 March. Washington, DC: Government Printing Office.

Kaiser, Robert G. 1981. "Reagan's Defense Spending Could Turn into Economic Nightmare." *Washington Post,* 25 April.

Kimmel, Lewis H. 1959. *Federal Budget and Fiscal Policy, 1789–1958.* Washington, DC: The Brookings Institution.

Kochin, L. 1974. "Are Future Taxes Anticipated by Consumers?" *Journal of Money, Credit, and Banking* 6, August.

Krauss, Melvyn B. 1980. "What We Need Is a 'Defense Tax.'" *The Wall Street Journal,* 12 March.

Kurz, Mordecai, and Avrin, Marcy E. 1979. "Current Issues of the U.S. Pension System." Mimeo (June), available through the authors.

Kyle, Deborah M. 1981. "DOD Supports House Plan for Multiyear Procurement: Urges F–16 Multiyear Buy." *Armed Forces Journal,* September.

Lillard, L., and Willis, R. 1979. "Longitudinal Analysis of Earnings Mobility." *Econometrica.*

Lin, William; Johnson, James; and Calvin, Linda. 1981. *Farm Commodity Programs: Who Participates and Who Benefits?* Agricultural Economic Report No. 474. September. Washington, DC: Department of Agriculture.

Lippman, Thomas W. 1981. "U.S. Navy: Shipbuilding Industry's Lifeline." *Washington Post,* 30 August.

Lucas, R. 1976. "Econometric Policy Evaluation: A Critique." In *The Phillips Curve and Labor Markets,* ed. K. Brunner and Arnold J. Meltsner. Carnegie-Rochester Conference Series on Public Policy. New York: North Holland Publishing Company.

———, and Sargent, T. 1979. "After Keynesian Macroeconomics." *Quarterly Review* (Federal Reserve Bank of Minneapolis), April.

Luft, Harold S. 1979. "HMOs, Competition, Cost Containment, and NHI." Presented at the American Enterprise Institute Conference on "National Health Insurance: What Now, What Later, What Never?" October. Washington, DC: American Enterprise Institute.

———. 1978. "How Do Health Maintenance Organizations Achieve Their 'Savings'?" *New England Journal of Medicine* 298, 15 June.

Mieszkowski, Peter. 1978. "The Choice of Tax Base: Consumption versus Income Taxation." In *Federal Tax Reform,* ed. Michael J. Boskin. San Francisco, CA: Institute for Contemporary Studies.

Munnell, Alicia H. 1982. *The Economics of Private Pensions.* Washington, DC: The Brookings Institution.

National Endowment for the Arts. 1981*a*. "Audience Studies of the Performing Arts and Museums: A Critical Review." Research Division Report No. 9. November. Washington, DC: National Endowment for the Arts.

———. 1978*b*. "Statement of the National Council on the Arts on Goals and Basic Policy of the National Endowment for the Arts." 17 June. Washington, DC: National Endowment for the Arts.

Newhouse, Joseph P., et al. 1981. "Some Interim Results from a Controlled Trial of Cost Sharing in Health Insurance." *New England Journal of Medicine* 305, 17 December.

Niskanen, W. 1978. "Deficits, Government Spending and Inflation." *Journal of Monetary Economics* 4.

Nobrega, Fred T.; Krishan, Igbal; Smoldt, Robert; Davis, Charles; Abbott, Julie A.; Mohler, Eda G.; and McClure, Walter. 1982. "Hospital Use in a Circumscribed Community." *Journal of the American Medical Association,* February.

Oates, W. 1972. *Fiscal Federalism.* New York: Harcourt Brace.

Office of the Assistant Secretary of Defense (Comptroller). 1980. *National Defense Budget Estimates for FY 1981.* Washington, DC: Department of Defense.

———. 1981*a. Procurement Programs (P-1).* 15 January–10 March. Washington, DC: Department of Defense.

———. 1981*b. Program Acquisition Costs by Weapon System.* March. Washington, DC: Department of Defense.

———. 1980–1981. *Selected Acquisition Reports.* 31 December 1980, 31 March 1981. Washington, DC: Department of Defense.

Office of the Assistant Secretary of Defense (Public Affairs). 1981. "FY 1981 and FY 1982 Department of Defense Budget Revisions." News release no. 77–81, 4 March. Washington, DC: Department of Defense.

Office of Management and Budget. 1977*a*–1981*a. The Budget of the U.S. Government, Fiscal Year 1978, 1979, 1980, 1981, 1982.* Washington, DC: Office of Management and Budget.

———. 1981*b.* "Federal Government Finances." Memorandum. Washington, DC: Office of Management and Budget.

———. 1981*c. Fiscal Year 1982 Budget Revisions.* Washington, DC: Office of Management and Budget.

———. 1981*d. Fiscal Year 1982 Budget Revisions, Additional Details on Budget Savings.* Washington, DC: Office of Management and Budget.

———. 1982*a. Major Themes and Additional Budget Details.* February. Washington, DC: Office of Management and Budget.

———. 1981*e. Special Analyses, Budget of the United States Government, Fiscal Year 1982.* Washington, DC: Office of Management and Budget.

———. 1982*b. United States Budget and Brief, Fiscal Year 1983.* Washington, DC: Office of Management and Budget.

O'Toole, Thomas. 1981. "Russians Build 3-to-1 Edge in Some Arms, Agency Says." *Washington Post,* 6 September.

Panetta, Leon E. 1982. "Reconciliation: A Congressional Tool for Spending Restraint." In *Constraining Federal Taxing and Spending,* ed. Alvin Rabushka and William Craig Stubblebine. Stanford, CA: Hoover Institution Press.

Parsons, D., and Munro, D. 1977. "Intergenerational Transfers in Social Security." In *The Crisis in Social Security,* ed. Michael J. Boskin. San Francisco, CA: Institute for Contemporary Studies.

Penner, Rudolph G. 1981. "Budget Assumptions and Budget Outcomes." *The AEI Economist,* August.

Peterson, John. 1976. *Changing Conditions in the Market for State and Local Government Debt.* Prepared for the Joint Economic Committee of the Congress. 6 April. Washington, DC: Government Printing Office.

Phares, Donald. 1980. *Who Pays State and Local Taxes?* Cambridge, MA: Oelgeschlager, Gunn and Hann.

Pocock, J. E. Q. 1977. *The Political Works of James Harrington.* New York: Cambridge University Press.

President's Commission on Military Compensation. 1978. *Report.* April. Washington, DC: Government Printing Office.

President's Commission on Pension Policy, ed. 1981. *Coming of Age: Toward a National Retirement Income Policy.* February, June. Washington, DC: Government Printing Office.

Rabushka, Alvin. 1980. "Tax and Spending Limits." In *The United States in the 1980s,* ed. Peter Duignan and Alvin Rabushka. Stanford, CA: Hoover Institution Press.

———, and Ryan, Pauline. 1982. *The Tax Revolt.* Stanford, CA: Hoover Institution Press.

———, and Stubblebine, William Craig, eds. 1982. *Constraining Federal Taxing and Spending.* Stanford, CA: Hoover Institution Press.

Ranney, Austin, ed. 1981. *The American Elections of 1980.* Washington, DC: The American Enterprise Institute.

Sargent, T., and Wallace, N. 1975. " 'Rational' Expectations, the Optimal Monetary Instrument, and the Optimal Money Supply Rule." *Journal of Political Economy* 83, April.

Schambra, William A. 1981. "A Beginning from Old Principles." Typescript. Washington, DC: The American Enterprise Institute.

Schick, Allen. 1980. *Congress and Money: Budgeting, Spending and Taxing.* Washington, DC: The Urban Institute.

———. 1982. "Controlling the Budget by Statute: An Imperfect but Workable Process." In *Constraining Federal Taxing and Spending,* ed. Alvin Rabushka and William Craig Stubblebine. Stanford, CA: Hoover Institution Press.

Scitovsky, Anne A., and McCall, Nelda. 1980. "Use of Hospital Services under Two Prepaid Plans." *Medical Care* 18, January.

Senate Judiciary Committee. 1981. Report on S.J.Res. 58, 9th Congress, 1st Session. Report No. 97–151, 10 July 1981. Washington, DC: Government Printing Office.

Shepsle, Kenneth A. 1981. "Geography, Jurisdiction, and the Congressional Budget Process: A Memo to the Chairman of the House Budget Committee." Mimeographed. Center for the Study of American Business, Washington University, St. Louis, MO, December.

Shrum, Robert. 1982. "The Non-Constitutional Character of Proposed Federal Spending and Budget Limiting Amendments." In *Constraining Federal Taxing and Spending,* ed. Alvin Rabushka and William Craig Stubblebine. Stanford, CA: Hoover Institution Press.

Social Security Administration. 1981a. *Annual Report of the Board of Trustees of the Federal Old Age and Survivors Insurance and Disability Insurance Trust Funds.* Washington, DC: Government Printing Office.

———. 1981b. *Annual Report of the Board of Trustees of the Hospital Insurance Trust Fund.* Washington, DC: Government Printing Office.

——— and Health Care Financing Administration. 1981. *Summary of the 1981 Annual Reports of the Social Security Boards of Trustees.* July. Washington, DC: Government Printing Office.

Stiglitz, J., and Boskin, Michael J. 1977. "Some Issues in the New Public Finance." *American Economic Review,* February.

Storing, Herbert J. 1981. *The Complete Anti-Federalist.* Volume 1: *What the Anti-Federalists Were For.* Chicago, IL: University of Chicago Press.

Stubblebine, William Craig. 1982. "Senate Joint Resolution 58: A Balanced-Budget and Tax Limitation Amendment to the Constitution of the United States." In *Constraining Federal Taxing and Spending,* ed. Alvin Rabushka and William Craig Stubblebine. Stanford, CA: Hoover Institution Press.

Taylor, J. 1980. "Aggregate Dynamics and Staggered Contracts." *Journal of Political Economy* 88, February.

Tiebout, C. 1956. "The Pure Theory of Local Government Expenditures." *Journal of Political Economy,* October.

Torrey, Barbara Boyle. 1981a. "Demographic Shifts and Projections: The Implications for Pension Systems." In *Coming of Age: Toward a National Retirement Income Policy,* Appendix, ed. President's Commission on Pension Policy. June. Washington, DC: Government Printing Office.

———. 1981b. "Guns vs. Canes: The Fiscal Implications of an Aging Population." December. Mimeograph. Washington, DC: Office of Management and Budget.

Urban Institute. 1981. *The Future of State and Local Pensions: Final Report.* April. Washington, DC: The Urban Institute.

Webster, Pelatiah. 1791. *Political Essays on the Nature and Operation of Money, Public Finances, and Other Subjects.* Philadelphia, PA: Joseph Crukshank.

White, Leonard. 1961. *The Federalists: A Study in Administrative History.* New York: The Macmillan Company.

———. 1951. *The Jeffersonians: A Study in Administrative History 1801–1829.* New York: The Macmillan Company.

Wildavsky, Aaron. 1973*a*. "The Annual Expenditure Increment." Working Papers on House Committee Organization and Operation (No. 96–321), Select Committee on Committees, 93d Congress. June. Washington, DC: Government Printing Office.

———. 1973*b*. "The Annual Expenditure Increment—or How Congress Can Regain Control of the Budget." *The Public Interest* 33, Fall.

———. 1982. "Does Federal Spending Constitute a 'Discovered Fault' in the Constitution? The Balanced Budget Amendment." Paper prepared for the Carl Albert Center of Congressional Research and Studies, Conference on the Congressional Budget Process, February.

———. 1980. *How to Limit Government Spending.* Los Angeles/Berkeley, CA: University of California Press.

———. 1981*a*. "The Party of Government, the Party of Opposition, and the Party of Balance: An American View of the Consequences of the 1980 Election." In *The American Elections of 1980,* ed. Austin Ranney. Washington, DC: The American Enterprise Institute.

———. 1981*b*. "The Three-Party System—1980 and After." *The Public Interest* 64, Summer.

Zubkoff, Michael, ed. 1976. *Health: A Victim or Cause of Inflation?* New York: Prodist Publishing.

ABOUT THE AUTHORS

JAMES W. ABELLERA is managing editor of the *AEI Foreign Policy and Defense Review* at the American Enterprise Institute in Washington, D.C. He has served as a consultant to the Department of Defense, as staff economist with the Defense Manpower Commission, and is the author of articles and studies on military manpower issues, arms sales, international trade, popular consensus for defense spending, and the future of the U.S. and Soviet navies.

MARCY E. AVRIN, president of Avrin Economics, Inc., in Sacramento, California, is a research associate at the National Bureau of Economic Research. She is a former consultant to the President's Commission on Pension Policy and to the U.S. Department of Housing and Urban Development on state and local pension problems. Her 1981 publications include "Modelling Alternative Solutions to the Long-Run Social Security Funding Crisis," written with Michael Boskin and Kenneth Cone; and, with Thomas Woodruff, "Retirement Policy in an Income Distribution Framework."

MICHAEL J. BOSKIN, director of the Palo Alto Office, National Bureau of Economic Research, and of the NBER program on social insurance research, is a senior fellow at the Hoover Institution and professor of economics, Stanford University. A specialist in public finance, econometrics, and labor economics, and consultant to several government organizations, he edited three books for the Institute for Contemporary Studies—*The Crisis in Social Security* (1977), *Federal Tax Reform* (1978), and *The Economy in the 1980s* (1980). Author and coauthor of many journal articles, he coauthored with H. Aaron *The Economics of Taxation* (1980) for the Brookings Institution.

GEORGE F. BREAK, professor of economics at the University of California, Berkeley, is the author of *Financing Government in a Federal System* (1980) and coauthor of a number of other books on public finance and tax reform. His articles in 1980 include "Intergovernmental Fiscal Relations" in the Brookings publication edited by Joseph A. Pechman, *Setting National Priorities: Agenda for the Eighties;* and "Inflation and the Federal Income Tax" in the sixth volume of *Special Study on Economic Change,* U.S. Congress, Joint Economic Committee.

ALAIN C. ENTHOVEN is Marriner S. Eccles Professor of Public and Private Management at the Graduate School of Business, and professor of health care economics in the Department of Family, Community, and Preventive Medicine, School of Medicine, both at Stanford University. His many publications include a two-part article in *The New England Journal of Medicine* entitled "Health Plan: The Only Practical Solution to the Soaring Cost of Medical Care" (1980), "Consumer-Choice Health Plan" (1978), and "Consumer-Centered vs. Job-Centered Health Insurance" in *Harvard Business Review* (1979).

ROBERT W. HARTMAN is a senior fellow at the Brookings Institution. A consultant to a number of organizations, he is a member of the editorial board of the *Journal of Contemporary Studies.* His most recent book is the forthcoming *Federal Employees Pay and Retirement Benefits,* and he is coeditor with Arnold R. Weber of *The Rewards of Public Service: Compensating Top Federal Officials* (1980).

HERSCHEL KANTER, a member of the research staff of the Institute for Defense Analyses, is a former senior fellow of the Brookings Institution. He has held positions in the Office of the Secretary of Defense and the Bureau of the Budget, and for five years was director of the Institute for Naval Studies of the Center for Naval Analyses. He has published articles and studies on naval policy, the defense budget, and NATO's armaments cooperation.

MELVYN B. KRAUSS is a senior fellow at the Hoover Institution, Stanford University, and professor of economics on leave from New York University. A supply-side economist with experience teaching in several European nations, his publications include books on international trade, protectionism, the European economic community, and microeconomic theory. His most recent book, *Development without Aid,* concerns North-South problems and the Reagan administration's approach to developing nations.

ROGER P. LABRIE is a research associate in foreign policy and defense studies at the American Enterprise Institute for Public Policy Research, Washington, D.C. His main areas of interest are strategic weapons policy and arms control. Among his publications is the edited volume *SALT Handbook: Key Documents and Issues, 1972–1979.*

ARNOLD J. MELTSNER, professor of public policy in the Graduate School of Public Policy, University of California, Berkeley, is a former analyst with the Rand Corporation and the Research Analysis Corporation. A political scientist, he is the author of *The Politics of City Revenue* (1971), *Urban Outcomes* (1974) written with Aaron Wildavsky and Frank Levy, and *Policy Analysts in the Bureaucracy* (1976). He is on the editorial board of the *Journal of Contemporary Studies,* and he edited the Institute's 1981 publication *Politics in the Oval Office.*

RUDOLPH G. PENNER, director of Tax Policy Studies and a resident scholar at the American Enterprise Institute, is a former assistant director for economic policy at the Office of Management and Budget. He has served as deputy assistant secretary for economic affairs at the Department of Housing and Urban Development, and was senior staff economist at the Council of Economic Advisers. He is the author of a number of books and articles on taxing and spending issues, and contributes a monthly column to *The New York Times.*

ALVIN RABUSHKA, a senior fellow at the Hoover Institution, Stanford University, in 1981 was consultant to the White House Conference on Aging and director of the conference on "Constraining Federal Taxing and Spending." His many publications include the 1979 volume *Hong Kong—A Study in Economic Freedom; The United States in the 1980s,* edited jointly with Peter Duignan (1980); and *The Tax Revolt* (1982), written with Pauline Ryan.

ROBERT D. REISCHAUER, senior vice-president of the Urban Institute, helped to set up the Congressional Budget Office and from 1979 to 1981 served as its deputy director. Earlier, in the economic studies division of the Brookings Institution, he contributed to the annual analysis of the federal budget, *Setting National Priorities,* and was coauthor of *Reforming School Finance.* He is an economist working on intergovernmental fiscal relations and federal budget problems.

LAURENCE S. SEIDMAN, associate professor of economics at the University of Delaware, previously taught health economics in the Wharton School of Finance, University of Pennsylvania. He is the author of articles on government tax and expenditure policy, and his current field of instruction is public finance.

AARON WILDAVSKY, professor of political science at the University of California, Berkeley, was dean of the university's Graduate School of Public Policy from 1969 to 1977. He is the author of *How to Limit Government Spending* (1980) and *Speaking Truth to Power: The Art and Craft of Policy Analysis* (1979), and coauthor with Nelson Polsby of *Presidential Elections* (1980) and, with Hugh Heclo, *The Private Government of Public Money* (1981).

INDEX

PUBLICATIONS LIST*

THE INSTITUTE FOR CONTEMPORARY STUDIES

260 California Street, San Francisco, California 94111

Catalog available upon request

AMERICAN FEDERALISM: A NEW PARTNERSHIP FOR THE
REPUBLIC
Edited by Robert B. Hawkins, Jr.
> $7.95. 200 pages. Publication date: July 1982
> ISBN 0–917616–50–2
> Library of Congress No. 82–80329

Contributors: Lamar Alexander, Benjamin L. Cardin, Albert J. Davis,
Eugene Eidenberg, Daniel J. Elazar, Robert B. Hawkins, Jr., Alan F.
Holmer, A. E. Dick Howard, Michael Joyce, Paul Laxalt, John
McClaughry, W. S. Moore, E. S. Savas, William A. Schambra, Stephen
L. Schechter, Wm. Craig Stubblebine, David B. Swoap, Murray L.
Weidenbaum, F. Clifton White, Aaron Wildavsky, Richard S.
Williamson

BUREAUCRATS AND BRAINPOWER: GOVERNMENT
REGULATION OF UNIVERSITIES
Edited by Paul Seabury
> $6.95. 170 pages. Publication date: June 1979
> ISBN 0–917616–35–9
> Library of Congress No. 79–51328

Contributors: Nathan Glazer, Robert S. Hatfield, Richard W. Lyman, Paul
Seabury, Robert L. Sproull, Miro M. Todorovich, Caspar W.
Weinberger

THE CALIFORNIA COASTAL PLAN: A CRITIQUE
> $5.95. 199 pages. Publication date: March 1976
> ISBN 0–917616–04–9
> Library of Congress No. 76–7715

Contributors: Eugene Bardach, Daniel K. Benjamin, Thomas E.
Borcherding, Ross D. Eckert, H. Edward Frech III, M. Bruce Johnson,
Ronald N. Lafferty, Walter J. Mead, Daniel Orr, Donald M. Pach,
Michael R. Peevey

*Prices subject to change.

THE CRISIS IN SOCIAL SECURITY: PROBLEMS AND PROSPECTS
Edited by Michael J. Boskin
$6.95. 222 pages. Publication date: April 1977; 2d ed. rev., 1978, 1979
ISBN 0–917616–16–2/1977; 0–917616–25–1/1978
Library of Congress No. 77–72542
Contributors: Michael J. Boskin, George F. Break, Rita Ricardo Campbell,
Edward Cowan, Martin S. Feldstein, Milton Friedman, Douglas R.
Munro, Donald O. Parsons, Carl V. Patton, Joseph A. Pechman,
Sherwin Rosen, W. Kip Viscusi, Richard J. Zeckhauser

THE ECONOMY IN THE 1980s: A PROGRAM FOR
GROWTH AND STABILITY
Edited by Michael J. Boskin
$7.95 (paper). 462 pages. Publication date: June 1980
ISBN 0–917616–39–1
Library of Congress No. 80–80647
$17.95 (cloth). 462 pages. Publication date: August 1980
ISBN 0–87855–399–1. Available through Transaction Books,
Rutgers–The State University, New Brunswick, NJ 08903
Contributors: Michael J. Boskin, George F. Break, John T. Cuddington,
Patricia Drury, Alain Enthoven, Laurence J. Kotlikoff, Ronald I.
McKinnon, John H. Pencavel, Henry S. Rowen, John L. Scadding,
John B. Shoven, James L. Sweeney, David J. Teece

EMERGING COALITIONS IN AMERICAN POLITICS
Edited by Seymour Martin Lipset
$6.95. 524 pages. Publication date: June 1978
ISBN 0–917616–22–7
Library of Congress No. 78–53414
Contributors: Jack Bass, David S. Broder, Jerome M. Clubb, Edward H.
Crane III, Walter De Vries, Andrew M. Greeley, S. I. Hayakawa, Tom
Hayden, Milton Himmelfarb, Richard Jensen, Paul Kleppner,
Everett Carll Ladd, Jr., Seymour Martin Lipset, Robert A. Nisbet,
Michael Novak, Gary R. Orren, Nelson W. Polsby, Joseph L. Rauh,
Jr., Stanley Rothman, William A. Rusher, William Schneider, Jesse
M. Unruh, Ben J. Wattenberg

THE FAIRMONT PAPERS: BLACK ALTERNATIVES CONFERENCE,
SAN FRANCISCO, DECEMBER 1980
$5.95. 174 pages. Publication date: March 1981
ISBN 0–917616–42–1
Library of Congress No. 81–80735
Contributors: Bernard E. Anderson, Thomas L. Berkley, Michael J. Boskin,
Randolph W. Bromery, Tony Brown, Milton Friedman, Wendell
Wilkie Gunn, Charles V. Hamilton, Robert B. Hawkins, Jr., Maria
Lucia Johnson, Martin L. Kilson, James Lorenz, Henry Lucas, Jr.,
Edwin Meese III, Clarence M. Pendleton, Jr., Dan J. Smith, Thomas
Sowell, Chuck Stone, Percy E. Sutton, Clarence Thomas, Gloria E. A.
Toote, Walter E. Williams, Oscar Wright

THE FEDERAL BUDGET: ECONOMICS AND POLITICS
Edited by Aaron Wildavsky and Michael J. Boskin

$8.95 (paper). 411 pages. Publication date: July 1982
ISBN 0−917616−48−0
Library of Congress No. 81−86378
$19.95 (cloth). 411 pages. Publication date: July 1982
ISBN 0−917616−49−9

Contributors: James W. Abellera, Marcy E. Avrin, Michael J. Boskin, George F. Break, Alain C. Enthoven, Robert W. Hartman, Herschel Kanter, Melvyn B. Krauss, Roger P. Labrie, Arnold J. Meltsner, Rudolph G. Penner, Alvin Rabushka, Robert D. Reischauer, Laurence S. Seidman, Aaron Wildavsky

FEDERAL TAX REFORM: MYTHS AND REALITIES
Edited by Michael J. Boskin

$5.95. 270 pages. Publication date: September 1978
ISBN 0−917616−32−4
Library of Congress No. 78−61661

Contributors: Robert J. Barro, Michael J. Boskin, George F. Break, Jerry R. Green, Laurence J. Kotlikoff, Mordecai Kurz, Peter Mieszkowski, John B. Shoven, Paul J. Taubman, John Whalley

GOVERNMENT CREDIT ALLOCATION: WHERE DO WE GO FROM HERE?

$4.95. 208 pages. Publication date: November 1975
ISBN 0−917616−02−2
Library of Congress No. 75−32951

Contributors: George J. Benston, Karl Brunner, Dwight M. Jaffe, Omotunde E. G. Johnson, Edward J. Kane, Thomas Mayer, Allan H. Meltzer

NATIONAL SECURITY IN THE 1980s: FROM WEAKNESS TO STRENGTH
Edited by W. Scott Thompson

$8.95 (paper). 524 pages. Publication date: May 1980
ISBN 0−917616−38−3
Library of Congress No. 80−80648
$19.95 (cloth). 524 pages. Publication date: August 1980
ISBN 0−87855−412−2. Available through Transaction Books, Rutgers−The State University, New Brunswick, NJ 08903

Contributors: Kenneth L. Adelman, Richard R. Burt, Miles M. Costick, Robert F. Ellsworth, Fred Charles Iklé, Geoffrey T. H. Kemp, Edward N. Luttwak, Charles Burton Marshall, Paul H. Nitze, Sam Nunn, Henry S. Rowen, Leonard Sullivan, Jr., W. Scott Thompson, William R. Van Cleave, Francis J. West, Jr., Albert Wohlstetter, Elmo R. Zumwalt, Jr.

408

NEW DIRECTIONS IN PUBLIC HEALTH CARE: A PRESCRIPTION
FOR THE 1980s
Edited by Cottom M. Lindsay
$6.95 (paper). 279 pages. Publication date: May 1976;
3d ed. rev., 1980
ISBN 0−917616−37−5
Library of Congress No. 79−92868
$16.95 (cloth). 290 pages. Publication date: April 1980
ISBN 0−87855−394−0. Available through Transaction Books,
Rutgers−The State University, New Brunswick, NJ 08903
Contributors: Alain Enthoven, W. Philip Gramm, Leon R. Kass, Keith B.
Leffler, Cotton M. Lindsay, Jack A. Meyer, Charles E. Phelps,
Thomas C. Schelling, Harry Schwartz, Arthur Seldon, David A.
Stockman, Lewis Thomas

OPTIONS FOR U.S. ENERGY POLICY
$6.95. 317 pages. Publication date: September 1977
ISBN 0−917616−20−0
Library of Congress No. 77−89094
Contributors: Albert Carnesale, Stanley M. Greenfield, Fred S. Hoffman,
Edward J. Mitchell, William R. Moffat, Richard Nehring, Robert S.
Pindyck, Norman C. Rasmussen, David J. Rose, Henry S. Rowen,
James L. Sweeney, Arthur W. Wright

PARENTS, TEACHERS, AND CHILDREN: PROSPECTS FOR CHOICE
IN AMERICAN EDUCATION
$5.95. 336 pages. Publication date: June 1977
ISBN 0−917616−18−9
Library of Congress No. 77−79164
Contributors: James S. Coleman, John E. Coons, William H. Cornog, Denis
P. Doyle, E. Babette Edwards, Nathan Glazer, Andrew M. Greeley,
R. Kent Greenawalt, Marvin Lazerson, William C. McCready,
Michael Novak, John P. O'Dwyer, Robert Singleton, Thomas Sowell,
Stephen D. Sugarman, Richard E. Wagner

PARTY COALITIONS IN THE 1980s
Edited by Seymour Martin Lipset
$8.95 (paper). 480 pages. Publication date: November 1981
ISBN 0−917616−43−X
Library of Congress No. 81−83095
$19.95 (cloth). 480 pages. Publication date: November 1981
ISBN 0−917616−45−6
Contributors: John B. Anderson, David S. Broder, Walter Dean Burnham,
Patrick Caddell, Jerome M. Clubb, E. J. Dionne, Jr., Alan M. Fisher,
Michael Harrington, S. I. Hayakawa, Richard Jensen, Paul Kleppner,
Everett Carll Ladd, Seymour Martin Lipset, Arthur D. Miller, Howard
Phillips, Norman Podhoretz, Nelson W. Polsby, Richard M. Scammon,
William Schneider, Martin P. Wattenberg, Richard B. Wirthlin

POLITICS AND THE OVAL OFFICE: TOWARDS
PRESIDENTIAL GOVERNANCE
Edited by Arnold J. Meltsner
$7.95 (paper). 332 pages. Publication date: February 1981
ISBN 0−917616−40−5
Library of Congress No. 80−69617
$18.95 (cloth). 332 pages. Publication date: April 1981
ISBN 0−87855−428−9. Available through Transaction Books,
Rutgers−The State University, New Brunswick, NJ 08903
Contributors: Richard K. Betts, Jack Citrin, Eric L. Davis, Robert M.
Entman, Robert E. Hall, Hugh Heclo, Everett Carll Ladd, Jr., Arnold
J. Meltsner, Charles Peters, Robert S. Pindyck, Francis E. Rourke,
Martin M. Shapiro, Peter L. Szanton

THE POLITICS OF PLANNING: A REVIEW AND CRITIQUE OF
CENTRALIZED ECONOMIC PLANNING
Edited by A. Lawrence Chickering
$5.95. 367 pages. Publication date: March 1976
ISBN 0−917616−05−7
Library of Congress No. 76−7714
Contributors: B. Bruce-Briggs, James Buchanan, A. Lawrence Chickering,
Ralph Harris, Robert B. Hawkins, Jr., George W. Hilton, Richard
Mancke, Richard Muth, Vincent Ostrom, Svetozar Pejovich, Myron
Sharpe, John Sheahan, Herbert Stein, Gordon Tullock, Ernest van
den Haag, Paul H. Weaver, Murray L. Weidenbaum, Hans
Willgerodt, Peter P. Witonski

PUBLIC EMPLOYEE UNIONS: A STUDY OF THE CRISIS IN
PUBLIC SECTOR LABOR RELATIONS
Edited by A. Lawrence Chickering.
$6.95. 251 pages. Publication date: June 1976; 2d ed. rev., 1977
ISBN 0−917616−24−3
Library of Congress No. 76−18409
Contributors: A. Lawrence Chickering, Jack D. Douglas, Raymond D.
Horton, Theodore W. Kheel, David Lewin, Seymour Martin Lipset,
Harvey C. Mansfield, Jr., George Meany, Robert A. Nisbet, Daniel
Orr, A. H. Raskin, Wes Uhlman, Harry H. Wellington, Charles B.
Wheeler, Jr., Ralph K. Winter, Jr., Jerry Wurf

REGULATING BUSINESS: THE SEARCH FOR AN OPTIMUM
Edited by Donald P. Jacobs
$6.95. 261 pages. Publication date: April 1978
ISBN 0−917616−27−8
Library of Congress No. 78−50678
Contributors: Chris Argyris, A. Lawrence Chickering, Penny Hollander
Feldman, Richard H. Holton, Donald P. Jacobs, Alfred E. Kahn, Paul
W. MacAvoy, Almarin Phillips, V. Kerry Smith, Paul H. Weaver,
Richard J. Zeckhauser

SOCIAL REGULATION: STRATEGIES FOR REFORM
Edited by Eugene Bardach and Robert A. Kagan
$8.95 (paper). 420 pages. Publication date: March 1982
ISBN 0−917616−46−4
Library of Congress No. 81−85279
$19.95 (cloth). 420 pages. Publication date: March 1982
ISBN 0−917616−47−2
Contributors: Lawrence S. Bacow, Eugene Bardach, Paul Danaceau, George
C. Eads, Joseph Ferreira, Jr., Thomas P. Grumbly, William R.
Havender, Robert A. Kagan, Michael H. Levin, Michael O'Hare,
Stuart M. Pape, Timothy J. Sullivan

TARIFFS, QUOTAS, AND TRADE: THE POLITICS
OF PROTECTIONISM
$7.95. 332 pages. Publication date: February 1979
ISBN 0−917616−34−0
Library of Congress No. 78−66267
Contributors: Walter Adams, Ryan C. Amacher, Sven W. Arndt, Malcolm D.
Bale, John T. Cuddington, Alan V. Deardorff, Joel B. Dirlam, Roger
D. Hansen, H. Robert Heller, D. Gale Johnson, Robert O. Keohane,
Michael W. Keran, Rachel McCulloch, Ronald I. McKinnon, Gordon
W. Smith, Robert M. Stern, Richard James Sweeney, Robert D.
Tollison, Thomas D. Willett

THE THIRD WORLD: PREMISES OF U.S. POLICY
Edited by W. Scott Thompson
$7.95. 334 pages. Publication date: November 1978
ISBN 0−917616−30−8
Library of Congress No. 78−67593
Contributors: Dennis Austin, Peter T. Bauer, Max Beloff, Richard E. Bissell,
Daniel J. Elazar, S. E. Finer, Allan E. Goodman, Nathaniel H. Leff,
Seymour Martin Lipset, Edward N. Luttwak, Daniel Pipes, Wilson E.
Schmidt, Anthony Smith, W. Scott Thompson, Basil S. Yamey

UNION CONTROL OF PENSION FUNDS: WILL THE NORTH
RISE AGAIN?
$2.00. 41 pages. Publication date: July 1979
ISBN 0−917616−36−7
Library of Congress No. 78−66581
Author: George J. Borjas

WATER BANKING: HOW TO STOP WASTING
AGRICULTURAL WATER
$2.00. 56 pages. Publication date: January 1978
ISBN 0−917616−26−X
Library of Congress No. 78−50766
Authors: Sotirios Angelides, Eugene Bardach

WHAT'S NEWS: THE MEDIA IN AMERICAN SOCIETY
Edited by Elie Abel
$7.95 (paper). 296 pages. Publication date: June 1981
ISBN 0−917616−41−3
Library of Congress No. 81−81414
$18.95 (cloth). 300 pages. Publication date: August 1981
ISBN 0−87855−448−3. Available through Transaction Books,
Rutgers−The State University, New Brunswick, NJ 08903
Contributors: Elie Abel, Robert L. Bartley, George Comstock, Edward Jay
Epstein, William A. Henry III, John L. Hulteng, Theodore Peterson,
Ithiel de Sola Pool, William E. Porter, Michael Jay Robinson, James
N. Rosse, Benno C. Schmidt, Jr.

THE WORLD CRISIS IN SOCIAL SECURITY
Edited by Jean-Jacques Rosa
$9.95. 245 pages. Publication date: May 1982
ISBN 0−917616−44−8
Contributors: Onorato Castellino, A. Lawrence Chickering, Richard
Hemming, Martin C. Janssen, Karl Heinz Juttemeier, John A. Kay,
Heinz H. Muller, Hans-Georg Petersen, Jean-Jacques Rosa, Sherwin
Rosen, Ingemar Stahl, Noriyuki Takayama

JOURNAL OF CONTEMPORARY STUDIES
$15/one year, $25/two years, $4/single issue. For delivery outside the
United States, add $2/year surface mail, $10/year airmail
A quarterly journal that is a forum for lively and readable studies on foreign
and domestic public policy issues. Directed toward general readers as
well as policymakers and academics, emphasizing debate and
controversy, it publishes the highest quality articles without regard
to political or ideological bent.

The Journal of Contemporary Studies is a member of the Transaction
Periodicals Consortium. Institute for Contemporary Studies books
are distributed by Transaction Books, Rutgers University, New
Brunswick, NJ 08903.